DATA JOURNALISM
Mapping the future

The front cover shows a simple mapping of conversations between a set of Twitter users from a one-hour sample of Tweets from Jacqui Taylor's timeline. Tweet authors and mentions are included. The green arc shows the selected user is more active in the conversation, while the red arc shows the selected user is more passive. Graph created by Ian Taylor, CTO of FlyingBinary, using D3.

DATA JOURNALISM
Mapping the future

EDITED BY
JOHN MAIR,
RICHARD LANCE KEEBLE
with
PAUL BRADSHAW
TEODORA BELEAGA

Published 2013 by Abramis academic publishing

www.abramis.co.uk

ISBN 978 1 84549 616 6

© John Mair and Richard Lance Keeble 2013

Printed and bound in the United Kingdom

Typeset in Garamond 11pt

Abramis is an imprint of arima publishing.

arima publishing
ASK House, Northgate Avenue
Bury St Edmunds, Suffolk IP32 6BB
t: (+44) 01284 700321

www.arimapublishing.com

Contents

Acknowledgements

This is the tenth in the Abramis series of "hackademic" texts created by Professor Richard Lance Keeble and John Mair in 2008. Thanks for this volume go to:

The authors and contributors who have been unstinting in creating their work and who have given their work pro-bono (as did the editors on all the books). They suffer a torrent of emails from the editors reminding them of looming deadlines. Most respond. Some fell at the first hurdle, which is a great pity (for them).

We have twenty contributors in this volume; three or four failed to deliver which is a pretty good success rate. Commissioning and chivvying works. We also need to thank warmly:

Richard and Pete Franklin of Abramis, who support and publish the series in double-quick time with great aplomb and little fuss. Whilst Paul Bradshaw and Teo Beleaga have been very supportive throughout.

Lastly, our families who have lived this and other "hackademic" projects for too long. They are the real heroes.

John Mair, Oxford
Richard Lance Keeble, Withcall, Lincolnshire
November 2013

The editors

John Mair has taught journalism at the Universities of Coventry, Kent, Northampton, Brunel, Edinburgh Napier, Guyana and the Communication University of China. He has now edited ten "hackademic" volumes over the last five years on subjects ranging from trust in TV, the health of investigative journalism, reporting the "Arab Spring" to three volumes on the Leveson Inquiry. He and Richard Lance Keeble invented the sub-genre. John also invented the Coventry Conversations which attracted 350 media movers and shakers to Coventry University and the podcasts of those have been downloaded five million times worldwide. Since then, he has launched the Northampton Chronicles, MediaMondays at Napier and most recently the Harrow Conversations at Westminster. In a previous life, he was an award-winning producer/director for the BBC, ITV and Channel Four and a secondary school teacher.

Richard Lance Keeble has been Professor of Journalism at the University of Lincoln since 2003. Before that he was the executive editor of the *Teacher*, the weekly newspaper of the National Union of Teachers and he lectured at City University, London, for 19 years. He has written and edited 26 publications on a wide range of subjects including peace journalism, literary journalism, journalism ethics, practical reporting skills, George Orwell, the coverage of US/UK militarism and the links between the intelligence services and Fleet Street. He is also the joint editor of *Ethical Space: The International Journal of Communication Ethics* and the winner of a National Teacher Fellowship in 2011 – the highest prize for teachers in higher education. He is chair of both the George Orwell Society and Louth Male Voice Choir.

Paul Bradshaw is a Visiting Professor at City University London, publishes the Online Journalism Blog and is the founder of the investigative journalism crowd sourcing site Help Me Investigate (shortlisted for 2010 Multimedia Publisher of the Year). He is described by *Press Gazette* as one of the country's "most influential journalism bloggers" and by the *Telegraph*'s Shane Richmond as "the UK's Jeff Jarvis". He also runs an MA at Birmingham City University.

Teodora Beleaga is a Digital Analyst at Edelman, the largest independent PR firm in the world. Before that she honed her data skills with leading direct marketing company Wunderman, part of the WPP group. She completed the MA in Interactive Journalism at City University London, for which she was awarded an AHRC (Arts and Humanities Research Council) bursary. During her studies, she was attached to the *Guardian*'s Data Store where she secured a front a page within less than a week under the guidance of James Ball, currently the newspaper's Data Editor. In her spare time, Teodora volunteers for the Open Spending Blog at the Open Knowledge Foundation.

Section 1:
What precisely is data journalism?

John Mair

This book is a glance into a secret new world; a piece of modern cultural anthropology. Data journalism (DJ) is much in evidence in the modern media but little known or written about. We hope to change it and encourage all students and teachers of journalism to become more numerate and data savvy. The text is by necessity a primer, an introduction: those whose interest is aroused are advised to dig deeper into the limited literature or better throw themselves into the DJ practice pond to learn more. A competent data journalist should not want for work in the next decade or more.

First, though, what precisely is data journalism? Jonathan Hewett runs a major, pioneering course in it at City University London. He traces the genesis and recent history of DJ as an academic subject: certainly the alumni of his course have gone on to populate the modern data rich newsrooms and this volume.

Simon Rogers is in many senses another grand-daddy of data journalism. He founded and headed the data team at the *Guardian* in London until last year when he jumped ship to Twitter. The *Guardian*, as on may other things digital, has pioneered and produced some of the very best work on DJ in the British media. Rogers argues that data journalism is like the punk movement – anybody with a laptop and the right programs can do it! Maybe he is right but for now the journalism professionals are making the best infographics aided by the deep pockets of Big Media..

Bella Hurrell and John Walton are data specialists at BBC News Online, one of the more respected and visited news websites in the world. They show how

DJ or "visual journalism" as the corporation inelegantly titles it, can improve understanding by explaining complex stories through real people and their circumstances. Precisely what television and radio do so well and have done for decades especially in set piece programmes such as the Budget and General Elections. Hurrell and Walton rightly put the audience and their understanding at the centre of their on-screen work.

Teodora Beleaga is a graduate of the Hewett School and Coventry University (disclaimer: she was taught by John Mair there). She thinks of people as walking data sets generating more and more data from waking to sleeping. The art for her of the DJ is to work out the salience of that data and to put it into form understandable to a non-nerd audience. She does this everyday in her day job as a marketing analyst for Edelman, the global PR firm.

Learning in progress: From computer-assisted reporting to data journalism, via freedom of information, open data and more

Data journalism has evolved out of computer-assisted reporting (CAR) in the USA – in part. Jonathan Hewett traces the development and teaching of data journalism in the UK, including the impact of freedom of information (FoI), open data and journalism education

Using the term "data journalist" only five years ago would have produced puzzled faces. "Journalists like us who use data in our reporting, you mean?" may have been the reasonable retort from some reporters, such as finance news specialists. Others may have made a connection with spreadsheets, databases and computer-assisted reporting (CAR). At university journalism departments in the UK, the response would have been similar, I suspect. But five years on, "data journalism" is appearing in job advertisements, the names of university courses, discussions about the future of journalism – and even in book titles...

Data journalism has its roots – or many of them – in CAR, going back to the 1960s in the USA. But even if they had heard of this computer-assisted reporting stuff, how many UK journalists were using spreadsheets for data analysis by (say) 2008 – at least, outside of financial and business journalism? How many people were actually teaching it here?

Tough times for investigative work

The short answer is very few. The challenges faced by investigative journalism – the main focus for CAR – form one factor. "Many would argue that the glory days of investigative journalism in the UK are well beyond us now," Arjan Dasselaar suggested (2005: 221), attributing this to cuts in editorial budgets, fierce competition and legal liabilities. David Leigh, then investigations editor at the *Guardian*, bemoaned "difficult and frustrating times for investigative journalism in Britain" (Meek 2005).

Dasselaar's survey noted also "some distrust towards new methods of information gathering, such as the internet". While the BBC's *Panorama* programme employed "computer researchers, journalists seem to consider going out and talking to people as superior to using Google". Others felt that "information on the internet must be untrue, for otherwise it would have been picked up already" (ibid: 224) – a point well made, given recurring errors attributable to "facts" taken from websites apparently without checking (Orlowski 2007).

Signs of change were already evident in 2005, as more journalists grasped the opportunities offered by the internet, particularly financial reporters accessing records: "The advent of the internet has revolutionised this branch of journalism," noted Dasselaar (op cit: 224). Even so, it was off the scale to anticipate the scale of a shift that five years later led to news organisations such as the *Guardian* dealing with huge volumes of data requiring detailed analysis. These included the Afghan war logs (92,201 rows of data), the Iraq war logs (391,000) and the US embassy cables (251,287) released through WikiLeaks (Rogers 2013a: 71).

Nerds plus words add up in the USA
Journalists on the other side of the Atlantic were far ahead of their UK counterparts. Already by 1999, a growing network of reporters, editors and journalism educators could look back on substantial developments in CAR over the previous ten years (Paul 1999). *When Nerds and Words Collide* reviewed progress since the 1989 creation of the National Institute for Advanced Reporting and the Missouri Institute for Computer Assisted Reporting (which became NICAR, the National Institute for CAR). Education and training formed a recurring theme in that report: notably how to train practising journalists and integrate CAR into journalism education at universities.

Even by the mid-2000s, the lack of such networks in the UK for sharing ideas, skills and discussions was another pointed contrast with the situation in the USA – and, indeed, with many other European countries such as the Netherlands, Denmark, Sweden and Germany. Again, this might have reflected the state of investigative journalism in the UK, which provided only 10 out of 450 delegates at the Global Investigative Journalism Conference in far-off Amsterdam in 2005 (Meek 2005).

Some CAR training was taking place in the UK, however, particularly through the Centre for Investigative Journalism (CIJ). Established in 2003, it had close links with the USA – hardly surprising as it was founded by a journalist from the States. Gavin MacFadyen had worked as a producer of investigative documentaries on both sides of the Atlantic – including on *World in Action*, Granada Television's campaigning series – and became the CIJ's director. The CIJ's first summer school in July 2003 offered what may have been the first intensive training conference in the UK (albeit with participants from outside the UK, too) on investigative techniques for journalists. It included a half-day introductory CAR course, plus advanced classes, explaining: "CAR is an increasingly important tool that enables journalists to add depth to their stories by accessing, making sense and presenting relevant government, financial, and social statistics" (CIJ 2003).

Transatlantic training triumphs

The influence of US journalism's experience in CAR was clear from the seven trainers who led the CIJ sessions. They all came from or had close links with NICAR and/or its parent body, Investigative Reporters and Editors (IRE), and included already experienced data practitioners such as Brant Houston, Aron Pilhofer and Jennifer LaFleur. The leading role played by NICAR can be inferred from the 40 to 50 seminars a year it ran during 1994–99, and the estimated 12,000 journalists who attended its 300 conferences and seminars in its first ten years (Houston 1999: 7).

Houston became managing director of NICAR in 1993 (before it gained that name), having been database editor at the *Hartford Courant* and won awards for his investigative work. His book *Computer Assisted Reporting: A Practical Guide*, into a third edition by 2003 (Houston 2003), became a key resource drawing on "what many of us had learned about training" and providing "at least one road map for classes in newsrooms and journalism schools" (Houston 1999: 6).

Pilhofer was working as database editor at the Center for Public Integrity in Washington DC, and later led the development of data and interactive journalism at *The New York Times*. LaFleur had worked as database editor at the *San Jose Mercury News* before becoming IRE's first director of training. She went on to be CAR editor at the *Dallas Morning News* and director of CAR at non-profit investigative newsroom ProPublica. As early as 1989, she had analysed the use of computers as part of her master's degree at the University of Missouri School of Journalism (home to IRE and NICAR) (LaFleur 1999: 25).

The beginner's CAR workshop at the 2003 CIJ summer school focused on "more effective searching techniques, resources and data on the internet, downloading data, and doing basic analyses using spreadsheet software such as Microsoft Excel". An "intermediate track" involved moving "from filtering and sorting data in Excel to calculating rates and ratios for news stories, cross-tabulating data and generating graphics" before "showing how to select and filter information in a database manager and introducing users to summarising data effectively to find trends and story ideas" (CIJ 2003).

More complex techniques of data analysis were covered in an "advanced track" with "techniques of summarising data and using relational databases to compare different files of information to see connections that could lead to new stories", and used Microsoft Access. It also offered participants the opportunity to "learn how to build their own databases when there is no electronic information or when governments or businesses refuse to release electronic data. Lastly, the track will include an overview of the new and increasing use of mapping (GIS) software to visualise the results of data analysis" (ibid).

Freedom of information, better journalism?

Such CAR training became a core feature of CIJ summer schools, along with another theme relevant to data journalism: the use of freedom of information (FoI) legislation. Passed in 2000, the FoI Act came properly into force on 1 January 2005 and was fundamental to the development of data journalism in the UK. For the first time, journalists had a legal right to request information held by public bodies, which now had to respond (although not necessarily by providing the information requested). This was a huge advance on the preceding code of practice on access to government information, introduced in 1994 as an alternative to FoI legislation (Brooke 2004). Drawing on her background as a reporter in the USA, Heather Brooke wrote an influential book on using FoI in the UK, *Your Right to Know*, partly out of her "frustration with the relationship between the citizen and the state in Britain, which was not as egalitarian as in America" (Brooke 2013). Data and CAR techniques were becoming well-established among US investigative reporters in the 1990s, Brooke says:

> The main reason was that the datasets were available. A typical story was to get hold of a list of school bus drivers and cross-reference it with a list of sex offenders or other offences. They are both public records in America, with no privacy law, so you could find out whether any of the school bus drivers were paedophiles or had other convictions (ibid).

The appliance of science to reporting

In contrast to the UK – and its lack of public data – the US federal FoI Act had operated since 1967. The timing seems coincidental, but it was same year in which Philip Meyer and colleagues at the *Detroit Free Press* produced a Pulitzer Prize-winning investigation into the causes of riots in the city, often cited as the beginning of CAR. Meyer saw the potential to apply social science techniques to journalism, having studied them the previous year while on a Nieman fellowship at Harvard. A course he took there also introduced him to computing in the form of an IBM 7090 mainframe machine (Meyer 1999: 4). In Detroit, Meyer deployed quantitative survey research, helped by two university professors, a team of 30 interviewers for field work – and a computer programmer. (This was not the first use of computing in support of journalism – in 1952, a Remington Rand Univac machine helped US television network CBS predict election results (Chinoy 2010).)

Having demonstrated "the application of the scientific method to the practice of journalism" (Meyer 1999: 4), he started to pass on his skills to other reporters in the same newspaper group as he developed his statistical and computing abilities. Published in 1973, his *Precision Journalism* – subtitled *A Reporter's Introduction to Social Science Methods* (Meyer 1973) – and its 1991 successor became landmarks in CAR. Meyer did not use public records in his investigative journalism until 1972 (Meyer 1999: 4), but his work converged with FoI in the use of computing tools and statistical techniques for analysis. As computers and software became more ubiquitous and easier for non-specialists to use, so US news organisations began to appoint dedicated database editors.

Grappling with hygienic spreadsheets

Interest in the UK seems to have remained very limited until more journalists began to realise the opportunities provided by FoI. From 2005, Heather Brooke trained hundreds of journalists in FoI techniques with the National Union of Journalists and elsewhere – and while she mentioned the value of obtaining information in the form of spreadsheets, she was not teaching analysis using them (Brooke 2013). She was also putting FoI through its paces herself as a freelance journalist – and learning CAR techniques to deal with the resulting data. One striking success published during the first year of FoI was an investigation with *The Times*. The resulting "justice by postcode" story, published on the front page, revealed huge disparities in conviction rates around the UK (O'Neill, Gibb and Brooke 2005). It also highlighted the greater experience in data analysis that journalists elsewhere in Europe had developed.

"I talked to the FoI officer at the Crown Prosecution Service about when they switched to electronic data. I got three years' worth of data in Excel spreadsheets – which was great, but it was 42 different sets of records from different CPS areas," Brooke recalls (2013; O'Neill and Brooke 2005). To help with the analysis, she turned to Tommy Kaas, who had run CAR training sessions at CIJ summer schools. He had set up the Danish International Center for Analytical Reporting (DICAR), which evolved from the Association of CAR in Denmark, set up in 1997 with other CAR pioneers such as Nils Mulvad, who taught CAR at the Danish School of Journalism.

A tipping point for CAR and data journalism

The fourth CIJ summer school (2006) was a turning point for CAR and data training. CIJ director Gavin MacFadyen noted a "surge in interest in computing. The rooms where those skills were being taught were packed and that's the first time that's happened. ... The whole landscape has changed and journalists see the value of using electronic tools that we've taken for granted and don't really know much about" (Brooke 2006). CAR trainers at the summer school – mostly from the USA – were starting to use data about the UK, obtained from UK public bodies under UK FoI legislation, to demonstrate what could be done:

> One of my very first FoI requests was for London councils' inspection reports on restaurant hygiene. Most of them were electronic datasets, which I didn't really know how to handle properly. It was around that time that Aron Pilhofer was over, and I gave him my restaurant inspection data. "This is really great for teaching," he said. "I'm going to use this for our CAR classes in London." He showed us different ways of analysing it using Excel – but also what the limits were, and how you could switch over to Access and write SQL queries to drill down into the data and find out very specifically which were the dirtiest restaurants in London. I think that was a

real transitional point because it was teaching using real data from this country rather than America, and obtained from FoI (Brooke 2013).

Another US CAR trainer, David Donald (then training director of IRE), was encouraged: "I think you'll begin seeing many more in-depth investigative stories that will be based on using CAR," he said (Brooke 2006). To support that growth, and to share tips and ideas among interested journalists, a mailing list called BICAR emerged – inspired by the successful equivalents at DICAR in Denmark and NICAR in the USA. It was set up by Martin Stabe, then at journalism weekly *Press Gazette*, after post-CIJ summer school discussions in a pub with Brooke and freelance investigative journalist Stephen Grey. Alas, their enthusiasm seemed to outrun the wider interest among journalists for such a project, as Stabe recalls:

> It never really amounted to much – there were almost no messages and it fizzled out quickly. There just wasn't the volume of material or people to make that viable, and I seemed to spend more time administering the server it ran on than actually having any content. I like to think that it was just ahead of its time (Stabe 2013).

Journalism education and training

Data-related work was also developing at City University London, where the CIJ was based and Brooke had become involved in teaching. I introduced FoI as part of the postgraduate Newspaper Journalism course at City in 2005; every student researched an FoI project to generate their own original story for publication. Some City students also worked with Brooke on other FoI/data projects, too. They included Elena Egawhary (BBC *Newsnight* and *Panorama*), James Ball (later data editor at the *Guardian*), and Alex Wood (who went on to work as a data journalist at the BBC World Service).

A stuffy computer room hosted a dozen or so participants for a key training event for UK data journalism in July 2007. Two hugely experienced trainers, Aron Pilhofer (database editor at *The New York Times*) and David Donald (by then data editor at the Center for Public Integrity in Washington), ran an intensive three-day "training the trainers" programme at City University London. Subtitled "how to teach computer-assisted reporting", the course – arranged through MacFadyen and the CIJ – aimed to "show how CAR is successfully taught so that more CAR training can take place here and more home-grown, UK-based journalists can take advantage of these skills". An outline of the course noted not only the importance of CAR – but also the lack of training in data-related skills and stories in the UK:

> Computer-assisted reporting (CAR) has led many reporting advances the past 20 years in the United States, Europe and elsewhere. It's both a method to discover stories that otherwise would go unreported and a way of adding depth and context to existing stories. Historically, the United

Kingdom has offered little training in these techniques for experienced journalists and novices alike (CIJ 2007).

What may have been the first such course in the UK – geared explicitly towards increasing the teaching of CAR and data, and their future development – brought together a number of people who were making their mark in data journalism and its training or education, or were to do so subsequently, including:

- Heather Brooke – FoI expert; went on to teach CAR and data at City University London.

- Martin Stabe – then new media editor at *Press Gazette*; later head of interactive news at the *Financial Times*.

- Cynthia O'Murchu – *Financial Times* reporter; later, investigative reporter on stories such as the data-intensive exposé of the EU Structural Funds (jointly with the Bureau of Investigative Journalism), and deputy interactive editor.

- Stephen Grey – freelance investigative reporter; former editor of *The Sunday Times* Insight team; had investigated the CIA's secret "extraordinary rendition" programme, analysing the details of more than 12,000 flights. Later he became special investigative correspondent at Reuters.

- Adrian Monck – then head of the Journalism Department at City University London; encouraged the development of the MA Investigative Journalism. Later, managing director, head of communications and media, at the World Economic Forum.

- Jonathan Hewett – then (and now) leading the MA Newspaper Journalism programme at City; later set up the Interactive Journalism MA with a dedicated module on data journalism.

- Francis Irving – then a programmer with MySociety; main developer of FoI site WhatDoTheyKnow and later chief executive of Scraperwiki.

- Elena Egawhary – then completing the Newspaper Journalism course at City; later became BBC researcher on *Panorama* and *Newsnight*, and data trainer.

- James Anslow – then a lecturer on BA Journalism at City; later developed modules with a more digital focus.

- Mike Holderness – freelance journalist; ran training courses in online publishing and databases with the NUJ.

Also that summer, two university courses for postgraduates were preparing to welcome their first investigative journalism students. Both included the use of CAR techniques, and elements – such as data-mining or scraping – of what one might now call data journalism, and were led by experienced investigative journalists (Waterhouse 2011; O'Neill 2011a). At the University of Strathclyde, in Glasgow, Eamonn O'Neill set up an MSc Investigative Journalism after studying the development of courses at universities in the USA. Investigative classes had been "available on American campuses since at least the 1950s and possibly earlier" (O'Neill 2011b). The Investigative Journalism MA at City University London was run by Rosie Waterhouse, formerly with BBC *Newsnight* and *The Sunday Times*. She was able to build also on the teaching experience at City, including the CIJ and its director, Gavin MacFadyen; the investigations editor of the *Guardian*, David Leigh; David Lloyd, former head of news and current affairs at Channel Four, and Heather Brooke. While these two courses represented an important step in journalism education in UK universities, and were followed by a BA in Investigative Journalism at Lincoln, it would be misleading to suggest that investigative journalism had previously been absent from the curriculum.

At Sheffield, for example, Mark Hanna had developed an investigative module for journalism undergraduates, the first to include a requirement to use FoI (Hanna 2008). At City, some courses included investigative research techniques and FoI, and Leigh and MacFadyen had already run a specialist investigative option. But such developments were relatively recent; O'Neill suggests that the UK "did not offer investigative journalism classes until the mid-late 1990s" (2011b). An earlier Investigative Journalism MA, at Nottingham Trent University, had been launched in 1997 (Hanna 2000) but ran into difficulties. It ceased after a number of dissatisfied students left the course (Adams 2001).

More online, more open data
Journalism education was also reflecting the industry's shift to the web, with courses such as the Online Journalism MA started by Paul Bradshaw in 2009 at Birmingham City University. He had noted data's significance for journalists, and had been teaching students to use Yahoo Pipes to aggregate, filter, mash and map since 2006. By 2010 he was also teaching data journalism to established reporters and news organisations' trainees (Bradshaw 2013), and made an introduction to data part of the core MA journalism curriculum at City.

Did the timing help the later courses to fare better? FoI was becoming better established and continuing to help journalists break stories. It was also at the heart of one of the biggest stories of the period in 2009, on MPs' expenses, even though the core material was ultimately leaked before it was due to be released (with redactions) under FoI legislation.

The open data movement was gathering pace, too. Technology journalists Charles Arthur and Michael Cross had kicked off a "Free Our Data" campaign aimed at changing government policy (Arthur and Cross 2006). The data.gov.uk site eventually followed in January 2010, expanding to offer more than 9,000 datasets by October 2013. Spurred on also by the commercial possibilities, David Cameron made a series of commitments on open data after he became prime minister in May 2010 – complementing the momentum that FoI had provided for data journalism.

Although the MPs' expenses files were obtained electronically, it was not a database that the *Telegraph* obtained – it was a mass of PDF files. That meant the investigating journalists "could mostly still operate like old-style reporters", says Brooke (2013), cross-referencing names, addresses and other details – even if spreadsheets were involved (Winnett and Rayner 2009: 220).

Dealing with data from FoI requests had been an essential part of James Ball's route towards data journalism in 2007-2008, when he worked with Brooke as a student on the Investigative Journalism course at City:

> Lots of the early stuff I was doing was standardising FoI responses, getting them into a spreadsheet, and doing … doing everything the hard way actually, because I hadn't been taught lots of things that I would now do to make the process easier. … But this was before anyone was interested in data journalism (Ball 2013).

WikiLeaks – and a journalism MA goes interactive

In 2010, the year after MPs' expenses, and more significantly for data journalism, came the huge WikiLeaks releases of war logs from Iraq and Afghanistan, and of cables from US embassies around the world. "It was a big deal for us – and it also made newsrooms see data people differently," says Simon Rogers, who had launched the *Guardian*'s data blog the previous year (Rogers 2013b). Working on the war logs and cables also proved formative for Rogers' successor as data editor, Ball, first at the Bureau of Investigative Journalism and then at WikiLeaks (Ball 2013).

Ball was soon teaching his successors at City University London, first on the MA Investigative Journalism. Data experience from the course helped Conrad Quilty-Harper gain a job at the *Telegraph* in 2010, where he became interactive news editor. The next step in data journalism at City was the MA Interactive Journalism, which I set up in 2011. This included a separate module dedicated to data journalism, led by Ball and Bradshaw, with input from Rogers – at the same time as his team grappled with data from the August riots that took place in London and other cities.

The Interactive Journalism course now has its third cohort, 16-strong. Alumni from the previous two years have gone on to data work at *The Times* and *Sunday Times*, the *Guardian*, *Financial Times*, *Manchester Evening News*, at investigative site *Exaro* and on Trinity Mirror's data journalism team (set up in 2013 to work with its regional newspapers). The course also includes a specialist module on strategic social media, community and online engagement, and many alumni are working in this area, as well as in more traditional reporting or editing roles.

No longer an embarrassing reminder

A more comprehensive picture of data journalism as a developing theme in British journalism – alas beyond the scope of this chapter – would also need to take account of:

- training sessions run elsewhere (eg with Journalism.co.uk) by Bradshaw, Kevin Anderson (ex-*Guardian* and BBC) and others;
- work by the Open Data Institute and the Open Knowledge Foundation (OKF) (and its School of Data project), including efforts for more – and more accessible, reusable – open data;
- collaborative input from computer scientists and developers such as Tony Hirst of the Open University (and "data storyteller" at OKF);
- data-related services developed outside mainstream journalism, ranging from UpMyStreet, PlanningAlerts and OpenlyLocal to MySociety's FixMyStreet, GIS and mapping initiatives;
- interest in fact-checking and data-informed visual material in journalism;
- data in business/financial journalism, social media, sharing and analytics;
- closer cooperation between journalists and developers, the evolving Hacks/Hackers movement and the annual MozFest supported by the Mozilla Foundation;
- the development of data journalism across Europe, including the European Centre for Journalism's extensive work;
- free online resources, including MOOCs (massive open online courses) in data visualisation and data journalism;
- web-based services for scraping and coding (eg Scraperwiki), and for analysis and visualisation;
- data journalism at broadcasters, news agencies, magazines and specialist media;
- continued links with CAR and data journalists in the USA and beyond.

"The time has come to abandon 'computer assisted reporting'," Meyer asserted in 1999. "CAR is an embarrassing reminder that we are entering the 21st century as the only profession in which computer users feel the need to call attention to themselves" (1999: 4). It remains work in progress, draws on more diverse foundations and aspirations – and its prospects are flourishing. So is "data journalism" a worthy successor?

References

Adams, Catherine (2001) Inside story, *Guardian*, 13 March. Available online at http://www.theguardian.com/education/2001/mar/13/highereducation.uk, accessed on 30 October 2013

Arthur, Charles and Cross, Michael (2006) Give us back our crown jewels, *Guardian*, 9 March. Available online at http://www.theguardian.com/technology/2006/mar/09/education.epublic, accessed on 30 October 2013

Ball, James (2013) Interview with Jonathan Hewett, 25 October 2013, London

Bradshaw, Paul (2013) Interview with Jonathan Hewett, 14 October 2013, London

Brooke, Heather (2004) *Your Right to Know*, London: Pluto Press

Brooke, Heather (2006) Investigate! *Journalist*, August/September, National Union of Journalists. Available online at http://heatherbrooke.org/2006/article-future-of-investigative-reporting/, accessed on 27 October 2013

Brooke, Heather (2013) Interview with Jonathan Hewett, 18 October 2013, London

Centre for Investigative Journalism (2003) Programme for CIJ Summer School, 18-20 July 2003, London

Centre for Investigative Journalism (2007) Programme for Training the trainers: How to teach computer-assisted reporting, 23-25 July 2007, London

Chinoy, Ira (2010). *Battle of the Brains: Election-Night Forecasting at the Dawn of the Computer Age*. Dissertation, University of Maryland

Dasselaar, Arjan (2005) United Kingdom, Van Eijk, Dick (ed.) *Investigative Journalism in Europe*, Amsterdam: Vereniging van Onderzoeksjournalisten pp 213-226

Hanna, Mark (2000) British investigative journalism: protecting the continuity of talent through changing times. Paper presented to the International Association for Media and Communication Research, Singapore, 18 July

Hanna, Mark (2008) Universities as evangelists of the watchdog role: Teaching investigative journalism to undergraduates, De Burgh, Hugo (ed.) *Investigative Journalism*, Abingdon and New York: Routledge, third edition pp 157-173

Houston, Brant (1999) Changes in Attitudes, Changes in Latitudes, Paul, Nora (ed.) *When Nerds and Words Collide: Reflections on the Development of Computer Assisted Reporting*, St Petersburg, Florida: Poynter Institute for Media Studies pp 6-7

Houston, Brant (2003) *Computer Assisted Reporting: A Practical Guide*, Boston: Bedford/St Martin's, third edition

LaFleur, Jennifer (1999) Evangelizing for CAR, Paul, Nora (ed.) *When Nerds and Words Collide: Reflections on the Development of Computer Assisted Reporting*. St Petersburg, Florida: Poynter Institute for Media Studies pp 25-27

Meek, Colin (2005) Analysis: Computer-assisted reporting leaves UK journalists in the slow lane, Journalism.co.uk, 5 October. Available online at http://www.journalism.co.uk/news/analysis-computer-assisted-reporting-leaves-uk-journalists-in-the-slow-lane/s2/a51543/, accessed on 25 October 2013

Meyer, Philip (1973) *Precision Journalism: A Reporter's Introduction to Social Science Methods*, Bloomington and London: Indiana University Press

Meyer, Philip (1991) *The New Precision Journalism*, Bloomington and Indianapolis: Indiana University Press

Meyer, Philip (1999) The Future of CAR: Declare Victory and Get Out, Paul, Nora (ed.) *When Nerds and Words Collide: Reflections on the Development of Computer Assisted Reporting*. St Petersburg, Florida: Poynter Institute for Media Studies pp 4-5

O'Neill, Eamonn (2011a) Digging Deeper: Reflecting on the Development and Teaching of Investigative Journalism in a University Setting in the United Kingdom, Mair, John and Keeble, Richard Lance (eds) *Investigative Journalism: Dead or Alive?* Bury St Edmunds: Abramis pp 291-307

O'Neill, Eamonn (2011b) Written evidence, *The Future of Investigative Journalism*, London: House of Lords Select Committee on Communications pp 425-429

O'Neill, Sean and Brooke, Heather (2005) Prosecutors in dock over disparity in convictions, *The Times*, 23 November p. 6

O'Neill, Sean, Gibb, Frances and Brooke, Heather (2005) Justice by postcode: The lottery revealed, *The Times*, 23 November p. 1

Orlowski, Andrew (2007) Braindead obituarists hoaxed by Wikipedia: Only fools and journos, The Register, 3 October. Available online at http://www.theregister.co.uk/2007/10/03/wikipedia_obituary_cut_and_paste/, accessed on 30 October 2013

Paul, Nora (ed.) (1999). *When Nerds and Words Collide: Reflections on the Development of Computer Assisted Reporting*, St Petersburg, Florida: Poynter Institute for Media Studies

Rogers, Simon (2013a). *Facts are Sacred: The Power of Data*, London: Faber and Faber/Guardian Books

Rogers, Simon (2013b) Interview with Jonathan Hewett, 22 October 2013, San Francisco/London (via Skype)

Stabe, Martin (2013). Email exchange with Jonathan Hewett, 30 October 2013, London

Waterhouse, Rosie (2011). Can you Teach Investigative Journalism? Methods and Sources, Old and New, Mair, John and Keeble, Richard Lance (eds) *Investigative Journalism: Dead or Alive?* Bury St Edmunds: Abramis pp 284-290

Winnett, Robert and Rayner, Gordon (2011) *No Expenses Spared*, London: Random House

Note on the contributor

Jonathan Hewett is Director of Interactive and Newspaper Journalism at City University London. His research interests include social media, data journalism, and the teaching and learning of journalism. Jonathan has led and taught on journalism programmes since 1997. He welcomes suggestions, corrections and other constructive feedback, plus offers of help, funding, coffee and chocolate to J.C.Hewett@city.ac.uk or @jonhew.

Why data journalism is the new punk

Simon Rogers argues that data journalism draws on the great tradition of punk to celebrate the "anyone can do it" philosophy

This is a chord … this is another … this is a third. NOW FORM A BAND. So went the first issue of British punk fanzine, *Sideburns*, in 1977 in the "first and last part in a series". It might be 35 years old, but this will do nicely as a theory of data journalism in 2012. Why? Arguably punk was most important in its influence, encouraging kids in the suburbs to take up instruments, with little or no musical training. It represented a DIY ethos and a shake-up of the old established order. It was a change. Crucial to it was the idea: anyone can do it.

Is the same true of data journalism? Do you need to be part of a major news operation, working for a big media company to be a data journalist? Now is the time to examine this. In May 2010, we published a piece on how journalists would be flooded with a "tsunami of data". A few years on and data journalism is part of the fabric of what we, and many other news organisations do.

What is it? I would say data journalism incorporates such a wide range now of styles – from visualisation to long-form articles. The key thing they have in common is that they are based on numbers and statistics – and that they should aim to get a "story" from that data. The ultimate display of that story, be it words or graphics, is irrelevant, I think – it's more about the process. There are even different streams now – short-form, quick-and-dirty data visualisations of the kind we do every day on the Datablog, right through to complex investigations and visualisations such as our riots data analysis or the kind of projects which made the shortlist of the Data Journalism Awards, from around the world. So, can we still say that anyone can do data journalism; in the first and last part in a series. Would this work?

1) This is a dataset. 2) Here's another. 3) Here are some free tools. NOW BE A DATA JOURNALIST

OK, it lacks a certain 1976 grittiness, but the theory is there. You don't have to be a developer or a coder to be a data journalist. We asked our Twitter followers what they thought. A couple stand out to me: "Maybe everyone can do it, but not everyone can do it well." "Like so many other things, done well is a mix of art and science." Mutual disregard for shared constructs of authority? Shared overarching aim of revealing reality away from the facade? But is that enough? The thing about data journalism is that there are so very many "chords" – just the free ones could fill several training manuals: Google fusion tables, Tableau, Gephi, OutWit Hub, Google Refine … Can anyone really do it?

Dan Sinker knows about both data and punk: he heads up the Knight-Mozilla News Technology Partnership and is a former editor of Punk Planet. He says there are some parallels – with a crucial difference.

> While I agree with the premise – it's never been easier to do this stuff than it is right now – I think there are a few steps beyond just learning three chords when doing data journalism. For one, Legs [McNeil, who coined the word "punk"] didn't really say a band needed to be *good* but I'd like to think we'd require that for data journalism. The theory goes that the punk bands we remember best are the ones that were good – but there needed to be a whole lot of kids experimenting and sounding awful before they got there. For what it's worth, I like the fact that there are many just trying stuff out, even if it is forgettable – because some of it will be amazing.

Data journalism – the great leveller

In fact, data journalism is a great leveller. Many media groups are starting with as much prior knowledge and expertise as someone hacking away from their bedroom. Many have, until very recently, no idea where to start and great groups of journalists are still nervous of the spreadsheets they are increasingly confronted with. It's rare for the news site reader to find themselves as powerful as the news site editor, but that's where we are right now – and that power is only increasing as journalists come to rely more and more on their communities for engagement and stories. Says Sinker:

> Where I think there are more parallels are in the fact that this is a young community (in years if not always age), and one that's actively teaching itself new tricks every day. That same vitality and excitement that motivated punk, it's motivating news hackers right now.

Meanwhile, more and more news teams are discovering that data equals stories and bulking up their teams. Some would say it's just an extension of work they've always done, but that's to ignore the huge shift in power the web has created. "Some people think that this stuff is instant," says Sinker. "Even though there are incredible tools now, there is still a learning curve." Out there in the world, there are lots of people who have just formed a band and got on with it – despite the obstacles.

Take the data team at *La Nación*, recently shortlisted for the Data Journalism awards for their work on transport subsidies. When the team started, it was sparse, to say the least, says Florencia Coelho.

> We had no web programmer or CAR [computer assisted reporting] people in our newsroom. We gathered an interactive designer and we self taught Tableau with their free training videos in what we called our Tableau days, in a Starbucks at a shopping mall in Buenos Aires.

The team is still not exactly huge – but it is easily the best data journalism site in South America and one of the most innovative around. It's not all about investigative reporting. First, all reporting probably counts as investigative journalism, but if you want to play semantics, then I will see your "investigative" and raise you "analytical". Not all data journalism has to bring down the government – it's often enough for it to shine a light in corners that are less understood, to help us see the world a little clearer. And if that's not investigative, what is?

Democratisation of data

There's a great democratisation of data going on. Rather than the numbers belonging to the experts, they belong to all of us – and data journalism is part of that reclaiming of the facts. Even at the OECD, users' voices are part of the process, making up the core analysis that lies at the heart of the Better Life Index on wellbeing. And, just to be clear – data journalism doesn't have to mean data visualisation. It is not about producing charts or intricate graphics – the results of data journalism just happen to lend themselves to that. Sometimes a story is best told in images and infographics, other times it works as words and stories. It's the ultimate in flexible formats.

But, when it comes to visualisations, what really comes across from this analysis of Visual.lys most viral infographics is how sometimes the simplest things can flood the web. Single charts are likely successful because they are easy to consume; the viewer only needs to learn how to read one "chunk" of visualisation to get the whole story. Simplicity lends itself to quick understanding and sharing, whereas complexity can prevent a viewer from reaching those points. Curiously, mixed charts, which is what we commonly think of as the typical form of an infographic, is the least successful here, perhaps because they take more mental work to consume completely, again pointing to simplicity and brevity as strengths in visual communication.

As the post points out, however, sometimes things done messily can still be hits – it's the information that's vital. People are willing to forgive a lack of perfection; they are much less forgiving for those who get the facts wrong. Data visualisation experts will always say: allow the data to choose the visualisation, that it's crucial for the visualisation to fit the numbers – and not the other way around. That question equally applies itself to whether something needs a visualisation in the first place.

As Joe Strummer stressed: People can do anything

Of course, for some people, this will never be journalism. But then, who cares? While they are worrying about the definitions, the rest of us can just get on with it. Punk eventually turned into new wave, new wave into everyday pop and bands that just aren't as exciting. But what it did do is change the climate and the daily weather. Data journalism is doing that too. In the words of Joe Strummer: People can do anything.

Note on the contributor

Simon Rogers is Data Editor at Twitter in San Francisco. He was previously 15 years at the *Guardian* – and he created its Datablog. He is also the author of *Facts are Sacred* (Faber and Faber, 2013).

How does that affect me? Making data personally relevant for your audience

Bella Hurrell and John Walton report on ways in which interactive applications can be used creatively to provide audiences with a wealth of personal data – such as about their class background, pay, the Budget and the price they pay for fuel

Data journalism – broadly making stories from numbers – has been with us for some time. It comes in many forms: investigative reporting, data visualisation and Freedom of Information requests, to name but a few. But data journalism has another branch to it, one that is sometimes overlooked. For want of a better phrase we have decided to call it "personal relevance". It's a storytelling technique used by BBC News to give the online, TV and radio audience a way of finding out something interesting about themselves and their lives.

There's a cliché in journalism that "people like stories about people" but it's also true to say that people also really like stories about themselves. They like to know where they fit in compared with everyone else and luckily stories with large datasets behind them are providing journalists with more and more opportunities to thrust their audience into the heart of a story by showing them exactly that.

Why personal relevance?

There is a danger that as practitioners of data journalism we have a tendency to talk to each other about preferred ways of telling and presenting stories and by so doing we lose sight of the needs and desires of our audience. While our readers, users or viewers are interested in the stories that come from data, we know that some bar charts and other traditional visualisations can be a real turn-off for many of them. Traditional presentations can sometimes be more reminiscent of a school maths textbook rather than a way of providing engaging and interesting news coverage.

So we need to work hard to make our users care about the stories as much as we do. This is important because an ability to communicate numbers and statistics to our audience is a key part of the BBC's journalism. It would be very hard, if not impossible, to understand the modern world without being able to follow at least some of the stories that flow from the reams of statistics churned out by governments and businesses.

We have found that users care most when the story tells them something about themselves – hardly rocket science, you might say. But what we hope to do in this chapter is to show what we mean by personal relevance, and describe how we use this insight when putting together our graphics and our interactives. We will look at several case studies from projects that we, and our colleagues in the BBC's Visual Journalism team, have worked on which have helped our audience find out more about, among other things, their class background, pay, the Budget and the price they pay for fuel.

Budget calculator

The Budget calculator is one of our oldest calculators, the ancestor of personal relevance, and we have been producing a version every year for the past decade. It is always one of our most popular stories around the annual Budget coverage. It had a facelift in 2012, simplifying it and making the interface more appealing. This year we did a version designed to work on a mobile for the first time.

When we can show how much better or worse off an individual or household may be after the Budget, it can help people grasp how the news is affecting them directly. For instance, the Chancellor, George Osborne, unveils a plethora of numbers; millions of pounds here, billions of pounds there, statistic follows statistic in his speech to a boisterous House of Commons. He tells the gathered MPs about national growth forecasts, borrowing projections and departmental budgets, not forgetting inflation, fuel duty, National Insurance, income tax and corporation tax.

Of course, covering the fine detail of all these measures is extremely important for journalists and their audience but it can be hard for any of us to work out from these facts and figures, both negative and positive, exactly how we are going to be affected by the chancellor's plans. This is especially the case when rival politicians, think-tanks and commentators will all have their own particular verdict, typically conflicting, on the Budget – how do we pick the bones from that?

It's good to know if public spending is going up or down or to know if borrowing is stable – but concepts like these can feel a little abstract. Yet if you tell the calculator how much you drink, how much you smoke and how much you earn, in return you will get a pretty good insight into how many pounds the chancellor has put into, or taken out of, your pocket. What's more, for every figure you enter into the calculator, you will immediately get a figure back in return. It won't tell you how the rest of the nation is faring – that's the part of the story that the calculator isn't cut out for – but it will give everyone who uses it a helpful handhold as they attempt to grasp one of the most important and complicated political stories of the year.

Fuel price calculator

Moving on from the Budget, but still firmly focused on the pound in your pocket, is another personal relevance calculator, based this time on how much you spend to fill up your car. The price of fuel changes on an almost daily basis and it always generates news stories with substantial traffic and comments. So it dawned on us that a fuel price calculator seemed to have good potential as a new personal relevance app. We imagined a tool that could be used by our audience via their mobile phone at a petrol pump anywhere in the world to check how the price they were paying compared with the national average and to prices in other countries.

But we realised a one-off calculator would not be a good use of resources as it would very quickly look out of date when attached to subsequent news stories. So we needed something that was easily updateable – both in terms of sourcing the data and updating the tool. The first step after having an idea is to find out if the data exists. In an ideal world there would be one single, reliable, regularly updated international dataset, but that is often not the case. After researching available data we decided to go with nine sources (including local BBC correspondents) covering 35 countries, an EU average and nine US regions. Why so many different sources? We wanted a good spread of countries so it would appeal to our global users on our two international editions and those who would come to it through one of our 28 World Service language sites.

We also incorporated three varieties of tank size into the fuel calculations because people drive different cars in different countries. We had to combine the price data with currency conversion data as we wanted to use relevant currencies for each country. Depending on the story we also translate our interactives and tools into a number of different languages – so it needed to be built with this in mind too.

Building for mobiles

Crucial to the success of calculators or tools of this type is an attractive, intuitive design with a simple interface and a limited number of stages before the audience reach their goal. Instant feedback, as a user progresses, can also be a great hook to retain engagement and make sure that the user makes it all the way through to the end. The fuel price calculator was the first project of this type that we designed "responsively" from the outset. Responsive design is a term that means using one code base to develop content that then displays in the most appropriate way for your device, be it desktop, tablet or mobile.

In design terms, this means starting with mobile first and then moving up to the full desktop experience, while ensuring that nothing essential is left out of a mobile version. This approach has lengthened the design and development phases of all projects, and can present real headaches in terms of older browsers, but it is absolutely essential given how the audience is shifting to mobile in very large numbers.

Social media and sharing

What do we want our audience to get out of the fuel calculator? We want them to know how the price they pay compares with others. But "You pay 2p more a litre than the EU average" isn't that exciting, for most people. However, if you are told: "You're paying £5 more than average in your country to fill your car up or £75 more than you would in Venezuela," it helps put things into a more wallet-sized "how-does-it-affect-me-really" perspective. So central to each calculator is the surprising and informative key fact a user gets, telling them how they fit into the story.

The development of social media has given an additional dimension to this technique. We noticed a few years ago that users had begun independently to share this information about themselves on Facebook and Twitter. Now we actively build sharing into all our calculators, supplying a link back to the interactive feature, stimulating debate and boosting online reach.

Great British class calculator

It is a widely held, if slightly antiquated, belief that the British are obsessed with social class. However, the popularity of our next example, the Great British Class Calculator, would seem to suggest that this is as true today as it ever was. The idea for the project was based on the premise that the traditional divisions of upper, middle and working class seem out of date in the 21st century. So the BBC's Lab UK – a digital team enabling the BBC audience to take part in "citizen" science – teamed up with sociologists from the London School of Economics and Universities of York and Manchester to analyse the modern British class system. Together, they came up with a 140-question online survey that generated more than 161,000 responses from the public. It was from this huge mass of data that our calculator was constructed.

It asked the user five simple questions ranging from their annual income, to whether they owned property, to what kinds of people they socialised with including nurses, farm workers, teachers or scientists. The result put the user in one of seven social classes. Some are familiar, like the "established middle class" and "traditional working class". But there are also new ones such as the "precariat", the most deprived group, who live in old industrial areas, or "emergent service workers".

The calculator tapped into a not-so-secret British obsession about how we measure up to others, generating millions of page views and plenty of newspaper column inches and airtime both on radio and TV. In fact, a significant amount of traffic originated outside the UK, suggesting that interest in the concept of class has an international dimension too. The project also presented us with an opportunity to cover the story in a multi-platform way that was really useful for our audience. When covering the story in our main TV news bulletins at 6pm and 10pm, the BBC correspondent used the online calculator via an iPad while he was interviewing members of the public. So a wider TV audience – perhaps many who rarely used the news website – had their interest piqued and then went online to find out how they fitted into the story. The class calculator is the most shared story on the news site so far this year (2013) and in June it won a data journalism award at Global Editors Network, in the category of data driven apps. This tool is a powerful demonstration of how valuable it can be to harness the power of personal relevance. By making some academic research directly relevant to the whole of the UK population, it took the story to millions rather than the few thousand who might have read a straight story about new interpretations of class.

A different approach would have been to create interactive visualisations around the numbers of the UK population in each different class. But we had to make a choice about how we could tell the story best and we knew that a calculator or app would be the most effective approach for connecting with our audience.

At the other end of the scale

The examples of calculators we have given so far are all very complex projects. They involve large groups of people, sometimes from several different organisations, with a large variety of skillsets to help put them together. Sometimes a personal relevance calculator may require many calculations as well as an analysis of thousands or hundreds of thousands of responses to surveys, or the bringing together of diverse datasets from a variety of sources, to make them work. Although every web app is going to need input from developers, designers and journalists, it's important to bear in mind if you are planning to embark on a similar project that it does not have to be very complex to offer your audience something interesting and insightful. So, here's an example of something more low key. It's a project from 2012, called Where Are You on the Global Pay Scale?

In short, readers were given the chance to compare their own wages with the rest of the world, and see how they compared with everyone else. It was produced in conjunction with our colleagues from BBC Radio 4's *More or Less* programme. They sourced the data on average wages from the International Labour Organisation (ILO), who had done the heavy lifting in terms of gathering all the data together. From the reader it only demanded two pieces of information: their country and their salary. Having entered that they could immediately see if they came out ahead of the average in their own country and, perhaps most interestingly, how they fared in comparison with the rest of the world.

The visual device to show this was a simple bar chart, on top of which the user's own figure was displayed. It was a popular piece and if the responses to it on Twitter were anything to go by, it gave people a wider sense of what people earn in their own country, and around the world. Data was provided for more than 70 countries and, although this is by no means comprehensive, it did lengthen the lifespan of the project, definitely helped broaden its audience – and meant the story was picked up and passed on by people right across the world.

Who are the audience?

A data journalist's approach to reporting stories should be defined by the audience or readers they serve. The BBC News website works closely with the BBC's international and domestic TV and radio output with the ambition of telling data stories in a joined-up way across all output. We set out to make our content relevant and appealing to a domestic and international audience, as well as most age groups and a wide social and economic demographic.

We can't do this with every story, visualisation or interactive application of course but it is our aim to make our content easy to understand and appealing to the widest number of people possible. Other media organisations will have a different audience and the tone and complexity of their content will be different as a result.

The future of personal relevance

The BBC is by no means the only organisation to tell data stories in this way. An interactive feature long admired by the data team here is *The New York Times*'s The Jobless Rate for People Like You from 2009, a simple and engaging presentation of recession unemployment. The feature allows the reader to explore unemployment data, moving from a monolithic national rate of 8.6 per cent, towards discovering how "people like you" are affected. It enables the user to filter the data by age, sex and education level to reveal differential rates. So for female college graduates over 25, the figure is less than half of the national average, while the rate for black men under 24, who didn't finish high school, is nearly 50 per cent.

And recently, the interactive team at the *Guardian* produced a timely and effective personal relevance calculator, Climate Change – How hot will it get in my lifetime? Climate change is an important story that can sometimes struggle to attract the interest of the audience, since many may feel they have heard all the arguments already. The *Guardian* app breathed new life into the debate, engaging the audience in a way that traditional forms of coverage can sometimes struggle with.

It is likely that our audience will increasingly come to expect us to tell stories in this way, in the coming years. But that's not to say that personal relevance is the storytelling tool for every tale. It has its limits. It may make people aware of how an issue affects them, but it may not always present them with the wider picture of how other people, or the nation may be affected. In that sense these types of news apps are typically best used when they support or are supported by traditional news reporting. However, if we enable our audience to find out, rather than imagine, how stories affect them, they will be better placed to make sense of a busy and confusing world, and we will have done our jobs as data journalists.

References

BBC News: Budget calculator: How will the 2013 Budget affect you? Available online at http://www.bbc.co.uk/news/business-17442946

BBC News: Fuel price calculator: How much do you pay? Available online at http://www.bbc.co.uk/news/business-21238363

BBC News: Great British Class calculator: What class are you? Available online at http://www.bbc.co.uk/news/magazine-22000973

BBC News: Where Are You on the Global Pay Scale? Available online at http://www.bbc.co.uk/news/magazine-17543356

New York Times: The jobless rate for people like you. Available online at http://www.nytimes.com/interactive/2009/11/06/business/economy/unemployment-lines.html?_r=0

Guardian: Climate Change: How hot will it get in my lifetime? Available online at http://www.theguardian.com/environment/interactive/2013/sep/27/climate-change-how-hot-lifetime-interactive

Note on the contributors

Bella Hurrell is Assistant Editor of the BBC News Visual Journalism team. She has worked with designers, developers and journalists for a number of years creating interactive content, infographics and data visualisations. She started her career in journalism working in local TV and radio, joining the BBC as a researcher on its first election website in 1997. Since then she has held a range of editorial roles at BBC News Online.

John Walton is the editorial lead for the data team, which is part of the BBC's Visual Journalism department. He has worked in web interactives for over a dozen years. His interest in data began while producing election results coverage for the BBC News website. In 2010 he was a fellow on the Knight-Wallace journalism programme at the University of Michigan.

- The BBC News Visual Journalism team was set up in 2012 and is made up of TV and online designers, web developers and journalists. The team's purpose is to create compelling and shareable visual storytelling for BBC News across TV, desktop, tablets and mobiles.

In a decade or less, could not all reporters be required to be data literate?

As data journalism is growing in visibility across the world, Teodora Beleaga invites us to take a step back and examine what data journalism is and why we should care

Each year 82 million people pass through the Waterloo tube station in London. According to Transport for London (TfL),[1] this qualifies Waterloo as their busiest tube station. Stop. Read this again. Can you picture 82 million people in transit within the space of a tube station and across the time span of one calendar year? Are you able to dispute TfL's claim? Does it mean anything to you?[2] This is where data journalism comes into play.

From the moment we wake up to the moment we go back to sleep we are constant generators of streams and streams of data. Our world has been rewired both to ensure and accommodate this constant data generation process and its exponential growth. From a simple card payment, to the revelations by NSA contractor, Edward Snowden about the PRISM program for mass surveillance, our privacy is invaded to an extent it has never been before – and this is a given for our society. Who reads any of the terms and conditions we are prompted with when installing a new app, for example? The thinking is simple: "I want to see this, therefore I click OK."

In a recent debate organised by the *Guardian* in partnership with Adobe, marketers who routinely collect and analyse such data (Disclaimer: As a Digital Analyst, I analyse similar yet anonymised data on a daily basis.) were challenged by a privacy law specialist on the legalities of such practices. Their response was to direct this person politely to their company's legal department. The point being, we live in a culture where, unless prompted to the dangers of our data generation patterns, we are not concerned with how much personal and sensitive data we hand over to companies and institutions. Moreover, their analysts (disclaimer again, my day job) are not concerned with the sensitivity of the data they operate with. This is the job of the legal department. And, with the

Raw Data Now movement and the increasing release of data seen across disciplines over the past five years, it is also the job of the 21st century journalist.

For despite this sheer volume of data, as journalists it remains our duty to investigate and report it accurately using current and future technologies at hand. But how does journalism, a discipline closer to the study of linguistics, arts and social sciences, adapt itself to join mathematics, statistics and computer science in an attempt to tackle this immense world of Big Data?

What is data journalism?

Reduced to its most basic feature, data journalism, or data-driven journalism, as it is also referred to within the industry and the academy, is the practice of telling stories with data. As Simon Rogers, launch editor of the Data Blog at the *Guardian*, explained for Harvard's Nieman Journalism Lab: "It's using the numbers to get a story and to tell a story" (2010). Yet with endless data gathering, interrogation and analysis methods, with discipline overlaps across information visualisation, statistical modelling, and computer science to name but a few, and not to mention the even more recent emergence of the data scientist, it becomes very easy to get confused about what data journalism *actually* is. In the *Data Journalism Handbook*, Paul Bradshaw (2012) says:

> I could answer, simply, that [data journalism] is journalism done with data. But that doesn't help much [since] both "data" and "journalism" are troublesome terms. ... What makes data journalism different to the rest of journalism? Perhaps it is the new possibilities that open up when you combine the traditional "nose for news" and ability to tell a compelling story, with the sheer scale and range of digital information now available.

It already, then, follows that data journalism is as much about finding and delivering the news as it is about scientifically filtering it through the informational noise.

As such data journalism finds itself at the crossroads between the disciplines of reporting and computer science, which is one of the reasons why it is closely associated and even identified in some instances with CAR (Computer-Assisted Reporting). Liliana Bounegru explains how CAR overlaps with data journalism in her foreword to the *Data Journalism Handbook*: "[Some argue that] CAR is a technique for gathering and analysing data as a way of enhancing (usually investigative) reportage, whereas data journalism pays attention to the way that data sits within the whole journalistic workflow" (Bounegru et al 2012). A classic example is Caplan and Mayer's reading of the 1967 Detroit riots which "showed that, contrary to popular belief, there was no correlation between economic status or educational levels and propensity to riot" (Younge 2011).

This was one of the first instances when a computer was used to tell a story, as Meyer himself explains: "After our Detroit study was published, we found considerable variation in the interpretation of what we had done – for many journalists, it seemed our key contribution was using a computer to do journalism. That might seem odd if you can't remember a time when there were no personal computers" (2011). Therefore, despite being a data-driven example in the most practical sense that interview data was collected, imported and analysed (using a program written by the authors) to inform a story – that "police brutality, overcrowded living conditions, poor housing and lack of jobs" were the main riot drivers –*it* is remembered as one of the early, classic examples of CAR.

To flip the statement that data journalism finds itself at the crossroads between the disciplines of reporting and computer science, the following definition of data journalism reinforces the fundamental values of the fourth estate employed by its practice. "Data journalism is a form of rich media with an additional dimension: it implies a return to the factual, to the investigative. It's about interrogating the data, finding and formulating the relationships. Data Journalism is a tool of democracy," said French Professor Alain Joannés (2011: 44-45).[3] To give a local example, when WikiLeaks released the Iraq War Logs in October 2010, OWNI, a French non-profit media innovation company, created an app that allows users to analyse the logs, create their own data stories and also keep track of their analyses across all 483,201 documents. "For each entry, the site locates the event on a map, allows comments from account holders and provides links to news articles from the *Guardian* and *The New York Times* about the conflict published on the date of the report. It also allows people to gather points based on how many logs they analyse, adding a competitive aspect" (Goodman 2010). The democratisation of news is thus complete.

The data journalist: A Jack or Jill of all trades
Such complex undertakings, like the OWNI War Log Project, require skills beyond those typically asked of journalists. As Emily Bell, Director of the Tow Centre for Digital Journalism at the Columbia Journalism School in New York, explains in a special report on the future of media for the *Columbia Journalism Review*, "five years ago data journalism was a very niche activity conducted in just a handful of newsrooms," (2012) most of which belonged to the financial services market, including Reuters, Bloomberg and Dow Jones. Today, as data journalism goes mainstream, "to be a journalist who handles data can mean a variety of things, from being a statistics number cruncher or creative interaction designer to being a reporter who uses data skills … The roles are still emerging, but very rarely are there teams of information scientists and mathematicians sitting inside news organisations working out how to use these new resources for the best effect" (ibid). Yet, as the example above suggested, "as soon as you put a journalist, a programmer and a designer together amazing things can happen" (Bouchart 2012).

Furthermore, while Bell's assessment that roles are still emerging within the practice of data journalism holds true for newsrooms across the world, stories such as the simultaneous release of the Afghan War Logs by the *Guardian*, *New York Times* and *Der Spiegel* have inspired activist developers to turn to journalism.

A great example is the Hacks and Hackers grassroots movement. Under the motto "rebooting journalism"[4] Hacks and Hackers sees journalists and developers across the world joined together by a passion for the future of news. Adam Tinworth captured this distinct gathering on his blog following the one year anniversary meet-up of Hacks and Hackers London:

> The hackers are the real techies. They are the people who play with code and consider it fun. The journalists? They're just users of tools, not builders of them, looking for new ways of plying their trades with those new tools the hackers are creating. Most people in that room who are working journalists can't code their way out of a wet paper bag – myself included. But they are the sort of people who want journalism to keep moving forward, to keep pace with the digital revolution and find new ways of expressing itself (2011).

Fast-forward a couple of years and the journo-developer is already embedded among more traditional reporters in newsrooms across the world, with the *Guardian* and *The Times* in the UK being great examples of this practice and their interactive long-form stories of Firestorm[5] and My Year with Malala[6] being testimony to this.

Although they are just a year apart, and another year from the date this book is going to print, these accounts of both emerging roles and reporters working alongside developers could not be more distinct, for the requirement of data journalists today is increasingly close to Nate Silver type skills[7] – as a collection of data journalist job ads published by Toni Hirst on his blog relays (Note: All the ads below were posted in 2013.):

> You will be expected to combine a high degree of technical skill – in terms of finding, interrogating and visualising data – with more traditional journalistic skills, like recognising stories and producing content that is genuinely useful to consumers (*Trinity Mirror*).

> The ideal candidate will have experience with database management, data analysis and web application development. (We use Ruby for most of our server-side coding, but we're more interested in how you've solved problems with code than in the syntax you used to solve them.) Experience with the full lifecycle of a data project is vital, as the data journalist will be involved at every stage: discovering data resources, helping craft public records requests, managing data import and validation, designing queries and working with reporters and interactive designers to produce investigative stories and interactive graphics that engage readers while maintaining AP's standards of accuracy and integrity (*Associated Press*).

> Wrangling data is an everyday part of this job, so you are a bit of a ninja in Excel, SQL, Open Refine or a statistics package like Stata or R. You are conversant in HTML and CSS. In addition, you will be able to give

examples of other tools, languages or technologies you have applied to editing multimedia, organising data, or presenting maps and statistics online ... While you will primarily coordinate the production of interactive data visualisations, you will be an all-round online journalist willing and able to fulfil other roles, including podcast production, writing and editing blog posts, and posting to social media (*Financial Times*) (Hirst 2013).

Thus, from journo-developers to statistician journalists, the 2013 data journalist is in effect a Jack or Jill of all trades, bursting with reporting skills, knowledge of analysis techniques and coding experience. From scraping to building and designing, this data journalist has experimented with open data across the board, while also accumulating traditional shoe-leather reporting skills. Yet with the discipline itself still to fully hold its own, it is perhaps no wonder that data journalism roles emerge from such distinct areas.

So why should we care?

The *Data Journalism Handbook* includes a chapter on why data journalism is important. It features "leading [data journalism] practitioners and proponents" including Philip Meyer and Sir Tim Berners-Lee, whose accounts you can read below. Yet, as it is the case with many important subjects, such as global warming or nano-technology for example, is the underlying argument for their validity as a discipline a good enough reason for reporters to care?

> When information was scarce, most of our efforts were devoted to hunting and gathering. Now that information is abundant, processing is more important. We process at two levels: (1) analysis to bring sense and structure out of the never-ending flow of data and (2) presentation to get what's important and relevant into the consumer's head. Like science, data journalism discloses its methods and presents its findings in a way that can be verified by replication (Meyer 2012).

> Data-driven journalism is the future. Journalists need to be data-savvy. It used to be that you would get stories by chatting to people in bars, and it still might be that you'll do it that way some times. But now it's also going to be about poring over data and equipping yourself with the tools to analyse it and picking out what's interesting. And keeping it in perspective, helping people out by really seeing where it all fits together, and what's going on in the country (Berners-Lee 2012).

On a different note, Bell argues about the potential danger of an industry-wide failure should we refuse to recognise the importance of data journalism. "The industry shot itself in the foot 15 years ago by failing to recognize that search and information filtering would be a core challenge and opportunity for journalism," writes Bell. "This time, there is an awareness that data will be similarly significant, but once again the major innovations appear destined to come from outside the field" (2012). Furthermore, Bradshaw plays on the fourth estate argument of a journalist's duty to hold power to account by arguing for data as a key to serving such a purpose. "Data itself is increasingly the 'power' to be held to account, with journalists investigating its flaws, uses and abuses, and giving a voice to the data which is 'voiceless'" (Bradshaw 2013). As a result, much like the arguably still ongoing digital revolution the data revolution is set to transform newsrooms from the ground up.

Conclusion

In 1997 the BBC news website was created. Mike Smartt, creator and former Editor-in-Chief of BBC News Online, said: "Initially, in the BBC, the journalists rejected the idea for two reasons: (1) the money that was used to finance it was obviously coming from radio and television, so there was some resentment, and (2) the internet was seen, amongst the people in the more traditional media, as competition"[8] (2010). Additionally, the website was run by a handful of geeks sat in the back of the newsroom. Fast-forward 10 years and all BBC reporters are required to file copy online – the web is at the heart of the newsroom.

Could it then follow that, in a decade or less, all reporters will be required to be data literate? Will data be sat at the heart of each newsroom? And, if so, can we afford not to care?

Notes

[1]. See http://www.tfl.gov.uk/corporate/modesoftransport/londonunderground/1608.aspx

[2] What if you knew that the amount of people in transit over a year at Waterloo Tube Station equals the entire population of Germany, which incidentally is 1.3 times the entire population of the UK?

[3] Personal translation. Original text in French reads: "Le data journalisme appartient en rich media, avec une dimension supplémentaire: il implique une retour au factuel, a l'investigation. Il s'agit d'aller chercher de données, de trouver des relations, de mettre en forme. Le data journalisme est un outil de démocratisation"

[4] See http://hackshackers.com/about/, accessed on 11 October 2013

[5] See http://www.theguardian.com/world/interactive/2013/may/26/firestorm-bushfire-dunalley-holmes-family, accessed on 11 October 2013

[6] See http://features.thesundaytimes.co.uk/public/malala/, accessed on 11 October 2013

[7] Nate Silver is a statistician journalist who gained recognition during the November 2008 US Presidential Elections by accurately calculating the winners of 49 out of 50 states. He went on to accurately predict the November 2012 US Presidential Election and also the US Senate races. He currently heads his brand blog FiveThirtyEight at ESPN as Editor-in-Chief, having previously licensed the blog to *The New York Times*, where it was published as FiveThirtyEight: Nate Silver's Political Calculus

[8] http://teodorabeleaga.com/2010/05/04/73/, accessed on 11 October 2013

References

(2012) Why Is Data Journalism Important? Gray, Jonathan, Chambers, Lucy and Bounegru, Liliana (eds) *The Data Journalism Handbook*, O'Reilly Media. Available online at

http://datajournalismhandbook.org/1.0/en/introduction_2.html#sthash.e9uVDyRV.d
puf, accessed on 19 October 2013

Bell, Emily (2012) Journalism by numbers, *Columbia Journalism Review*, September.
Available online at
http://www.cjr.org/cover_story/journalism_by_numbers.php?page=all, accessed on 15
October 2013

Bouchart, Marianne (2012) Data Journalism Workshop, City University London, March.

Bounegru, Liliana (2012) Data Journalism in Perspective, Gray, Jonathan, Chambers,
Lucy and Bounegru, Liliana (eds) *The Data Journalism Handbook*, O'Reilly Media. Available
online at http://datajournalismhandbook.org/1.0/en/introduction_0.html, accessed on
15 October 2013

Bradshaw, Paul (2013) Ethics in Data Journalism: Automation, Feeds and a World
without Gatekeepers, Online Journalism Blog, 20 September. Available online at
http://onlinejournalismblog.wordpress.com/2013/09/20/ethics-in-data-journalism-
automation-feeds-and-a-world-without-gatekeepers/, accessed on 19 October 2013

Bradshaw, Paul (2012) What is Data Journalism? Gray, Jonathan, Chambers, Lucy and
Bounegru, Liliana (eds) *The Data Journalism Handbook*, O'Reilly Media. Available online at
http://datajournalismhandbook.org/1.0/en/introduction_0.html, accessed on 15
October 2013

Goodman, Emma (2010) WikiLeaks' Iraq War Logs: A Week On, Editors Weblog, 29
October. Available online at http://www.editorsweblog.org/2010/10/29/wikileaks-
iraq-war-logs-a-week-on, accessed on 17 October 2013

Hirst, Tony (2013) So what is a data journalist exactly? A view from the job ads ...,
OUseful Blog, 31 May. Available online at http://blog.ouseful.info/2013/05/31/data-
journalism-jobs-in-the-air/, accessed on 19 October 2013

Joannés, Alain (2011) Communiquer en rich media et data journalisme (trad.
Communicating in rich media and data journalism), *Archimag*, May pp 44-45

Meyer, Philip (2011) Riot theory is relative, *Guardian*, 9 December. Available online at
http://datajournalismhandbook.org/1.0/en/introduction_0.html, accessed on 17
October 2013

Smartt, Mike (2010) The Birth of Online News. Talk at Coventry University, May.

Tinworth, Adam (2011) Sex, Lies and the Tools of the Trade, One Man and His Blog,
25 August. Available online at
http://www.onemanandhisblog.com/archives/2011/08/sex_lies_and_the_tools_of_the
_trade.html, accessed on 19 October 2013

Younge, Gary (2011) The Detroit riots of 1967 hold some lessons for the UK, *Guardian*,
5 September. Available online at
http://www.theguardian.com/uk/2011/sep/05/detroit-riots-1967-lessons-uk, accessed
on 17 October 2013

Note on the contributor

Teodora Beleaga is a digital analyst at Edelman, the largest independent PR firm in the
world. Before that, she honed her data skills with leading direct marketing company,
Wunderman, part of the WPP group. She completed the prestigious MA in Interactive
Journalism at City University London, for which she was awarded the AHRC (Arts and

Humanities Research Council) Bursary in full. During her studies, she was attached to the *Guardian*'s Data Store where she secured a front page story within less than a week under the guidance of James Ball, currently the newspaper's Data Editor. In her spare time, Teodora volunteers for the Open Spending Blog at the Open Knowledge Foundation.

Section 2:
Tips from the experts on developing data journalism skills

Richard Lance Keeble

According to Paul Bradshaw, there are too many myths surrounding data journalism which are hindering its development. In the first chapter in this section – focusing on data journalism skills, he writes:

> Fear and hope are the engines of myth – and data journalism inspires both. It is a myth that data journalism is resource-intensive: data journalism can save resources. It is a myth that data journalism involves digging – it can just as equally be about reacting quickly to new information. And it is a myth that a data journalist needs to know everything from scraping to data visualisation: a data journalist is unlikely to fit the unhelpful stereotype of the lone investigative reporter.

In challenging those myths, Bradshaw highlights five elements of many data journalists' workflows that have nothing to do with technical skills, and everything to do with good organisation and basic editorial nous. "These are tips that make it more likely that data comes to you, allow you to react quicker to developing stories, avoid things that might slow you down, and produce better journalism that reaches more people with less effort."

Worried about all the jargon surrounding data journalism? Next Nicola Hughes reveals everything you really wanted to know about developing DJ skills – but were afraid to ask. She writes:

> A big part of a data journalist's job is equipping oneself with tools to clean, structure and analyse the primitive form of data eking out of crumbling

bureaucratic systems. Data provided by traditional sources are more often than not made for presentation: PDFs or Excel formats. It is not structured for analysis, visualisation or story-finding. So any journalist wading through the flood of data needs to be equipped with the necessary skills and tools for doing any or all of the above in a timely fashion.

This, she says, can involve using proprietary software such as Microsoft Excel or ABBYY FineReader, knowledge of freely available tools such as Google Fusion Tables and Open Refine or building solutions from scratch using code. "Each individual data journalist's toolbox will be individual, as will their idea of a data-driven story."

Increasingly, static representations of data are being superseded by interactive visualisations. Jacqui Taylor explains the science behind data infographics – and urges everyone to Go For It! Journalists, she argues, can augment all that they do with data visualisation by understanding the science of the human visual system. This will ensure that their designs are intuitive and compelling.

Daniel Ionescu, editor of the Lincolnite news site, next provides a speedy guide for journalists on finding data and tools for visualising it – with minimum coding skills required. Thus his overview includes the Government Data Portal and the Office of National Statistics – and a useful list of tools to assist visualisations and data mapping. Pupul Chatterjee follows on from this offering some tips on how to read data sets and work with them on transport-related stories.

Ændrew Rininsland, news developer at *The Times* and *Sunday Times*, ends this section arguing that anyone "willing to learn D3 will find they are given an unparalleled ability to create visualisations that bring data alive".

Data journalism workflow: Confronting the myths

Paul Bradshaw challenges some of the myths surrounding data journalism and provides some basic tips for reporters on how to develop their basic editorial nous

Fear and hope are the engines of myth – and data journalism inspires both. It is a myth that data journalism is resource-intensive: data journalism can save resources. It is a myth that data journalism involves digging – it can just as equally be about reacting quickly to new information. And it is a myth that a data journalist needs to know everything from scraping to data visualisation: a data journalist is unlikely to fit the unhelpful stereotype of the lone investigative reporter.

To address those myths I want to explain five elements of many data journalists' workflows that have nothing to do with technical skills, and everything to do with good organisation and basic editorial nous. These are tips that make it more likely that data comes to you, allow you to react quicker to developing stories, avoid things that might slow you down, and produce better journalism that reaches more people with less effort. They begin with newswires.

Set up data newswires

Most newsrooms take a newswire of some sort – national and international news from organisations such as the Press Association, Reuters, Associated Press, or others. These days most newsrooms also monitor social networks as secondary newswires: local tweets; updates from politicians, celebrities, experts or sportspeople. Data journalism is no exception. If you want to find stories in data, it helps to know what data is coming out, when it comes out.

You can find data newswires in all sorts of places. The most obvious is a national statistics agency such as the Office of National Statistics (ONS) in the UK. There are also international statistics bodies like Eurostat in the EU. Local, regional and national government and departments are another.

Regulators and auditing bodies, charities and nonprofits, professional bodies and unions, political parties and thinktanks all regularly collect data. Remember that many of these have agendas so if they won't let you look at the original data, or provide details on the methods used to gather it, then you should be sceptical and report that. Commercial research companies collect data for a range of clients, too.

Academic institutions and journals are another useful source of possible data alerts. Even if the data isn't published or you don't have access to the full journal it will give you an author name that you can chase up for more details.

The final two areas to look for data news are corporations and open data initiatives. Corporations gather data on their customers, market and performance. Some of this will be published in annual reports, but they are likely to be talking about other information in press releases and specialist trade press coverage. In the field of open data OpenSpending opens up spending data from dozens of countries around the world. OpenCorporates has data on millions of companies in jurisdictions from Abu Dhabi to Tanzania, and new projects are springing up all the time.

Be a librarian

Once you have your data newswires, you will start setting datasets which aren't necessarily newsworthy but which you think might come in useful later. You might also stumble across useful datasets as you pursue other stories. For example, you may find a dataset with the population of every local authority – this will be useful for any future story where you want to turn absolute numbers into the rate per person. Or you might find a dataset which gives the addresses of every GP surgery, or hospital, or school in a particular region or country. That's going to enable you to map those in a future story.

Unless you want to have to search for those things all over again – against a deadline – a good habit to develop is bookmarking that data effectively. Social bookmarking tools such as Delicious and Pinboard are ideal for this. Unlike bookmarking on your browser, you can access them from any computer, tablet or mobile phone. And also unlike traditional bookmarking, you can file them in multiple ways, using tags. And if you are willing to pay a few pounds per year, you can even use Pinboard to save a copy of bookmarked web pages which might later disappear.

When you use a social bookmarking tool you save web pages or online documents as you come across them, adding tags to help describe them. For example, you might tag one dataset with the words "data", "LA" (for local authorities), and "populations". You might tag another "data", "health", "GP" and "addresses". This tagging makes it very easier to find the data later when you need it. If you need data on housing you might go to your social bookmarking account and search for bookmarks tagged with both "housing" and "data". You can often create URLs that link to these too – on Delicious for example those bookmarks would be at delicious.com/yourusername/data+housing. On Pinboard they would be at pinboard.in/u:yourusername/t:data/t:housing. That also makes it easy to share links or background research with other people – although you can also make individual bookmarks private if you prefer.

Anticipate problems

A particularly useful habit of successful data journalists is to think ahead in the way you request data. For example, you might want to request basic datasets now that you think you will need in the future, such as demographic details for local patches. You might also want to request the "data dictionary" for key datasets. This lists all the fields used in a particular database. For example, did you know that the police have a database for storing descriptions of suspects? And that one of the fields is shoe size? That could make for quite a quirky story. Likewise, if you know that the gifts and hospitality register requires politicians to say whether they took a partner to a particular event that adds an extra angle you may not have considered.

Cost codes are another useful dataset to have. Birmingham City Council's monthly published data on spending, for example, includes which directorate made the payment, but also the cost centre code for each one. Knowing what they mean means you can get a much more specific idea of who spent the money and what it was for. You can also use that information to request further data. If you know the cost code for the mayor's travel expenses, for example, you might make a Freedom of Information for entries against that code, and so on.

Another problem you can try to anticipate is possible objections to a request that you might make. The Freedom of Information Act is full of exemptions for everything from confidentiality to official secrets. Some of these are absolute and cannot be argued, while others must meet a public interest test, or make a strong argument of potential harm. One very common exemption is that the information would cost too much to collect. If you think any of these exemptions might be used to refuse your request then try to anticipate them in your request. If you think cost might be raised, point out that they are obliged to help you rephrase the request to get it under the cost limit (for example, by narrowing the scope or time period covered).

If you think privacy issues might be raised, offer to have the data with names and identifying information removed (if that's not crucial to your story). If you think commercial interests might be an issue, read up on the official guidance on that exemption and remind them of their obligations under that (for example, they need to demonstrate the harm that might result), or suggest that they might still supply some of the information.

Heather Brooke's *Your Right to Know* (London: Pluto Press 2007, second edition) and Brendan Montague and Lucas Amin's *FoIA Without the Lawyer* (London: Centre for Investigative Journalism, 2012) are excellent reference books on these areas – but also look at the FoI requests being made on WhatDoTheyKnow.com and pick up tips from the good ones.

Lower the barriers to collaboration – and seek out collaborators

There is a cultural battle taking place in journalism right now between journalists who want to "own" a story, and the "open" culture of collaborative online networks. Data journalism – with its reliance on a range of skills –lends itself particularly to collaborative methods. The *Guardian*'s use of crowdsourcing to invite users to look at MPs' expenses; its use of a Flickr photo pool to allow designers to share their visualisations of data shared on the datablog; and its creation of an API which more than 8,000 web developers have registered to use are all examples of creating value by opening up assets which could never be fully exploited in-house.

Ask yourself how you might do the most with a particular data story. Can you publish the data the story is based on, and invite others to find things you might have missed? Or invite people to contribute their own visualisations? The more generous you are with your own resources, the more likely others are going to be generous with their skills and time.

Think about communities of people who might help you do better journalism. If you need data scraping, for example, the Scraperwiki mailing list is useful to follow and engage with. The NICAR-L mailing list is particularly useful for asking questions about computer assisted reporting, FoI and spreadsheets. If you are really geeky you can try contributing to the forums on StackOverflow.

Is there a statistician at a local university you can turn to when you are not sure of the validity of data? Do you have the contact details for the person who deals with data at the local fire service? Is there a non-government body that might be collecting data, like a charity, or academic? Contacts have always been vital in journalism, and data journalism is no different.

Think like a computer

The final workflow tip is all about efficiency. Computers deal with processes in a logical way, and good programming is often about completing processes in the simplest way possible. If you have any tasks that are repetitive, break them down and work out what patterns might allow you to do them more quickly – or for a computer to do them. For example, if you are cleaning some data what's the pattern in that process? Is there a way to automate that? Or is that a problem someone has already solved? Search for the problem and if there are tools that already tackle them. There is a tool called Mr People which will clean up names in a dataset.

Look for patterns in data to help you work with them. Codes might always begin with the same characters, or be the same length – that can help you sort them, clean them or understand them. Dates have a particular pattern; so do phone numbers and postcodes, web links and email addresses. Use that to your advantage. Scrapers (programs that comb web pages for data and store them in a form which allows you to ask it questions) take advantage of exactly the same patterns. If you see a series of web pages which display information in the same way then it should be possible to write a scraper which looks for that pattern and stores the information within it.

That pattern can range from the obvious structure of a webpage table, to a series of job listings that always have the job title in bold, and then the location in italics, and so on. In PDFs the pattern might be in the position of the information (always being in the same place on a page) to the way it is expressed (dates are always three pairs of digits separated by a slash; money is always a series of numbers preceded by a "£"; a relevant sentence might always contain a key phrase such as "ethnic minority" or "special educational needs").

If you are scraping a series of pages the structure might be in the web addresses too: in one case, detailed in my book *Scraping for Journalists* (see https://leanpub.com/scrapingforjournalists), I was able to scrape data on free school meals in Scottish schools because I noticed that the hundreds of web pages they were published on had exactly the same URL apart from a six-digit ID code at the end: find a list of those codes and you could cycle through them, adding each to the basic URL and scraping the information on it.

But finally, data often contains dozens of possible leads and stories, so be systematic and focused, and don't get distracted. Having flow charts and lists helps me in this regard. For example, my "inverted pyramid of data journalism" includes the following processes:

- Compile, Clean, Context, Combine, Communicate. That reminds me that for any story I need to compile the data, clean it, put it into context, combine it with other data, and then communicate the results.

- The second part of the pyramid – on communicating the story – involves six possibilities: Visualise, Narrate, Humanise, Personalise, Socialise, Utilise. The first three are traditional ways of telling stories in print and broadcast journalism. But the others are new: we can now create personalised stories ("How does the budget affect you?"); social stories ("Share your position in the world's population with your friends!"; "Help us find out what expenses your MP claimed"); and stories-as-tools ("Click here to generate an FoI request to find out more about this spending").

Another flow chart I created maps out the possible routes to compiling data: this ensures I don't miss any options in getting hold of the data I need – or writing a story about the lack of data itself.

Finally, a "chart chooser" by A Abela details the different types of story you might want to tell with data – and the relevant charts to go for. A story about composition ("50 per cent of charity money is going on marketing") is likely to be told with a pie chart or treemap. If it's over time ("Marketing spend has risen from 25 per cent to 50 per cent over the last three years") then a stacked area chart is a good choice.

Other types of stories might be about comparison ("Ambulance service staff have a much higher sick rate than other parts of the health service"), relationships ("Young black men are much more likely to be stopped and searched") or distribution ("These GP surgeries have prescription patterns which stick out as unusual compared with where most others lie").

Conclusion: The importance of thinking clearly about processes

These models, flow charts, heuristics, help you do jobs quickly. We often internalise them as we go about our jobs – but some professions, such as the health system, make them explicit to avoid missing key steps. Making them visible also helps you identify blind spots and think critically about your own processes. Ultimately, that's key – because we haven't yet worked out what best practice is. Having good workflow habits to begin with makes it much easier to find out.

Note on the contributor

Paul Bradshaw is a Visiting Professor at City University London, publishes the Online Journalism Blog and is the founder of the investigative journalism crowdsourcing site Help Me Investigate (shortlisted for 2010 Multimedia Publisher of the Year). He is described by *Press Gazette* as one of the country's "most influential journalism bloggers" and by the *Telegraph*'s Shane Richmond as "the UK's Jeff Jarvis". He also runs an MA at Birmingham City University.

A beginner's guide to data journalism and data mining/scraping

Worried about all that jargon surrounding data journalism? Here Nicola Hughes reveals everything you really wanted to know about developing DJ skills – but were afraid to ask

Journalism in the age of data

Journalists need to be data-savvy... [it's] going to be about poring over data and equipping yourself with the tools to analyse it and picking out what's interesting. And keeping it in perspective, helping people out by really seeing where it all fits together, and what's going on in the country (Sir Tim Berners-Lee, founder of the internet).[1]

The world wide web has disrupted many industries and the news industry is no exception. In the struggle to reformat news output for a digital age the internal structure of the organisation has somewhat lagged behind. The real internal disruptions appear to be from the creation of roles such as social media editor, newsroom developer and the data journalist.

So what is a data journalist? Using Tim Berners-Lee's definition, a data journalist is someone who pours over data, equipped with tools to analyse it and pick out what is interesting. Let's break this definition down so we can understand just how complex it can be. Data is information, not only numbers. Data is what all journalists have always worked with: court orders, police records, even press releases. The internet has allowed a steady stream of information to flow between networks of machines. Governments, in a drive for efficiency, have turned from paper to a digital output, making it easier for their data to be made accessible to our machines. However, all this does not mean the data made available is always useable.

A big part of a data journalist's job is equipping oneself with tools to clean, structure and analyse the primitive form of data eking out of crumbling bureaucratic systems. Data provided by traditional sources are more often than not made for presentation: PDFs or Excel formats. It is not structured for analysis, visualisation or story-finding. So any journalist wading through the flood of data needs to be equipped with the necessary skills and tools for doing any or all of the above in a timely fashion. This can involve using proprietary software such as Microsoft Excel or ABBYY FineReader, knowledge of freely available tools such as Google Fusion Tables and Open Refine or building solutions from scratch using code. Each individual data journalist's toolbox will be individual, as will their idea of a data-driven story.

Finding what is interesting in a tide of data is dependent on what set of data the journalist can access using the tools in his or her box. Because I code I can access datasets hundreds of millions of rows in size. Software can't do this so a journalist who does not code cannot either. What drives the data journalist is also the editorial priorities of the news organisation. Getting stories from data involves understanding what constitutes a good story. For some it may be an exploratory map, others want investigations to generate headlines, the more community savvy newsrooms might want to create a narrative around user-generated-content. Looking at all the combinations of data formats, tools and editorial directions you will not find two data journalists of the same ilk. In fact, looking across newsrooms, across print, web and broadcast, and across broadsheet and tabloid formats you will not find two data journalists who appear to be of the same species. To understand how this has evolved we need to look to ancestor of the data journalist: the computer-assisted-reporter.

Born in the USA

Data, before it was made sociable or leakable, was the beat of the computer-assisted-reporters (CAR). They date as far back as 1989 with the setting up of the National Institute for Computer-Assisted Reporting in the United States. Data-driven journalism and, indeed, CAR has been around long before social media, Web 2.0 and even the internet. One of the earliest examples of computer assisted reporting was in 1967, after riots in Detroit,[2] when Philip Meyer used survey research, analysed on a mainframe computer, to show that people who had attended college were equally likely to have rioted as were high school dropouts. This turned the public's attention to the pervasive racial discrimination in policing and housing in Detroit. Even today, the US is leading the way in digital journalism and data-driven story-telling.

For example, at the end of 2004, the then *Dallas Morning News* analysed the school test scores of the Texas Assessment of Knowledge and Skills and uncovered one school's alleged cheating on standardised tests. This then turned into a story on cheating across the state. The *Seattle Times*'s report in 2008, logging and landslides, revealed how a logging company was blatantly allowed to clear-cut unstable slopes. Not only did they produce an interactive but the beauty of data journalism (which is becoming a trend) is to write about how the investigation was uncovered using the requested data. Newspapers in the US are clearly beginning to realise data is a commodity for which you can buy trust from your consumer. The need for speed appears to be diminishing as social media gets there first, and viewers turn to the web for richer information. News in the sense of something new to you, is being condensed into 140 character alerts, newsletters, status updates and things that go bing on your mobile device. News companies are starting to think about news online as exploratory information that speaks to the individual (which is Web 2.0). They are no longer the gatekeepers of information but the providers of depth, understanding and meaning in an age where there is too much information.

Open data

The UK government launched its open data website, data.gov.uk, in September 2009. So what is meant exactly by "open data"? There is, in fact, an open definition for open data. It states:

> A piece of data or content is open if anyone is free to use, reuse, and redistribute it — subject only, at most, to the requirement to attribute and/or share-alike (Open Knowledge Foundation).

This appears to be more about online licensing and ownership than it has to do with journalism and at face value it does. However, the ideology behind reusing online data to build websites and utilities has championed developers and data enthusiasts to work with data and in many ways provide services akin to traditional media organisations.

MySociety was founded as far back as September 2003. Its mission is to "help people become more powerful in the civic and democratic parts of their lives, through digital means". They are responsible for the site TheyWorkForYou, which helps citizens find all the details regarding their local MP as well as how they voted on certain topics. They created an online space, WhatDoTheyKnow, for sending and viewing FoI requests. Both of these are useful to every journalist, not just a data journalist. The Open Knowledge Foundation began in May 2004 in Cambridge. It runs data portal software, CKAN, used by many governments for their open data projects and OpenSpending aims to track every government financial transaction across the world. They even run School of Data, a resource and courses to acquire tools to use data effectively. In September 2012, the Open Data Institute, founded by Sir Tim Berners-Lee and Professor Nigel Shadbolt, secured £10 million over five years from the UK government. It houses open data start-ups including OpenCorporates, a database of information on 60 million companies worldwide and counting.

The push to make data open, available and ultimately useful is being championed outside the UK newsroom. But maybe having inventors and developers at the forefront of open data will make data journalism easier to adopt within a newsroom. It also supplies a direct benefit to forward thinking newsrooms. The open data movement in the UK has fostered the interest of computer programmers in civic media and engagement. Being based mostly upon ideology, the conventional form of outreach is the "hack day" – pairing programmers and interested parties to create online tools. This has provided a base of self-taught and self-motivated individuals which newsrooms can hire to form digital teams focused on web input and output. Now you know a bit more about the term "data journalism", let's look at what it entails.

Computer assisted reporting

In a newsroom the data journalist will be considered the "numbers person". What is traditionally used for headlines and copy is a ranking; the worst performing hospitals, the most dangerous roads, the banks giving the biggest bonuses, etc. This is very simple to do using a filter, however it may not always be the right thing to do. Say, for example, we are looking at hospital deaths. An absolute number is not a measure of performance. If we get the top ten hospitals by the largest number of deaths we will be ranking the hospitals by number of patients with a bias towards hospitals that have specialist units for cancer, heart disease and other high mortality rate conditions. For comparisons sake we have to normalise by the total patients and also build an indicator depending on the mortality rate of the condition. Composite indicators are directly comparable and the government is responsible for calculating these. However, you should always read about how these are computed. If you are given absolute numbers then you can understand where there could be a ranking bias. Ask yourself: "Am I just measuring the total possible volume?" considering the total possible patients who could die, the total traffic on the road where there could be an accident, the total number of employees who could get a bonus.

Another aspect to consider is the distribution of the data. If the data is normally distributed then the top ten worst performers should be a certain distance away from the mean (three standard deviations in fact). So if the average mortality rate is 1.0 and the worst performers is 1.9 and the best performers is 0.1 then what you are seeing in the ranking of the worst performers is a performance relative to the variations expected. Someone is always going to perform "badly" when an indicator is calculated from performance within a system with natural variation. Thus the idea of shutting down hospitals which perform badly will mean we end up with only one hospital. If, however, your top ranking hospital for mortality rates was 4.0 and the second worse was 1.8 then just producing a ranking is missing the story. That hospital is a significant outlier and questions need to asked regarding its performance.

A spreadsheet-based piece of software can work out the normalised data, its ranking and its distribution. It cannot tell you when you need to normalise or look at the distribution. Computers assist reporters. It is still up to the data journalist to provide the understanding, pre- and post-analysis. A numbers person does not just know when to use a median and when to use a mean. The skill of a data journalist lies not in being able to make the calculation but knowing when one is needed. Computers do not interpret meaning, they do what you tell them whether it is sensible or not. It is the interpretation that makes a story. Whether you are writing or visualising a story based on data if you do not have the correct understanding the output will be deeply flawed.

Going native

Understanding basic statistics is a skill vital to any journalist working with data. Do not be intimidated by statistics. It is easier than you think. The two previous examples will get you a long way and there are many resources to help you get started. I would recommend reading *The Tiger That Isn't* (2007), by Michael Blastland, creator of the BBC Radio 4 programme *More or Less* and taking Statistics: Making Sense of Data taught by Toronto University (see http://www.topfreeclasses.com/course/7262/Statistics-Making-Sense-of-Data). As a data journalist, your understanding and sense of data is just as valuable as your abilities, if not more. A news organisation can always hire a statistician or a developer. A key role for a data journalist is knowing what is possible, generating ideas and knowing when to dig deeper.

I trained as a broadcast journalist and began my career as a digital producer at CNN International. I took the major (and somewhat crazy) step of leaving CNN to learn to code. I worked as a data journalism advocate for the UK start-up ScraperWiki. The role started in 2011 where I was first exposed to a HTML tag and the true contents of a webpage. That same year I won a competition held by the Mozilla Foundation and funded by the Knight Foundation to put forward-thinking digital communicators into newsrooms throughout the world. What came to be known as the OpenNews Fellowship awarded me a placement with the *Guardian* interactive team. After completing my fellowship I then got hired as a data journalist at *The Times*. I am now a developer/journalist, working with programmers, production editors and a statistician to bring the newspaper founded in 1785 into the digital future.

I wouldn't say computer programming is a necessary skill for a data journalist. It is however the most sought after skill in a newsroom and, as I found, the key to unlocking doors and getting your foot in. I would recommend anyone interested in becoming a data journalist to try your hand at it. I will spend the rest of this chapter expanding on the computer side of computer assisted reporting and explaining web scraping.

Before I start there are some caveats to my teaching. I am a Pythonist. My first coding language is Python. This is mostly due to the fact that the programmers at ScraperWiki are Python programmers. Coding languages are like languages derived from Latin, they all have structural similarities. There is no one easier than the other. The hardest one to learn is your first one. Once you are comfortable writing in one computer language, using another is a matter of translating syntax. Your decision as to which language to learn will be based on what you want to do with it. As with speaking languages, each computer language has its own culture behind it. In the next section I'll go through the jargon you will come across when you begin to learn to program and where each language fits in the newsroom.

Mining the web

First of all I am not a native web programmer. All of what I have learnt has been garnered from scraping information off a website and building some tools for demonstrations. So I will give you some basic knowledge from a journalistic point of view and some jargon which you might hear newsroom developers speak. So which end is which? One thing you will hear is front end and back end or client side and server side respectively. Very simply, these refer to what exists in the browser and what exists off the browser. Almost all newsroom developers will work client side and will code in JavaScript. JavaScript, HTML and CSS are all code native to the browser. HTML and CSS are mark-up and styling languages. They tell the browser what is a paragraph, what the font colour should be, etc. A browser interprets these to show you the webpage. All the actions you see such as drop-down menus and reveals plus interactives are almost always done in the native programming language JavaScript. If you are most interested in the visual side of data journalism then your language of choice is JavaScript and CSS.

If your interests lie more in database generation and analysis then you would be more of a back end data journalist. Your programming languages of choice would be either Python or Ruby plus the database query language SQL. Know that some news organisations have a preference and ask their programmers to use one or the other so if you have a target newsroom in mind check and see which language they prefer. The US started newsroom developing before the UK when Python was a popular language and so you will find more Python across the pond. Here you will find mostly Ruby houses. Ruby is more embedded in the web community having a web development package called Ruby on Rails. Python is more established in the scientific data community with lots of add-ons for machine learning and data analysis. Regardless of which of the two you choose they are both very similar and you can convert from one to the other with relative easy.

So what makes coding so powerful? The key to programming is that a lot of what you want to do has been done before. You are not building things from scratch but reusing code others have packaged for you. These are called libraries. A good analogy is apps for smartphones. A smartphone has very basic functions but become incredibly useful once you start installing apps. The same is true for coding and coding libraries. The basics are very basic but the power lies in using the libraries available. For instance, one of the scraping libraries in Python is called BeautifulSoup (Ruby has a library for scraping called Notogiri). Once you understand the syntax for using BeautifulSoup (like getting to know the navigation and functions in an app) you now have a new tool in your box that can be applied across the web. Libraries are built by the community of developers coding in that language and because JavaScript has a huge community there are tens of thousands of libraries. The one that set the data visualisation community buzzing is D3.js, the creator of which, Mike Bostock, went to work for *The New York Times*. Newsrooms are not just looking for writers *on* the web but builders *of* the web. They are beginning to realise that we can now build the medium for the message. Being able to write basic coding syntax and use a library will go a long way to understanding this shift in ideology.

Scraping a story together

If all data was open and all of the web structured correctly we would never need to scrape or send an FoI. We do not live in that utopia and probably never will but there are certain oases of well structured and freely available data which highlight the best case scenario for an overworked and underpaid data journalist. These are APIs. This stands for application programming interface and is a way for you to get direct access to information from a website. It involves making an "API call". This is usually in the form of an url structured in a certain way. Many popular APIs such as Twitter's require a key so they can limit the amount of calls one computer can make. Each site will have a simple way for getting keys and these are then added to the url for the API call. A good example of a well-structured, easy-to-use and journalistically useful API is the TheyWorkForYou API. Once you are understand JavaScript Object Notation (a series of one or more "lists" and "dictionaries") you can access all of the UK parliamentary information.

There is no easy solution to finding stories in data and there is no one way to becoming a data-driven journalist. I cannot teach you to program or to scrape a website in this book. Journalism is more a craft than an academic endeavour. The same can arguably be said for software engineering. You need to learn by experimentation and determination. All you the hardware you need is a computer. But like all good journalists looking to find something out you need to get away from your desk, find the right people and ask the right questions. If you would like to know more stop reading, go online and find your nearest HacksHacker meet-up, find every resource for learning your chosen language, find their meet-up, follow people building what you want to build and telling the type of stories you want to tell on Twitter. When you get stuck Google it, look on StackOverflow and tweet out. Even if you are not coding listen out for new tools in all the same spaces, especially School of Data and Data Driven Journalism. Never stop looking because you can never stop learning.

Conclusions: The great value of data-driven journalism

The area of data journalism provides journalists with a wonderful opportunity. A data journalist's value is based on analysis and exploring new areas of information within the timeframe of a newsroom cycle. It is bringing back the investigative side of journalism and marrying traditional journalistic outputs with the world wide web. This allows the data journalist to explore new avenues for story gathering and push the news output towards creative, multi-layered storytelling.

Data journalism is a role deeply involved with editorial and yet just as enmeshed with digital production and output. It is an exceedingly challenging role but to make a difference one has to expect to do things differently.

Note

[1] See
http://www.ted.com/talks/tim_berners_lee_the_year_open_data_went_worldwide.htm,
accessed on 30 October 2013

Note on the contributor

Nicola Hughes is a programmer-journalist, specialising in uncovering, structuring and analysing datasets for investigative news content. She worked at CNN International as a digital media producer, leaving her role to learn to code with tech startup ScraperWiki. She then became a Knight-Mozilla OpenNews fellow is 2012 where she was embedded at the *Guardian* interactive team. She has learnt to scrape and parse data in Python, manage databases using MySQL and display information online using JavaScript. She is currently working as a data journalist for The Times Newspapers Limited.

Data visualisation: Now for the science

Increasingly, static representations of data are being superseded by interactive visualisations. Here Jacqui Taylor explains the science behind data visualisations – and urges everyone to Go For It!

Not a day goes by without me seeing another data visualisation (or infographic if you prefer, I treat the two definitions as interchangeable) telling a story based on data. I'm aware that the sceptics exist, that their view is "this is just another pretty picture", and I assume if you hold that view you are already irritated by the title of this chapter.

Data journalism came into my world by accident: I'm a web scientist and had no previous experience of dealing with the heady world of journalism. Sometimes the happy accidents of life bring great rewards. At a data conference I was fortunate to meet Simon Rogers, who was at the time Editor of the "newish" *Guardian* Data Blog, and as all good data folks do we talked about possibilities. I offered to help out *pro bono* the next time he had a challenging dataset he needed to visualise and thus began the journey.

Two years on, we have created many key data visualisations for the *Guardian*, although arguably the most important one was the first. We visualised the "Human cost of 10 years of war in Afghanistan" by mapping every death using data provided by WikiLeaks. Even at the time we were all aware we were at the beginning of a new journey for data. I remember we discussed whether anyone would understand what we had presented and whether the essential story in the data would be communicated. The response we received stunned us all: millions of people around the world interacted with the visualisation and it proved to be very sticky, with people spending on average between 8-10 minutes with the data. This is a screenshot of the visualisation.

10 years of war in Afghanistan - the human cost

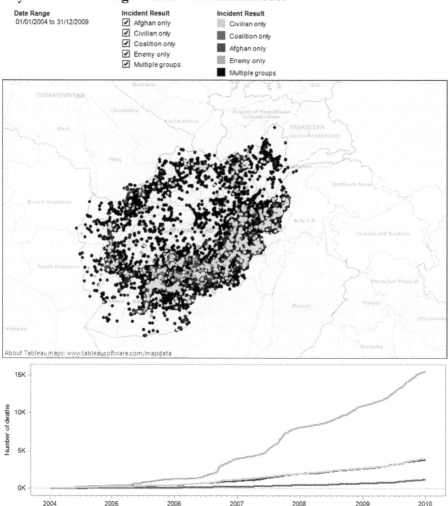

The grey scale image is a poor reflection of the interactive visualisation which captured people's imagination. The interactive live visualisation is available online at http://public.tableausoftware.com/views/AfghanistanDeaths02/DeathsinAfgh anistan. Even in this grey scale version, the deaths in the south of the country and the impact of the landmines on the "road to Basra" can be clearly seen, a major factor in the death toll.

Looking to the future of data journalism

Today, I don't have to persuade any student of journalism that they should have some basic data skills and ensure that they include a data specialist as a key contact to bounce ideas off. These are now essential supplementary skills in the journalistic world. Indeed, I expect that specialist teams like those who create the *Guardian* Data Blog will be a fixture of any media organisation as we move towards more evidence-based journalism. The value created by matching top flight journalism skills and evidencing the resulting stories has not yet been fully realised. We currently only have just over 20 per cent of the world's population online: this is set to rise to more than 80 per cent in the next few years. The result of this huge rise in potential audience and the engagement possible from utilising interactive visualisations is a largely untapped market.

What most people are unaware of is that the basic science related to our human interaction with visuals is incorporated during the design of the visualisation. Certainly, this the foundation of the way we at FlyingBinary build our data visualisations. From the beginning, and on an ongoing basis where we embed our visualisations on the web, we have put our cloud platforms to work analysing how we can refine the science to ensure the interactivity is the most compelling for our audience. Evidencing journalism is becoming a key way of further enforcing the message we are articulating and increasingly static representations of data are being superseded by interactive visualisation.

Impact of the generations
Currently Generation X (the baby boomers) are in a dominant position of leadership in our media organisations. However, this will change over the next five years as Generation Y become predominant in our workforce. Generation Y (or as they are sometimes known, the Millennials) are a highly visual generation and are increasingly comfortable with the use of visual presentations to present facts or data. As a result of this the science behind visualisation becomes ever more important.

From a future viewpoint it is important to consider the increasing Generation Z audience (those born after 1993). They also have key visual abilities but these are combined with kinaesthetic (movement, touch) capabilities. This audience shift will require us all to make increasing use of interactive visualisation capabilities in order that we serve this generation in a way which harnesses their biological capabilities. There are those of us who already know of the need to move from static visualisations to interactive visualisations to meet the needs (or more likely demands) of this new audience. We made this change at FlyingBinary two years ago, and have found that the science we apply to visualisations had to be updated to reflect the needs of this new audience.

We teach the Science of Data Visualisation as a one-day workshop as part of a series of training modules to develop the capabilities needed to ensure that the work produced is compelling for the newer audiences. I have chosen to outline in this chapter the science behind the work we do to reflect the needs of the Generation Z. A Generation Z audience has the combination of visual and kinesthetic skills and this has required us to revamp the essential training we give in these workshops. The links to the interactive visualisations are examples of the combination of visual and kinesthetic visualisations designed to engage with

Generation Z. At the moment many visualisations are serving up static capability and if you measure your audience engagement you will be able to track the data as it begins to decline. However, I recommend that you move to interactive visualisations now and capture the increasing new audience as well.

Introducing web science

The first science we apply is web science. It is unlikely that most of the readers will be familiar with this new discipline which was created just over four years ago by the original web scientist, Sir Tim Berners-Lee. Web science draws on existing areas of study, but requires new scientific methods and techniques to be developed. The web's diverse nature means that it has to be able to be considered from a broad range of perspectives both independently and in unison; for this reason, web science is an interdisciplinary subject that draws on many different academic areas.

Nothing like the web has ever happened in all of human history. The scale of its impact and the rate of its adoption are unparalleled. This is a great opportunity as well as an obligation. All of the data visualisations we develop are designed to be web-enabled whether or not they are eventually deployed on the web. When Sir Tim Berners-Lee appeared in the opening ceremony of the 2012 Olympics Games in London, our web science message was signalled around the Olympic Stadium: "It's for Everyone." This is another reason why the move to interactive visualisations is key: web science aims to be inclusive. The most flexible way of ensuring that this ideal is met is by using some key design principles to support the development of our data visualisations.

Understanding cultural differences

We use our social intelligence Big Data platform to understand audiences beyond our current reach. It is this work which has highlighted differences in the engagement of audiences with our visualisations, in particular geographies. Whilst this does not relate to the specific science we use to visualise data, it does underline important cultural differences we have found across the world which require us to design visualisations which translate across the cultures. However, there is a key cultural difference which needs to be decided upon at the outline design stage.

It is important to decide whether your main audience is likely to be in the West or East. In the West we read from left to right in contrast to the East where right to left is the norm. Essentially the design needs to consider which audience is targeted. In the detailed science I will explain why it is important to organise the data story to be on one page. With a single visualisation this is easy; however, multiple visualisations need to be positioned with panes on the screen using a left, right and top down sequence. This allows a Western user to follow the story you are relating intuitively.

Visualisation design principles

We often get questions on our data visualisation courses about how to decide how much data to present. Ultimately, you are looking to produce an intuitive design for a user who has no prior domain knowledge of the subject. We will aim to produce an uncluttered visualisation, minus any bling, with a "less is more" philosophy. However, it is important to recognise that some users will need additional support to assimilate the data story.

When you use interactive visualisations you can optimise the user experience by adopting a progressive reveal technique. This allows you to showcase the data story in stages rather like the traditional journalism techniques applied to data: headline, byline, body text etc. Additionally what this also does is make the engagement with the interactive visualisation very sticky, on average 8-10 minutes for our web facing visualisations. The "stickiness" of these visualisations is a direct result of giving the user the ability to explore the data in this way. A number of companies are pioneering this feature to drive traffic and, therefore, revenue through their websites. It is expected that as we move to an ever more open and social engagement model this will move beyond the early adopters and become the pervasive method of user engagement.

Impact of the human visual system

In the meantime there are a number of techniques you can use when designing your interactive visualisations which utilise the basics of our human biology to make them more intuitive and, therefore, more compelling. Our vision is by far our most powerful sense: approximately 70 per cent of the receptors in our body are related to our vision system. Given that Generation Y and Z both demonstrate high visual abilities, we can maximise the impact of visualisations by designing and displaying data in the most impactful way for these users.

The human visual system is able to discern patterns in a most powerful way. We use the combination of the power of our eyes to perceive those patterns and interpret them via the brain. This uses a key set of rules which ensures that we can unlock the power of data presented via a massively parallel process. This is a complex subject; however, an understanding of the basics of visual perception can transform the impact of a visualisation. If we do not engage our audience using the power of visual perception we run the risk of our message not being communicated. This is best illustrated:

```
3 2 4 5 0 7 6 8 9 4 3 0 1 2 3 4 5 9 8 7 6 4 5 6 7 0 9 2 3 4 5 6 7 8 7 2 4 3 6 3
7 8 2 0 2 4 4 5 0 0 2 2 4 6 5 8 9 4 3 0 1 2 3 4 5 4 8 7 6 4 9 8 7 6 4 5 6 7 3 2
3 0 1 2 3 4 5 4 8 7 6 4 9 5 6 7 0 2 3 4 5 6 7 8 1 2 4 3 6 7 8 5 0 8 4 4 5 0 0 2
2 4 6 5 8 1 3 2 4 5 0 7 6 3 2 4 5 0 7 6 8 3 4 3 0 1 2 3 4 5 2 8 7 6 4 5 6 7 0 5
2 3 4 5 6 7 8 9 2 4 4 3 0 1 2 3 4 5 3 3 8 7 6 4 5 6 7 0 9 1 6 7 0 2 3 9 5 6 7 8 1
2 4 3 6 7 8 5 0 8 4 4 5 0 0 2 2 4 6 5 8 3 2 4 5 0 7 6 8 3 9 3 0 1 2 3 4 5 2 8 7
```

As quickly as possible count the number of 9s which appear in the table of numbers above. I expect this took quite some time as attentive processing is slow because we carry out the task sequentially. How many 9s did you count? By contrast if I asked you to count the number of 9s in the table below you will likely get the correct answer very quickly.

3 2 4 5 0 7 6 8 **9** 4 3 0 1 2 3 4 5 **9** 8 7 6 4 5 6 7 0 **9** 2 3 4 5 6 7 8 7 2 4 3 6 3
7 8 2 0 2 4 4 5 0 0 2 2 4 6 5 8 **9** 4 3 0 1 2 3 4 5 4 8 7 6 4 **9** 8 7 6 4 5 6 7 3 2
3 0 1 2 3 4 5 4 8 7 6 4 **9** 5 6 7 0 2 3 4 5 6 7 8 1 2 4 3 6 7 8 5 0 8 4 4 5 0 0 2
2 4 6 5 8 1 3 2 4 5 0 7 6 3 2 4 5 0 7 6 8 3 4 3 0 1 2 3 4 5 2 8 7 6 4 5 6 7 0 5
2 3 4 5 6 7 8 **9** 2 4 4 3 0 1 2 3 4 5 3 8 7 6 4 5 6 7 0 **9** 1 6 7 0 2 3 **9** 5 6 7 8 1
2 4 3 6 7 8 5 0 8 4 4 5 0 0 2 2 4 6 5 8 3 2 4 5 0 7 6 8 3 **9** 3 0 1 2 3 4 5 2 8 7

How did you do? I expect you found this quite quick to do and by contrast with the first list of numbers you got the right answer. In both lists there are ten 9s. This second list was much easier because you used the visual perception functions of your visual system. Numbers to our visual system are just a series of squiggles whereas if we colour a particular number (in this case all the 9s) our brain can process the black 9s separately from all the other numbers coloured grey. This is called preattentive cognition.

Maximising preattentive cognition
In the field of visual science there are 17 preattentive cognition attributes but we can group these into categories: Colour, Position, Form and Motion. It would require an all-day workshop to understand how best to use all these categories in your visualisation design (and more particularly why). However, there are some key attributes which we use regularly in our work and I will focus on these. This is arbitrary distinction but will allow me to describe some of the basics of the science and work within the limits of a single chapter of this book.

We are all familiar with the use of size and position to encode data; for example, the use of line and bar charts to represent data visually. So I intend to cover how to encode data correctly with area, colour and shape to maximise the impact of your visualisations. I will explain this in the context of quantitative, ordinal and nominal data to ensure that the different treatment of each data type is explained in detail. I am limited to grey scale only images for this book. The reader should assume colour encoding for all examples unless explicitly stated.

Firstly we will look at data we are most familiar with when we are looking to visualise data, quantitative data, a set of numbers, for example: 1, 2, 3, 4, 5 or 3.2, 5.1, 6.0, 7.1, 9.9

Encoding quantitative data using area. I have used 8 circles to represent a large set of values. We are typically interested in general comparisons rather than exact distinctions, so a large range of sizes is acceptable, with no practical limit.

Encoding quantitative data using a colour ramp. I have used a continuously varying shades of a single colour to represent the full range of values being visualised. We are typically interested in general comparisons rather than exact distinctions.

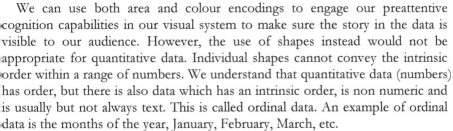

We can use both area and colour encodings to engage our preattentive cognition capabilities in our visual system to make sure the story in the data is visible to our audience. However, the use of shapes instead would not be appropriate for quantitative data. Individual shapes cannot convey the intrinsic order within a range of numbers. We understand that quantitative data (numbers) has order, but there is also data which has an intrinsic order, is non numeric and is usually but not always text. This is called ordinal data. An example of ordinal data is the months of the year, January, February, March, etc.

Again we can use both area and colour encodings although for ordinal data it is important to be able to distinguish clearly the different values of the encoded data. So for these reasons we use a smaller range of sizes for comparison purposes.

Encoding ordinal data using area. I have used four circles here but we have a practical limit of 5 circles to compare the area of the circles easily.

Encoding ordinal data using colour. I have used a palette of four shades of one colour to compare ordinal data for the same comparison reasons we use with area.

Finally for this chapter we will look at how we can best represent nominal data to ensure we are using the power of the human visual system. This last type of data is non numeric data with no intrinsic order, for example: apple, orange, blackberry and raspberry. For nominal data it is inappropriate to encode data using area because the size of the area would imply an order where none exists. We can, however, use colour as a method of choice to encode this data, but now we use the actual colour rather than the shade.

Encoding nominal data using colour. I have used a palette of eight colours which has a practical limit of ten colours.

Nominal data is an example of where shapes can be utilised for our visual perception to be utilised, as simple shapes can be pre attentively perceived in a way that complex shapes (e.g. numbers) cannot.

Encoding ordinal data using shape. I have used eight different shapes and whilst there is no practical limit to the number of shapes you can use, it is important to ensure that the shapes are sufficiently distinct to enable visual differences to be discerned.

Having done a quick tour of the encodings to use with different data types. I think that you will find it useful for your data visualisation work to have a list of the top three encodings for each of the types of data we have already considered. This gives a basic guide on the best choices to make to ensure you are maximising the capabilities of human visual perception when designing your visualisation.

Quantitative data: Top three encoding choices

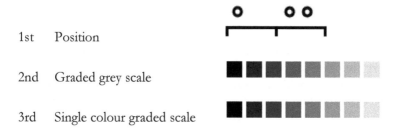

1st   Position

2nd   Length

3rd   Angle

Ordinal data: Top three encoding choices

1st   Position

2nd   Graded grey scale

3rd   Single colour graded scale

Nominal data: Top three encoding choices

1st   Position

2nd   Shape

3rd   Colour palette

As you can see in all three cases position is our number one choice for encoding data to harness the power of our visual perception. We should make different choices in our design if we have to use a second and/or third encoding, dependent on which type of data we are visualising.

Understanding short-term memory
I have dealt in some depth on visual perception which is linked to the iconic memory of our brain where the processing of what we see occurs. However, we also use both short term and long term memory when processing visual information. There are some key issues with our short term memory which we should take into account when designing interactive visualisations.

- It is limited in the information it can store.

- Only a portion is dedicated to visual memory.

- It is temporary storage.

We can only store about three chunks of information in our short term memory at any one time. Individual numbers in a table may constitute a chunk of memory, whereas a pattern of numbers represented graphically (e.g. by a bar on chart) can convey many numbers in one chunk. Whilst the good design principles we have already discussed are key to ensure an intuitive visualisation, an understanding of the limits of short term memory can be equally important when designing great interactive visualisations.

It is important to present related data as a set of data visualisations on a single page/screen, commonly called a dashboard. The dashboard allows the user to understand the related data stories, with no need to rely on their short term memory to process the data. Where possible group the detailed data into particular segments of the dashboard. This will allow the user to interact with the detailed components of the data story in an exploratory manner in a sequence which is most important to them. When you arrange data on a dashboard within a user's vision that data can be processed and understood extremely quickly.

An example of where this is done well is the roadmap we designed for the UK Open Data User Group, of which I'm a member, to showcase a new type of Open Data, demand led Open Data. This visualisation shows the engagement with the data community requesting government data to aid their work, research or interests.

As before, the grey scale limits the visual impact of the interactive visualisation we built. You can get the best appreciation with the online version at http://www.tableausoftware.com/public/gallery/open-data-request.

Open data request roadmap

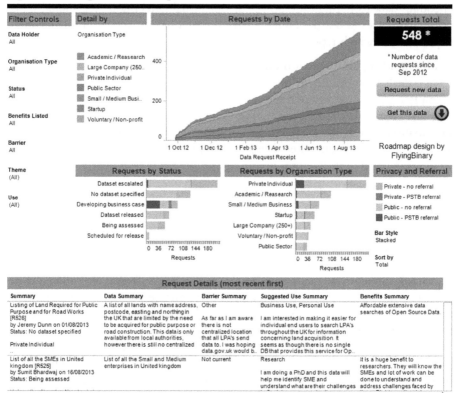

This visualisation has equally served interested citizens across the globe, not just the UK, with more than 5,000 views of the dashboard, and has profiled 548 requests for government data at the time of writing. It also provides a transparent view of the process of government, which we believe to be a world first.

The use of data as evidence for journalists to amplify their work has created a new communication medium. Data is a language which only a few will learn but we can use data visualisation to communicate this language of data to a global audience. However, we can augment all that we do with data visualisation by understanding the science of the human visual system. This will ensure that our designs are intuitive and compelling. I encourage you all to Go Viz!

Note on the contributor

Jacqui Taylor has 25 years of implementing technology across the world. She co-founded FlyingBinary after implementing a banking regulatory change programme. An appointment to the Open Data User Group recognised her as a web scientist of influence in the era of Big Data. A data innovator for smart city initiatives signals the next steps for her company and the Internet of Things which will transform all our daily lives. Jacqui trains advanced analysts on the science of data visualisation and is a regular speaker on cloud adoption, big data, smarter analytics and profiting from the web.

Sources and tools for data journalism

A speedy guide for journalists on finding data and tools for visualising it – with minimum coding skills required. By Daniel Ionescu

Government Data Portal

The central repository of public data relating to the UK is the HM Government Data Portal,[1] which hosts more than 10,000 datasets from all central government departments, as well as a range of public sector bodies and local authorities across the country. Most of the data available is free to download and use, and it is released under an Open Government Licence (OGL).[2] The OGL encourages the use, adaptation and re-use of information available under this type of licence, with the condition of acknowledging the source of the information, along with any attribution statement specified by the individual provider. When using multiple sources, a general acknowledgement of public data is acceptable. The rule of thumb is that if possible, and space allows it, a written notice or a link with credit is recommended when datasets are used in a visualisation or chart.

The main publishing body on the Government Data Portal is the Office for National Statistics (ONS, discussed separately). The Department for Communities and Local Government shares a range of useful datasets, some with historical data, relating to indices of deprivation in England, national housing stock, the housing market and house prices, together with household population projections, among others. The NHS Information Centre for Health and Social Care is another major publisher, with data on health surveys for England, Accident and Emergency attendance rates, obesity statistics, NHS dental activity, statistics on smoking, drinking and drug use, maternity and GPs. The Environment Agency shares data on flood zones, river water quality and pollution incidents, while the British Geological Survey holds records of earthquakes in the UK and worldwide, data on mineral resources and historical maps.

The Department for Transport publishes data on road safety, road casualties MOT tests and results (anonymised), while HM Revenue and Customs (HMRC) offers statistics on UK overseas trade, personal wealth, income tax data, and tax credits among other national indicators. It is worth also checking individual departments' websites, as some times not all the data is available in the same place, and it can be released on departmental sites before it reaches the Government Data Portal.

Wealth of datasets: The Office for National Statistics

The Office for National Statistics (ONS),[3] the UK's national statistics agency, shares on its website a wealth of datasets relating to the labour market, population, economy, business, population, crime and justice. Unlike some of the departmental datasets found on the HM Government Data Portal, the ONS releases data periodically at regular intervals and maintains a release calendar on its website, which can be useful for planning data-driven editorial. For example, labour market statistics, national and regional, as well as retail prices index and some economic indicators are released on a monthly basis, which can be used to generate stories on unemployment and benefits claims.

As with the Government Data Portal, most of the data from ONS is available in Excel or CSV format, for compatibility with visualisation tools. There are also a number of UK regional statistics bodies, often called observatories, maintained by local authorities. Such examples are the Lincolnshire Research Observatory[4] and the Cumbria Intelligence Observatory[5], which hold detailed breakdowns on population, economic and health data for the regions they cover, and can be useful for local and regional stories alike.

For detailed crime statistics, the Police.uk[6] website allows journalists to not only get a visual look at crime across the country and regions, but drill down to street level by types of crime. When the Ministry of Justice, Home Office and local police forces initially launched the tool, it was mainly a visual way for citizens to check the performance of their local policing team and get an overview of criminal activity in their area. But Police.uk has been improved in the past two years and can have a real value for data journalism, especially for local journalists. The data is now updated on a monthly basis, and users can draw on a map the area they wish to see crime statistics for, no longer limited by a radius around a postcode. The website gives a breakdown of the crime types recorded for areas selected, outcomes of police action, as well as comparison views with other areas or historical data. Additionally, the data can be downloaded in CSV format, meaning it can be used with external tools to overlay, for example, the relation between deprivation or poverty data from ONS and crime levels for certain areas in a city.

Similar to the UK, the United States government maintains its central data on Data.gov[7], which hosts datasets from individual US government agencies, as well as an extensive list of similar sites for other cities such as New York,[8] states, and countries such as Canada,[9] France, Kenya and Saudi Arabia. The US data portal also hosts links to a range of other organisations sharing data, such as the Organisation for Economic Co-operation and Development (OECD),[10] which shares core data from 34 member countries on demography, economy, education, environment, finance, health and transport. Similarly, the United Nations (UN)[11] has a comprehensive data portal hosting datasets on a range of topics, including fertility, energy use, and environment statistics, while the World Bank[12] shares datasets about development in countries across the globe. For detailed European data, Eurostat[13] from the European Commission holds detailed statistics and economic indicators datasets from countries across the continent along with a handy release calendar for editorial planning.

There are also a handful or datasets aggregators that can be useful when researching data sets. Such examples are Knoema,[14] which claims to be the largest public and open data repository in the world, Datahub[15], and Data 360,[16] which hosts a mix of datasets and data visualisations.

Data leads that journalists can follow-up to obtain the dataset for visualisation can also come from some other sources. Charities and non-profit organisations often gather data indicators to highlight various issues, such as homelessness, abuse or social mobility – all of which could be mapped or visualised by region in charts. Unions, think-tanks and political parties will also regularly collect data, as well as professional bodies and regulators, which release data quarterly, and some times monthly. Many universities also carry out research in various fields, and through journals and publications, data journalists can track down interesting datasets.

Beyond Excel: Essential tools for data journalists

While many data sources will offer machine-readable data to download in Excel, XML or CSV files formats, which can be opened with Microsoft Excel or similar software, journalists will often still find or receive data in PDF format. PDF files are easy to view on most platforms, but extracting the data from such files so that it can be adapted to visualisations can be difficult, because data cannot be easily copied and pasted in a spreadsheet. Tabula[17] is a free tool that allows journalists to upload text-based PDF files (not scanned documents), draw a box around the area of the data table needed, and the software will process tabular data in a spreadsheet-ready CSV format. To avoid this problem when requesting data via the Freedom of Information Act (FoI), it is recommended to request specifically that the data is shared in XLS or CSV format – although this might not always be received as such.

Extracting data from sources that do not offer an easily downloadable file format can be automated using Import.io[18] (falso free) instead of copy and pasting from web pages, which can be particularly time-consuming for journalists on a deadline. Import.io allows journalists to pull data from any website into a spreadsheet by selecting the rows and columns containing the information required. The application asks users to set up "connectors" for teaching the software where the data is on the page, between two to five examples,[19] and set up column names. Import.io can then mix data from different websites into a single searchable database for comparison.

Google offers three free tools that can be applied to data journalism. Google Spreadsheets, as part of the Google Docs[20] (free) suite allows journalists to open a dataset file and create simple charts, such as bar, line or pie charts, similar to the same process in Microsoft Excel, with several customisation options for colours, headings and scales. For more complex tables and mapping them, Google Fusion Tables[21] (also free) can produce zoom-able maps with data overlays. For this, the journalist needs to import a dataset file, which includes location data for latitude and longitude. Fusion Tables then auto-detects the location data in the table and plots the data on a map. Additional data layers, such a regional borders for health, police or local authorities in KML format[22] can be added.

With some practice and free tutorials,[23] complex and comprehensive visualisations can be achieved with Google Fusion Tables, and the results can be embedded directly onto online articles. Google Charts[24] lets journalists create interactive charts, also embeddable onto online articles, with a vast gallery of designs available, from the standard pie, donut and bar charts, to geo (map-based) charts, timelines, bubble charts and treemaps. The chart colours are customisable, so they match the look and feel of the host website, and hovering over data points in the charts can display additional information tooltips for users.

For simple and complex tasks: Data mapping tools

When venturing into complex data visualisations, CartoDB[25] (free for personal use) is a data-mapping tool that offers finer controls over the design of the mapped data and interactive pointers. The data maps generated with CartoDB can have a more distinctive style with existing presets or by creating a particular style, while the tool allows for multiple datasets to be merged easily to explore relations between multiple indicators. Another data map visualisation tool is Tableau[26] (free trial), which adds data layers on to maps, and can also display in the same interface different types of charts, such as bar charts below a map visualisation. GeoCommons[27] (free) is an open repository of data and maps for the world, down to a local level, which offers a range of tools to visualise and analyse data on maps. It can also animate data through time and space to highlight trends.

Datawrapper[28] (free) is one of the tools for journalists to create interactive charts and graphs that can be embedded directly into online stories. It supports editing of the dataset within the software, which makes it easier to change a label for a set. Datawrapper also ensures that labels on charts and graphs do not overlap when data values are very close, and labels small slices outside a pie chart. These features make the resulting charts easier to read and superior to most charts created using spreadsheet software. Many Eyes[29] (free) from IBM alternative tool for charts, which creates varied types of visualisations: word trees, word and tag clouds, phrase nets, as well as bar charts, bubble charts, scatterplots, matrix charts and treemaps, as well as a range of map-based visualisations. With both Datawrapper and Many Eyes, it is very important to make sure the data fed into the tool is formatted cleanly, and keep in mind data uploaded into Many Eyes will be publicly available for anyone to see.

Most of the data visualisation tools, whether used to create charts or maps, allow journalists to customise the colour scheme for data points. Many publications' graphics departments have strict guidelines on the colours used in illustrations, so obtaining from the equivalent colour codes for the web would help you match the title's look and feel for visualisations. If such a code is not readily available, journalists can customise their graphics with more distinctive colour schemes using Color Scheme Designer[30] (free).

For maximum accessibility, the tool also provides colour scheme modes that keep in mind people who have various types colour blindness, so that the effect of a chart or visualisation is not lost on them (Color Scheme Designer estimates that more than 85 per cent of the online-connected population has normal vision). Color Brewer[31] (free) is a similar colour scheme tool, which is meant to help data journalists choose map colours, based on the number of classes in the map, and also the nature of the data. Color Brewer can also account for colour-blind safe schemes, as well as print-friendly colour variations.

Conclusion: Why infographics are increasingly popular

Infographics are an increasingly popular way to display cherry-picked data points in easy-to-digest visualisations. The recent popularity of infographics has brought a range of tools for creating this type of data illustrations, with three of them standing out in particular for their design range and ease of creation. Infogr.am[32] (from free) creates interactive infographics with charts. Multiple charts of various types, including column, pie, bubble and hierarchy can be used into one single data visualisation.

The interactive infographics are shared through the service's website publicly. A paid pro account (£12) allows users to download the infographics as graphic files on a computer, and also share the animated interactive versions privately. For more graphic-led infographics, Piktochart[33] (free trial, then £18 per month) can help create themed visualisations with a drag-and-drop visual interface, similarly to Easel.ly[34] (free beta), which also has more than 100 templates to drag and drop elements and data into for infographics.

Taking some time to customise the elements of an infographic can make it stand out from many of the similar works using the same template.

Notes

[1]. HM Government Data Portal. See http://data.gov.uk, accessed on 14 August 2013

[2] Open Government Licence (OGL) See http://goo.gl/3fdwDZ, accessed on 14 August 2013

[3] Office for National Statistics (ONS). See http://www.ons.gov.uk, accessed 14 August 2013

[4] Lincolnshire Research Observatory. See http://www.research-lincs.org.uk, accessed on 15 August 2013

[5] Cumbria Intelligence Observatory. See http://www.cumbriaobservatory.org.uk, accessed on 15 August 2013

[6] Police.uk. See http://police.uk, accessed on 18 August 2013

[7] US Data.gov. See http://www.data.gov/, accessed on 18 August 2013

[8] NYC Open Data. See https://nycopendata.socrata.com, accessed on 18 August 2013

[9] Government of Canada Data. See http://data.gc.ca/eng, accessed on 18 August 2013

[10] OECD StatExtracts. See http://stats.oecd.org, accessed on 18 August 2013

[11] UN Data. See http://data.un.org, accessed on 18 August 2013

[12] World Bank Open Data. See http://data.worldbank.org, accessed on 19 August 2013

[13] Eurostat. See http://ec.europa.eu/eurostat, accessed on 11 September 2013

[14] Knoema See http://knoema.com/data, accessed on 11 September 2013

[15] The Datahub. See http://knoema.com/data, accessed on 11 September 2013

[16] Data 360. See http://www.data360.org/, accessed on 11 September 2013

[17] Tabula. See http://tabula.nerdpower.org, accessed on 4 October 2013

[18] Import.io. See http://import.io, accessed on 4 October 2013

[19] Marshall, Sarah (2013) Data scraping tool for non-coding journalists launches, Journalism.co.uk, 4 September. Available online at http://goo.gl/DmELBW, accessed on 24 September 2013

[20] Google Docs. See http://docs.google.com, accessed on 24 September 2013

[21] Google Fusion Tables. See http://www.google.com/fusiontables/Home/, accessed on 24 September 2013

[22] Rogers, Simon (2013) Borders and boundaries: 16 Google Fusion border files for you to use, SimonRogers.Net. Available online at http://goo.gl/z8Zo0B, accessed on 26 September 2013

[23] Hurley, Kathryn (2012) Fusion Tables Workshop. Available online at http://goo.gl/WmyQLh, accessed on 26 September 2013

[24] Google Charts. See http://developers.google.com/chart/?csw=1, accessed on 28 September 2013

[25] CartoDB. See http://cartodb.com, accessed on 26 September 2013

[26] Tableau Software. See http://www.tableausoftware.com/solutions/mapping-software, accessed on 26 September 2013

[27] GeoCommons. See http://geocommons.com, accessed on 6 October 2013

[28] Datawrapper. See http://datawrapper.de, accessed on 6 October 2013

[29] Many Eyes. See http://www-958.ibm.com/software/data/cognos/manyeyes/, accessed on 6 October 2013

[30] Color Scheme Designer. See http://colorschemedesigner.com, accessed on 29 September 2013

[31] Color Brewer. See http://colorbrewer2.org, accessed on 29 September 2013

[32] Infogr.am. See https://infogr.am/, accessed on 1 October 2013

[33] Piktochart. See http://piktochart.com, accessed on 1 October 2013

[34] Easel.ly. See http://www.easel.ly, accessed on 1 October 2013

Note on the contributor

Daniel Ionescu is a journalist and publishing entrepreneur (originally from Bucharest, Romania). He studied Journalism at the University of Lincoln and upon graduating founded with two of his colleagues a local news digital publication, The Lincolnite. The online publication won the special Chairman's Award in the Online Media Awards 2013 and has been shortlisted two years in a row in the Best Local News Website category. His interest in data journalism stems from his interest in making stories easy to understand and quick to read through data visualisations, as well as crunching and mapping the numbers, whether it's to find which neighbourhood has the highest crime levels, to covering local elections through interactive live graphics.

Using transport data for public information

Got the figures? Pupul Chatterjee provides some tips on how to read them and work with them on transport-related stories

Transport data – an introduction

Dealing with data sets for transport-related news stories can have two sides to it – having too much or too little data to begin with. In both cases, looking at the context in which the story is being told can entirely change the meaning. In the case of too much data, we need to decide which data sets might be useful for a particular story. Just as all the notes scribbled during a press conference don't go into a single news story, with data too, we need to decide what is useful and what needs to be discarded, to avoid confusion at later stages.

When there is too little data, there can be various interesting options to explore. Will a Freedom of Information (FoI) request help gather the data? Can we move away from the traditional styles of journalism and look at options such as crowd sourcing through social media? If a data set is very small, can it be used as a case study to look at the larger picture? This, however, again needs to be done keeping the context in mind.

Having an idea of what the audience for a particular news piece would be also helps to choose or decide the context. For instance, if a story is for national newspapers or television, talking about bus stops on a particular street of a city will never work. However, if the same story is carried in the local papers with street names, it will generate a lot of interest within the local communities and in the wider city areas. Buses, trains, flight delays are topics on which there is no lack of people complaining about various kinds of problems. So, while it might be easy to get lots of data through comments and crowd sourcing, constant fact-checking and going back and forth with it are vital to such stories.

Sources of transport data – where to begin?

National and local government authorities – these are often the best places to begin looking for data. Some government bodies that hold very interesting national data could be:

- Highways Agency
- Driver and Vehicle Licensing Agency (DVLA)
- Department for Transport (DfT)
- Office of the Rail Regulator (ORR)

At the local level:

- Transport departments of the local councils
- Traffic control rooms
- Local police force
- Airport authorities (Civil Aviation Authority for national data)
- Bus and train operators and their unions and regulators (sometimes these are governed by the local councils, some are private operators).

Being on their mailing lists (where possible) gives access to press releases that could otherwise be easily missed. Almost all of these bodies are very active on social media, especially Twitter. So having them on Twitter feeds/lists helps to keep an eye on the latest developments, announcements, annual surveys etc.

FoIs – Filing your own FoI requests (when press offices are not very forthcoming with data/ information), subscribing to RSS feeds related to your own areas of investigations from websites such as WhatDoTheyKnow (WDTK) lead to good data sources. This, however, often takes weeks (or months) and needs to be planned well in advance to meet deadlines. With FoIs we need to think inside the box or the filing cabinet or hard drive, rather than thinking outside the box. We need to think in terms of what information a government office might hold on a particular area (Rosenbaum 2013).

Local radio – drive time shows have travel stories almost every day, apart from the regular travel updates. While these may not be direct sources of large spreadsheets of data, they often point towards people and offices that will have them.

Activists and independent groups –independent groups such as Passenger Focus, Bus Users UK, or other advisory groups (some of which are run commercially, so data from them needs to be looked at differently) also release their own surveys. Here, we also need to look closely at the methodology adopted for those surveys, the sample sizes on which the surveys are based in order to secure an idea of scale and proportions being talked about. Often, revealing the sample sizes is a good way of making sure numbers are not misinterpreted.

Crowd sourcing through social media – as mentioned earlier, when there is a lack of data, exploring alternative and innovative ways of doing journalism (Lewis 2011) really works well for some stories (discussed later in detail in the next segment).

Got the numbers? How to read them and work with them?

There could be two ways of starting a data story – having a story idea in mind then going out to look for data or coming across a data set and then looking at it from different angles to see what could be the best possible news stories coming out of it. So after getting the data, we then start thinking of what to do with it. What could be the best ways to visualise the data? How do we keep it simple, interactive (for online platforms) and make sure we do not clutter it with too much information? How do we make sure we don't move away from the story? When dealing with numbers, the ways used to represent and interpret them can completely turn around a situation. For instance, one set of numbers could be read in two different ways:

a) "About 80 per cent of bus stops in the city have Real Time Information (RTI) screens"

So if we look at the 80 per cent, it seems that it is, on the whole, a very positive scenario and most bus stops seem to be operating well. However, the other side of it also means that 20 per cent, i.e. one fifth, of them don't have these screens. In such a case this could also be written as:

b) "Every fifth bus stop in the city runs without an information screen"

Very often the government or other authorities that we question as journalists, would try to convince us that option (a) is the best way to look at a data and (b) is not.

How to explore different tools to use the data?

In a few cases, taking a closer look at the data reveals more than one side to a story. A story on "car crimes" (incidents of thefts of vehicles and thefts from vehicles) was recently reported by a local radio programme. It later led to the local police claiming that the data was misinterpreted and placed out of the context (which is a very common claim and at times true). The data in the story talked about different parts of cities that had recorded higher crime rates. The post codes in the city centre showed higher crimes compared to other parts of the same cities. It could have led to the conclusion that if cars were parked in the city centre, they were more likely to be broken into. However, the local police said that all cities had higher "transient populations" in the city centre, i.e. more people who travel to the city centre for work, shopping etc, but very few actually lived there. They also suggested that the crime figures in the city centre should be compared against the population of the areas to give a sense of proportion to the numbers.

Datawrapper

Here is one of the data sets for this story:

Car crime rate breakdown by city

City	Number of offences (per 10,000 vehicles)
Manchester	505
Bradford	457
London	443
Leeds	420
Sheffield	389
Newcastle	318
Birmingham	313
Liverpool	287
Cardiff	285
Bristol	255
Nottingham	193
Hull	180
Middlesbrough	178
Leicester	155
Southampton	147
Oxford	147
Peterborough	143
Derby	130
Cambridge	112
Plymouth	101
Portsmouth	96
Carlisle	86
Norwich	85

We could compare these city figures against the national average (121 offences per 10,000 vehicles) and the national urban average of 242 offences. Here, choosing the right kind of visualisation can make all the difference to a story. One of the simplest ways could be this:

Cities with highest car crimes

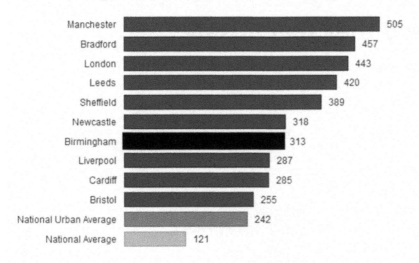

Manchester	505
Bradford	457
London	443
Leeds	420
Sheffield	389
Newcastle	318
Birmingham	313
Liverpool	287
Cardiff	285
Bristol	255
National Urban Average	242
National Average	121

Created with Datawrapper   Source: HonestJohn.co.uk. Get the data

If we use a pie-chart instead, it would make the data quite confusing to understand as it would be difficult to judge the difference, for instance, between the 443 offences in London against the 420 offences in Leeds. Choosing only the top 10 cities (out of the total of 24 in the initial data) and then comparing them to national averages is another way of making sure the visual elements remain simple. If aiming at the local media of a particular city (in this case Birmingham), highlighting the figures of that city or using colour coding to indicate are also useful. Visual elements like choosing the right colour combinations (using the colour wheel to decide what sets of colours go well with each other) also help make the end product better. More details on this story are available at http://brumtransport.com/birmingham-one-of-the-worst-in-the-country-for-car-crimes.

Infogra.am
Another simple tool for beginners is infogr.am – it also allows us to make charts and infographics. Again, we need to decide this by thinking what suits a story better. In many ways, datawrapper and infogr.am are similar in function. They can both be used for interactive graphics, can be embedded into blogs, websites etc, can be shared on social media platforms and even saved as static images as done here:

Percentage of passengers who said they feel unsafe

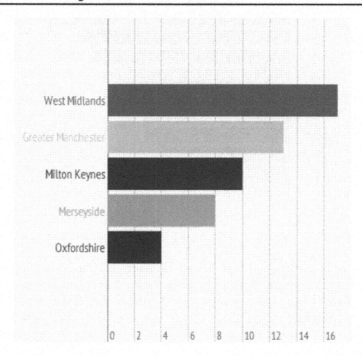

Data Source: Bus Passenger Survey 2013 by Passenger Focus

Create infographics

When using either of them, or most other mapping and visualisation tools, using various pointers to help a reader understand the data better is a good idea. For instance, adding a title to the chart itself, adding a very short explanation of what the data is about, mentioning the data sources, adding the spreadsheets used to put the data together (through the "get the data" option on datawrapper) are ways in which this can be done. In the case of interactive data, a few points on how to use the interactive elements (as almost always done with the *Guardian* datablog stories) are also important ways to make the story easier to understand and guide the reader through it.

More details on this story available at http://www.birminghammail.co.uk/news/local-news/fear-buses-west-midlands-worst-2729653 and http://brumtransport.com/west-midlands-passengers-the-most-unsafe.

74

Google fusion tables and mapping: What works?

For a story that has geographic locations at the heart of it or explains it better, Google fusion tables are good for making maps. However, in some cases, maps will work if only we have specific geographic locations (postcodes, geocodes etc) and a wider area may be difficult to mark on a map. For the story on bus stop RTI screens discussed earlier, this is a map that is based on crowd sourced data that was collected through bus users tweeting updates about their bus stops:

This is based on a very small data set, and hence a very simple spreadsheet with just four values on it – four of the bus stop locations being marked on the map. In such a case, the data is only a small sample study to indicate the condition of a few bus stops on a given day, during a given time. The results could be completely different on a weekend, or late at night, when the frequency of buses is really low in most cities. The idea here was to capture through the tweets (with all users using a pre-decided #phantombuses) the experiences of different passengers. Finding the correct locations/postcodes of the bus stops would be the first step, followed by putting them up on a spreadsheet. For an online platform, this works as an interactive map. Clicking on each of the four marked spots gives more details, for instance street names or any other values that we may choose to include in the spreadsheet.

If trying to plot streets etc of a particular city, Google fusion tables requires us to be as specific as possible. In this case, not mentioning Birmingham, UK led to some points in the map being plotted in Birmingham, Alabama in the US (Vane H, 2013). More details on this story available at: http://brumtransport.com/phantombuses-how-real-are-the-real-time-information-screen-announcements-at-bus-stops.

What doesn't?

Another transport data set, involving crimes on buses posed a problem of a different nature. Here the data sets talked about police operations carried out in wider areas of Birmingham. As such, there were no postcodes or geocodes that could be used to mark specific areas on the maps. (These were not even locations like the earlier example of bus stops, so that technique wouldn't work.) Most of the locations here were regions that the police patrols were monitoring, spread out or overlapping a few streets in different parts of the town. This led to yet another tool to be tried and tested – Scribble Maps, used to draw shapes on the map, to indicate roughly the geographic locations.

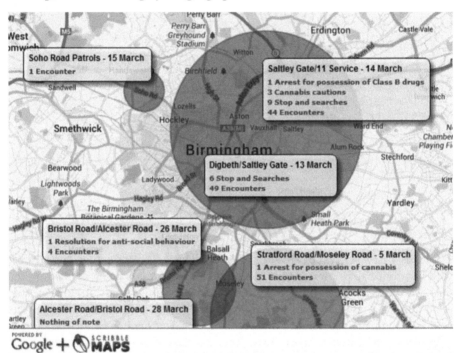

As seen in the map, there were two separate operations carried out in the Bristol Road-Alcester Road on 26 and 28 March. Also some streets in and around Moseley Road come within the Alcester road patrols. These locations could have been confusing using Google fusion tables and maps, and hence Scribble Maps for this data set might be more suitable.

Scribble Maps does allow the use of Google maps and pick up street locations even without post codes. We can then use various shapes, colours etc to mark what we want, using its features as if it were a Windows Paint software. However, it tends to be a bit fiddly when saving and editing changes to the map after it is created, especially if it needs to be embedded on an online platform.

One option here is to save it as an image file (after taking a screengrab etc) but then it does not remain an interactive map any more after this step.

Conclusion

Like any other kind of journalism, data journalism is also about finding an interesting way to tell a story – a story that could otherwise be lost in numbers or remain hidden in files and folders. The role of a data journalist, then, could be to make a dreary, dry set of numbers lively and fun to look at and easy to understand for the layperson, not just a statistician.

References

Rosenbaum, M. (2013) Freedom of Information: Be careful what you ask for, BBC Academy, 15 January. Available online at
http://www.bbc.co.uk/blogs/blogcollegeofjournalism/posts/Freedom-of-information-be-careful-what-you-ask-for, accessed on 3 October 2013

Lewis, P. (2011): Crowdsourcing the news, TedxTalks, Thessaloniki, November 2011. Available online at
http://www.ted.com/talks/paul_lewis_crowdsourcing_the_news.html, accessed on 29 September 2013.

Vane, H. (2013) Champions League: Reflection, See Ya Later alliDATA. Available online at http://seeyalaterallidata.wordpress.com/2013/03/01/champions-league-reflections, accessed on September 30, 2103.

Note on the contributor

Pupul Chatterjee runs Brum Transport (www.brumtransport.com), a transport news website in Birmingham. It was recently shortlisted for the *Guardian* Student Media Awards 2013. Before this, she was a transport news correspondent with the *Indian Express*. She also contributes to the Bham Datablog, Behind the Numbers – the regional datablog run by *Birmingham Mail* and the *Moseley B13* magazine. Twitter: @pupulchatterjee

d3.js and explanatory approaches to interactive data visualisation

Ændrew Rininsland argues that anyone "willing to learn D3 will find they are given an unparalleled ability to create visualisations that bring data alive"

Two varieties of software often appear when searching for the right tool to visualise data. On one hand are *exploratory* tools such as Tableau[1] or Google Fusion Tables[2], which allow a user to easily create interfaces for sorting or filtering data. Especially at the start of an investigation, these are important tools that often point journalists towards interesting stories. What happens once the journalist finds a story, however?

For quite some time, the next step has often been to write it up and make the exploratory tool available to readers, a practice popularised by the *Guardian* Data Blog (Aitamurto et al 2010: 11). This provides transparency and allows readers to personalise the story by filtering content down to the local level, but it has the potential to sacrifice the story in order to do so – after all, the relationship between data journalist and audience is such that the journalist is there to tell the audience why this data's interesting, and which parts are worth looking at (and, equally, not worth looking at).

On the other hand, some journalists have adopted *explanatory* tools that, instead of merely interfacing with data, allow journalists to pick it apart and show readers only the good bits. The JavaScript library for manipulating and presenting data, D3.js (hereafter just D3) popularises this approach by giving competent users a high-level means by which to bind data to web display components. In other words, it lets you map data on to whatever you want – whether that be a line, or a rectangle, or most other elements that a web browser can render – and then manipulate those objects using that data. While flexible enough to enable the creation of exploratory tools, D3 really shines when used to create visualisations that highlight the most important pieces of data. Beyond that, the D3 community is riding some of the most interesting trends and techniques in modern web development, making D3 proficiency an important skill for aspiring journo-coders and data journalists.[3]

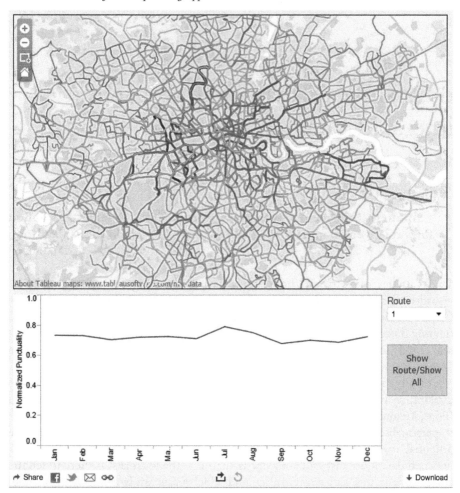

Fig. 1 – This exploratory Tableau-based interactive allows users to find out information about London bus routes. It follows the classic Visual Information-seeking Mantra of "Overview first, zoom and filter, then details on demand". Note that the user isn't directed to a particular end, and is required to use the tool to find relevant data. Source: Ændrew Rininsland (aendrew.com/content/waiting-tfl-bus-punctuality-transport-londons-network).

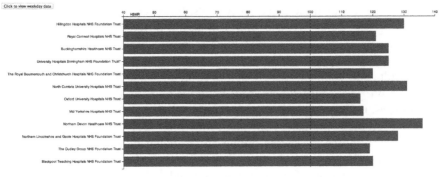

Fig. 2 – This explanatory D3-based graphic has two states: "weekday" and "weekend" (shown). While backed up by a dataset containing every NHS trust in the UK, only the 12 designated by Dr. Foster as possibly having issues are shown. Clicking between weekday and weekend highlights the issue of increased mortality at hospitals on weekends. Source: Ændrew Rininsland, *The Sunday Times* (features.thesundaytimes.co.uk/public/hsmr-top12).

Evolution or revolution?

The internet's development has had several distinct phases. Initially there was the static internet – Web 1.0 – which was constructed mainly using basic HTML pages and this persisted into the mid- to late-nineties. JavaScript, the language of D3, was created by Brendan Eich at Netscape in 1995 to allow the web-browser to be more interactive than before, and this was what drove many of the comically-bad webpage special effects that were characteristic of the early web[4] – in part, this was because early web browsers didn't really have any native languages for drawing shapes.

The lack of web-based drawing technologies forced visualisation artists to use static images or graphics technologies like Macromedia Flash (later Adobe Flash). Following the popularisation of server-side scripting languages (such as PHP, Ruby and others), the internet is thought to have entered a second iteration commonly referred to as Web 2.0. This new phase was marked by an emphasis on user-driven content and extensible, open source systems for managing it (Graham 2005). WordPress became wildly popular, and blogs started to appear *en masse*.

The new focus on web-based content creation systems resulted in the emergence of early interactive data visualisation, with IBM's Java-based ManyEyes in 2007 being one of the first examples of Web 2.0 user-driven visualisation tools. First Google Spreadsheets enabled basic interactive charts to be added to a story, then Google Fusion Tables allowed journalists to create complex, interactive maps from spreadsheet data. The *Guardian*'s use of

WikiLeaks data to map deaths in the Iraq conflict is a prime example of how powerful these tools can be in telling a story (see Rogers 2010).

The problem with these exploratory tools, however, is that they can be very intimidating for readers. A map with a thousand different-but-uniform-looking data points on it probably doesn't impress much upon the reader except its sheer scale. Even if the journalist had found a story in such a map, Fusion Table maps aren't really sophisticated enough to easily walk a user through the story.

Flash and Java, meanwhile, had continued to evolve as web graphics technologies, but were quickly starting to show their age. Not only did Flash not work on Apple's popular iOS platform (Jobs 2010), but it also added unnecessary resource overheard during an era when most web browsers were starting to be able to draw things natively.[5] Java, on the other hand, reached a tipping point in terms of security and stopped being available as a browser plugin in Mac OS X and eventually became blacklisted by Apple (Kelly 2013). By dropping its support for these two technologies, Apple drove the visualisation community to reevaluate how it displayed information.

As people stopped using the buggy, older versions of Microsoft Internet Explorer, drawing technologies such as SVG and Canvas became much more viable as a consequence. Not only did these newer technologies use less system resources than Java and Flash, but they were also great in terms of speed and stability. And critically, SVG also worked on mobile devices.

This spawned a whole raft of exploratory JavaScript-based drawing tools. Highcharts, Flot and The JIT were among the first, enabling data visualisation artists to easily create interactive, web-native versions of basic graphics like line graphs and pie charts. In the same vein, Google upgraded their visualisation tools to allow interactive visualisations in 2008. The downside is that these tools are very use case-driven and often not very extensible. What if you need to make a candlestick graph but your graphing library only supports basic bar graphs? Meanwhile drawing tools like Raphaël.js and ProcessingJS are really good for creating interesting visual content, but are inefficient because neither was really created with the intent of supporting sophisticated web-based data visualisation.[6]

Mike Bostock and Jeff Heer at the Stanford Visualization Group released Provis in 2009 to address this. This JavaScript library allowed data to be bound to various visual objects in the web-browser, and that data is used to manipulate the appearance of those objects. Provis was fairly successful and a community formed around it. In 2011, Bostock superseded Protovis with the first release of D3.js, which contained numerous improvements to the workflow established by Protovis.

Data-driven documents

D3 provides some convincing answers to quite a few contemporary problems in data visualisation:
• Portability

- ○ JavaScript, the language D3 is written in, is probably the single most versatile programming language on the Internet at the moment. Windows, Linux and Mac OS X all run JavaScript nearly identically.[7] Moving a D3 visualisation from the computer where it's being developed to the production server is as difficult as moving a few files into a web-accessible directory.

- Extensibility

  - ○ D3 can read most popular data formats such as CSV, TSV, XML and JSON. This versatility lets it communicate with most common webservices, meaning visualisations can easily consume live data.

- Scalability

  - ○ D3 visualisations are run on the "client-side", meaning the viewer's computer is the one that does all the processing work. This avoids laborious server-side data crunching, which can also help prevent many of the scalability issues inherent in high-traffic server-side code. While server-side code can still be used to generate the data set (as is often the case when using D3 to consume data from webservices), the tendency is to have precompiled static data sets. In other words, D3 visualisations are less likely to break under high server strain if done correctly.

- Hosting

  - ○ The D3 community commonly hosts its visualisations on GitHub Pages, the free cloud-based file hosting service provided by GitHub.[8] Doing this provides both free, cloud-based data storage and the popular, open source "git" distributed version control system. Another GitHub technology, Gists, are used by the community to create examples as a way of explaining how to use D3.[9] Bostock's "bl.ocks.org" tool acts as a convenient viewer for these. The upshot of this strategy is that publicly-hosted data doesn't need a complex server setup, can easily be hosted for free, and will scale regardless of traffic requirements.

- Mobile accessibility

  - ○ The vast majority of mobile and desktop web browsers now support Scalable Vector Graphics (SVG). This powerful graphics technology is fast and versatile, but perhaps a bit difficult to use. D3 simplifies the creation of SVG graphics substantially, while doing so from the perspective of exacting, pixel-perfect data visualisation.

- Cost

  - ○ D3.js is licensed under the popular open source BSD license, making it free to use, even for commercial purposes. One only needs a web-browser to begin creating D3 visualisations – projects such as Tributary let users experiment with D3 without having to ever configure a code editor.[10]

Further, its continued development is currently being subsidised by *The New York Times*, where Mike Bostock is Graphics Editor.[11]

D3 is useful because it solves many contemporary problems faced by data journalists in the newsroom, which often make it difficult to present their work in a unique or interesting manner. For instance, above I mention the difference between "server-side" and "client-side" code, with the former being processed by the big server computers which keep a news organisation's website up, and the latter being run on the news consumer's computer once received from the servers. Scalability is a huge issue for news organisations – a visualisation is often bombarded by huge amounts of traffic for a short time, after which it loses relevance but still must remain online for search engine reasons. If a server overloads and goes down while a piece is newsworthy, the audience impact is diminished considerably. D3's emphasis on cloud hosting through GitHub removes a lot of hardware requirements (especially if combined with a cloud-based script hosting service such as Scraperwiki), and allows visualisations to be embedded in news articles via iframes.

This simplicity also extends to how easily D3 visualisations can be made to look consistent across multiple platforms. So long as a browser can render SVG and run JavaScript, it will output a D3 visualisation in a similar fashion. Not only that, D3's SVG output can even be pasted into a text file and opened with Adobe Illustrator, enabling it to be useful for creating print graphics.

Brace yourself – some code stuff ahead

It's worth reiterating that d3.js is a *JavaScript library*, which means one uses the idioms D3 sets out when one writes JavaScript code, with the effect that many common tasks are simplified. A good example of this is how, in D3, you "select" specific objects on a page before then executing a sequence of operations on them:

```
var svg = d3.select('body').append('svg').attr('id', 'viz');
```

A lot of functionality is packed into the above bit of code:[12]

- First, D3's "select" method (that is, "d3.select()") is told to find "body" — in a webpage, "body" is the place where content is visible to the web browser.

- "select" passes the next method in that chain, "append," an object[13] pointing to the page's main content area.

- The job of "append" is to add an element to the end of whatever it's been given, and, having been given the "body" selection, it adds an "svg" area inside the webpage's main display area (that is, the "body").

- "Append" then changes the focus to the newly-appended "svg" element, and gives that updated object to "attr" (short for "attribute"), which sets an attribute of an element – in this case, setting its "id" attribute to "viz".

- This whole abstraction is computed, with a reference to it then stored in a variable named "svg" so it can be easily accessed later (this is the "var svg =" part at the very beginning).

An empty SVG container such as this is a common starting point for many visualisations.

If I lost you there for a second by throwing a bit of JavaScript at you, I apologise — I'll refrain from doing that again for the remainder of this chapter. The point is that D3 isn't so much a graphing library so much as a way of *binding data to display objects* — once you use another function to open up a dataset, using the idioms discussed above, you often then *select* that SVG container, and *append* a bunch of rectangles to it; then you could bind data (using, unsurprisingly, the "data" function) to those rectangles, setting the height (which is an *attribute*) to whatever value each rectangle had bound to it. Without going into further detail, you now have most of the elements necessary for a basic bar graph.[14] Other elements are often added in a similar manner: first something is *selected*, then items are *appended* to it, then the *attributes* of those items are manipulated in some manner. The "select, then modify" idiom described above is the most common in D3.

Exploring and explaining

As simple as I made this all appear,[15] it still involves significantly more code compared to simply dropping a spreadsheet into Google Drive and using the Google Visualisation API to render it as a bar graph or line chart. It's worth noting that the example above didn't do anything with scales, margins, axis lines, or have any interactivity whatsoever – all that is taken for granted with a tool such as Google Charts, but can't be with D3. If all that's needed is a basic bar chart (and *especially* if uncertain what that chart will look like once drawn), the Google Charts route is probably preferable. If you have a tonne of data and just want to chart it to see whether there are any trends or further bits of data to interrogate, D3 might not be the best choice – there are a whole host of tools better suited to that which are faster and less frustrating.

But what if you found one data point that's interesting – it might not be a maximum or a minimum, could possibly be right in the middle of the herd – and you want to point it out to the user in a way that's somewhat unusual? What if you want to put all your data into arbitrary categories, and then colour each category appropriately? What if you want the graph to grab a related data set and adjust itself accordingly whenever the user clicks on an element? Or what if you want to hook everything up to a live dataset, to enable your visualisation to update and always have the latest data?

Scott Murray, author of D3 guide *Interactive Data Visualization for the Web*, describes the difference between exploratory and explanatory visualisations as follows:

> D3 doesn't generate predefined or "canned" visualizations for you. This is on purpose. D3 is intended primarily for *explanatory* visualization work, as

opposed to *exploratory* visualizations. Exploratory tools help you discover significant, meaningful patterns in data. These are tools ... which help you quickly generate multiple views on the same data set. That's an essential step, but different from generating an *explanatory* presentation of the data, a view of the data that highlights what you've already discovered. Explanatory views are more constrained and limited, but also focused, and designed to communicate only the important points (Murray 2013: Chapter II; emphasis his).

Typically, if a visualisation needs a lot of dropdowns or other ways of filtering/constraining data, it's probably more of an exploratory visualisation. Explanatory visualisations don't typically follow Shneiderman's visual information-seeking mantra of "overview first, zoom and filter, then details on demand" (Shneiderman 1996), instead presenting the user with a rendered snippet of data that separately presents its context in the wider data picture. This extends beyond presentation, however – an explanatory visualisation generally won't stand on its own given it lacks the context created by a user's journey through an exploratory visualisation. An explanatory visualisation will often be accompanied by quite a lot of text, or at least a bunch of other visualisations intended to cement context.

Are explanatory graphics harder or easier than exploratory? In an interview with Data Stories, Mike Bostock discussed some of the challenges one is faced with when creating an exploratory graphic:

I think it's simply harder to do a good exploratory graphic, and that is because an exploratory graphic sort of implies that you're doing exploration, which means you're doing some amount of work to extract the insight from that graphic. Whereas if you have an explanatory or expository graphic, you're sort of presenting up front "Here's what's the conclusion," or "Here's the interesting insight from that data" ... The reason why exploratory is hard is because you have to find that balance where you have some initial insight you want to show in the overview, but there's also that really rich data set that facilitates further insights if you play with it. Not every data set has that level of depth to it. *Sometimes, you just want to show those initial insights as quickly as possible and not make people work for it* (Bertini and Stefaner 2013; emphasis mine).

On some level, this explains why the extra coding effort required to do an explanatory visualisation is worthwhile. But it also implies an obligation to visualise a story in the manner which best suits the data. Using an exploratory tool to communicate a concept that really should just be explained to the reader ultimately does the story a disservice. Additionally, each layer of interactivity requires bug testing, cross-browser testing and cross-device testing, *on top of* the usual journalistic rigour necessary to verify and fact check all the data within the visualisation. If this functionality is being hacked on top of some other

JavaScript library, the long-term development effort might be more than is necessary to build a D3 visualisation from scratch.

Further, D3's learning curve shallows out after the first few successful uses, and especially if one is familiar with JavaScript. While needing to learn JavaScript is probably the highest barrier to entry for most users, it's also a valuable skill for data journalists to have, given both that language's availability and its utility online.

Conclusion

In this chapter, I have discussed D3, the environment from which it arose, what use cases it is most relevant for, some common development idioms, and the differences between explanatory and exploratory data visualisation. D3 certainly has a much higher learning curve than most non-coder visualisation tools. However, those willing to learn D3 will find they are given an unparalleled ability to create visualisations that bring data alive, and, in having learned JavaScript to do so, will suddenly also have the ability to add interactivity to nearly any web project, using one of the internet's most useful and widespread programming languages.

Notes

[1]. Public version available at tableausoftware.com/public. Free to use

[2] Built into Google Drive, drive.google.com. Free to use

[3] Note that this chapter will provide a high-level overview of the technology and won't get too deep into how to actually use D3. For that, please see Murray (2013)

[4] For an overview of JavaScript's history, see Severance (2012)

[5] By this, it's meant that the web-browser itself can draw elements like curved lines and circles without having to resort to a third-party piece of code to do so

[6] That said, gRaphaël (available for free at g.raphaeljs.com) would eventually be released as an extension to Raphaël.js, intended to make the creation of simple graphs much easier

[7] Excepting the aforementioned buggy Internet Explorer

[8] See: http://pages.github.com/

[9] A really good way to learn D3 is to study and attempt to duplicate some of the examples provided by the community. See: https://github.com/mbostock/d3/wiki/Gallery

[10] See: http://tributary.io/

[11] See: http://bost.ocks.org/mike/#projects

[12] If you've never written any code, don't worry – this is the sole code example in this chapter

[13] I use the word "object" here in the computational manner used when mentioning, for instance, "Object-Oriented Programming". If not a coder, just imagine an "object" as "something that has stuff". If something is "selected", think of the resulting object as a "thing that has the properties of that which was selected". Clear as mud, right? Again,

don't worry – this is only a high-level overview. To really learn D3 or JavaScript, see "References" section

[14] Or, bind the data points to the vertices on a line and you have a line-graph instead. These basic examples understate D3's power, however; the object being manipulated can be much more complex, such as is the case with geographic shape data

[15] I'm joking

References

Aitamurto, Tanja, Esa Sirkkunen, and Pauliina Lehtonen (2011) Trends in Data Journalism. Available online at http://virtual.vtt.fi/virtual/nextmedia/Deliverables-2011/D3.2.1.2.B_Hyperlocal_Trends_In%20Data_Journalism.pdf, accessed on September 2013

Bertini, Enrico and Stefaner, Moritz (2013) Data Stories #22: NYT Graphics and D3 with Mike Bostock and Shan Carter, Data Stories. Available online at http://datastori.es/data-stories-22-nyt-graphics-and-d3-with-mike-bostock-and-shan-carter/#t=20:52.459, accessed on 30 September 2013

Graham, Paul (2005) Web 2.0. Available online at http://www.paulgraham.com/web20.html, accessed on 29 September 2013

Jobs, Steve (2010) Thoughts on Flash. Available online at http://www.apple.com/hotnews/thoughts-on-flash/, accessed on 29 September 2013

Kelly, Meghan (2013) Oracle issues fix for Java exploits after DHS warns of its holes, *VentureBeat Security*, 13 January. Available online at http://venturebeat.com/2013/01/14/java-fix-issued/, accessed on 29 September 2013

Murray, Scott (2013) *Interactive Data Visualization for the Web*, O'Reilly Media. Available online at http://chimera.labs.oreilly.com/books/1230000000345/index.html, accessed on 29 September 2013

Rogers, Simon (2010) WikiLeaks Iraq war logs: Every death mapped, *Guardian*, 23 October. Available online at http://www.theguardian.com/world/datablog/interactive/2010/oct/23/wikileaks-iraq-deaths-map, accessed on 29 September 2013

Severance, Charles (2012) JavaScript: Designing a Language in 10 Days, *Computer*, Vol. 45, No. 2, pp 7-8. Available online at http://www.computer.org/csdl/mags/co/2012/02/mco2012020007-abs.html, accessed on 29 September 2013

Shneiderman, Ben (1996) The Eyes Have It: A Task by Data Type Taxonomy for Information Visualizations, *Proceedings of the IEEE Symposium on Visual Languages*, pp 336-343. Available online at http://rw4.cs.uni-sb.de/teaching/infovis08/papers/theeyeshaveit.pdf, accessed on 29 September 2013

Note on the contributor

Ændrew Rininsland is a news developer at *The Times* and *Sunday Times*. He blogs at aendrew.com and can be found on Twitter via @aendrew. He is a contributor to The Times Digital Development Blog (timesdigitaldevelopment.tumblr.com) and the Hackney Citizen (hackneycitizen.co.uk).

Section 3:
Data journalism: The broader issues – locally, nationally and internationally

Richard Lance Keeble

For Andy Dickinson, testing the context, provenance and ownership – where data comes from and why – is a fundamental part of the data journalism process. If journalists are not critical of the data they use (and those that provide it), perhaps becoming over-reliant on data press releases, they risk undermining their credibility with data-churnalism or, worse still, data-porn!. As data journalism practice evolves, it would seem logical to explore ways that journalists reduce their dependency on other sources all together. In this first chapter of a section looking at the broader issues surrounding data journalism, the use of sensors, Dickinson suggests, offers a compelling solution.

Next, Gabriel Keeble-Gagnère argues that – in the light of the recent NSA revelations about mass surveillance by US and UK intelligence agencies – journalists, especially those dealing with sensitive topics, should become familiar with encryption techniques. And he provides an overview of the methods reporters can use to protect themselves from the snoopers. Keeble-Gagnère concludes with these rousing words:

> The Snowden leaks have revealed that there is, indeed, a war going on – an information war in which cryptography is a key weapon. The true role of journalism is to hold power to account; sadly, as we now know, a power that has evidently overstepped. It's time for journalists to fight back.

Journalists recently investigating the scandal of offshore tax havens have had to be particularly adept in DJ skills. Indeed, when an enormous cash of data emerged exposing the use of offshore tax havens by the world's rich and famous, an international consortium of journalists got to work in an unprecedented, complex, collaborative endeavour. Here Arthur Lashmar shows how they did it – and the extraordinary effects of the revelations.

From global scandal we shift to the hyperlocal. According to Damian Radcliffe, data journalism is still a nascent concept in the emerging hyperlocal media sector. But examples of activity do exist – particularly in the US – and steps can be taken to make it more mainstream, he argues.

Next, Tom Felle interviews a group of international data journalists and finds they all argue their work can play a crucial democratic role in holding the powerful to account. He concludes:

> Does data reporting have a public interest role? Can using data reporting assure transparency? Does it engage citizens, or is data journalism just creating a well-informed, technologically literate elite and leaving many citizens behind? Evidence suggests such journalism has a public interest and important democratic function. Around the world reporters are finding stories in the numbers, acting in the public interest, and producing better and stronger stories using digital data reporting methods. Data is fulfilling a traditional accountability role, albeit in a more nuanced way than perhaps one might have first imagined.

John Burn-Murdoch highlights the way in which journalists have used statistical methods to uncover a series of remarkable exclusives for the *Financial Times*.

Finally, in this section, Yaneng Feng and Qian Li compare the state of data journalism in China with its current position in Western media organisations. And they conclude: "It is essential for the Chinese government and media to encourage data journalism – and for society to embrace the change."

Making data journalism real

Andy Dickinson wonders if the growing field of sensor journalism offers an insight into what comes next for data journalism

During the 2008 summer Olympics, the Beijing Air Track project[1] took a team of photographers from Associated Press and used them to smuggle hand-held pollution sensors in to Beijing. Using their press access to the Olympic venues, they gathered pollution readings to test the Chinese government's data that a series of extreme emergency measures put in place in the run-up to the games had improved the city's notoriously poor air quality. They were not the only organisation to use sensors in this way. The BBC's Beijing office also used a hand-held sensor to test air pollution gathering data that appeared in a number of reports during the games (BBC News: 2008).

Clean air. Clean data

The Air Track project and AP's interactive report[2] are now cited as a "prime example of how sensors, data journalism, and old-fashioned, on-the-ground reporting can be combined to shine a new level of accountability on official reports" (Howard 2013). In contrast to the Chinese data, the level of transparency displayed in the way the data was collected[3] illustrates how sensors can play a part in reinforcing data journalism role in the process of accountability.

Testing the context, provenance and ownership – where our data comes from and why – is a fundamental part of the data journalism process. If we are not critical of the data we use (and those that provide it), perhaps becoming over-reliant on data press releases (Knight 2013), we can risk undermining our credibility with data-churnalism or, worse still, data-porn! (Oliver 2010). As data journalism practice evolves, whilst the basic critical skills will remain fundamental, it would seem logical to explore ways that we reduce our dependency on other sources all together. The Beijing project, with its use of sensors, offers a compelling solution. As Javaun Moradi, product manager for

NPR digital, succinctly put it: "If stage 1 of data journalism was 'find and scrape data', then stage 2 was 'ask government agencies to release data' in easy to use formats. Stage 3 is going to be 'make your own data'" (Moradi 2011).

Crowdsensing data

The three stages that Moradi identifies are not mutually exclusive. Many data journalism projects already include an element of gathering new data often done using traditional forms of crowdsourcing; questionnaires or polls. As much as involving the audience has its benefits (Bradshaw 2012), it is notoriously unpredictable and time-consuming. But as individuals we already make a huge amount of data. That isn't just data about us collected by others through a swipe of a loyalty card or by submitting a tax return online. It's also data we collect about ourselves and the world around us.

An increasing number of us strap sensors to ourselves that track our health and exercise and the "internet of things" (Ashton. 2009) is creating a growing source of data from the buildings and objects around us.[4] The sensors used by the AP team were specialist air pollution sensors that cost in excess of $400 – an expensive way for cash-strapped newsrooms to counter dodgy data. Since 2008 however, the price has dropped and the growing availability of cheap computing devices such as Raspberry Pi and Arduino[5] and the collaborative and open source ethic of the hacker and maker communities, have lowered the barriers to entry. Now sensors, and the crowd they attract, are a serious option for developing data driven reporting.

Hunting for (real) bugs with data

In 2013, New York braced itself for an invasion. Every 17 years a giant swarm of cicadas descend on the East Coast. The problem is that exactly when in the year the insects will appear is less predictable. The best indicator of the emergence of the mega-swarm (as many as a billion cicadas in a square mile) seems to be when the temperature eight inches below the ground reaches 64 degrees (18oC). So when John Keefe, WNYC's senior editor for data news and journalism technology, met with news teams to look at ways to cover the story, he thought of the tinkering he had done with Arduino's and Raspberry Pi's (Waite 2013). He thought of sensors.

Keefe could not find a source for the data that offered any level of local detail across the whole of New York. He took the problem of how to collect the data to a local hackathon, organised by the stations popular science show Radiolab, who helped create a "recipe" for an affordable, easy to make temperature sensor which listeners could build and send results back to a website 6 where they would map the information (Alba 2014).

Developing collaboration

Whilst sensors play an enabling role in both examples, underpinning both the Beijing AirTrack and Cicada projects is the idea of collaboration. The Beijing project was originally developed by a team from the Spatial Information Lab[6] at

Columbia University. Combining the access of the media with the academic process and expertise of the lab gave the project a much bigger reach and authority. It's a form of institutional collaboration that echoes in a small way in more recent projects such as 2012's Reading the riots.[7] The cicada project, on the other hand, offers an insight into a kind of community-driven collaboration that reflects the broader trend of online networks and the dynamic way groups form.

Safecast and the Fukushima nuclear crisis

On 9 March 2011, Joichi Ito was in Cambridge Massachusetts. He had travelled from Japan for an interview to become head of MIT's prestigious Media Lab. The same day a massive underwater earthquake off the coast of Japan caused a devastating tsunami and triggered a meltdown at the Fukushima Dai-ichi nuclear plant, starting the worst nuclear crisis since Chernobyl in 1986. Ito, like many others, turned to the web and social media to find out if family and friends were safe and gather as much information as he could about the risk from radiation (Kalin 2012).

At the same time as Ito was searching for news about his family, US web developer Marcelino Alvarez was in Portland scouring the web for information about the possible impact of the radiation on the US's west coast. He decided to channel his "paranoia" and within 72 hours his company had created RDTN.org, a website aggregating and mapping information about the level of radiation (Alvarez 2011).

For Alvarez and Ito the hunt for information soon developed into an effort to source geiger counters to send to Japan. Within a week of the disaster, the two had been introduced and RDTN.org became part of project that would become Safecast.org. As demand outstripped supply, their efforts to buy geiger counters quickly transformed into a community driven effort to design and build cheap, accurate sensors that could deployed quickly to gather up to date information.

Solving problems: Useful data

Examples such as WNYC's cicada project show how a strong base of community engagement can help enable data driven projects. But the Safecast network was not planned, it grew "from purposed conversations among friends to full time organization gradually over a period of time" (Safecast history 2013). There was no news conference to decide the when and the how it would respond or attempt to target contributors. It was a complex, self-selecting, mix of different motivations and passions that coalesced into a coherent response to solve a problem. It's a level of responsiveness and scale of coverage that news organisations would struggle to match on their own. In that context, Moradi believes that journalism has a different role to play:

> Whether they know it or not, they do need an objective third party to validate their work and give it authenticity. News organisations are uniquely

positioned to serve as ethical overseers, moderators between antagonistic parties, or facilitators of open public dialogue (Moradi 2011).

Building bridges

Taking a position as a "bridge" between those with data and resources and "the public who desperately want to understand the data and access it but need help" (Rogers 2011) is a new reading of what many would recognise as a traditional part of journalism's process and identity. The alignment of data journalism with the core principles of accountability and the purpose of investigative journalism, in particular, makes for a near perfect meeting point for the dynamic mix of like-minded hacks, academics and hackers, motivated not just by transparency and accountability. It also taps into a desire not just to highlight issues but begin to put in place solutions to problems. This mix of ideologies, as the WikiLeaks story shows (Ellison 2012), can be explosive but the output has proved invaluable in helping (re)establish the role of journalism in the digital space. Whether it is a catalyst to bring groups together, engage and amplify the work of others or a way to "advance the cause of journalism by means other than reporting" (Moradi 2011), sensor journalism seems to be an effective gateway to exploring these new opportunities

The digital divide

The rapid growth of data journalism has played a part in directing attention, and large sums of money, to projects that take abstract concepts like open government and "make them tangible, relevant and useful to real live humans in our communities" (Sopher 2013). It's no surprise, then, that many of them take advantage of sensors and their associated communities to help build their resources. Innovative uses of smart phones, co-opting the internet of things or using crowd funded sensor project like the Air quality egg.[8] But a majority of the successful data projects funded by organisations such as the Knight Foundation,[9] have outputs that are almost exclusively digital: apps or data dashboards. As much as they rely on the physical to gather data, the results remain resolutely trapped in the digital space.

As far back as 2009, the UK government's *Digital Britain* report warned: "We are at a tipping point in relation to the on-line world. It is moving from conferring advantage on those who are in it to conferring active disadvantage on those who are without" (BIS 2009: 11). The solution to this digital divide is to focus on getting those who are not online connected. As positive as this is, it's a predictably technological deterministic solution to the problem that critics say conflates digital inclusion with social inclusion (Livingstone and Lunt 2012). For journalism, and data journalism in particular, it raises an interesting challenge to claims of "combating information asymmetry" and increasing the data literacy of their readers on a mass scale (Gray et al 2012).

Insight journalism: Journalism as data

In the same year as Digital Britain report appeared, the Bespoke project dived into the digital divide by exploring ways to create real objects that could act as interfaces to the online world. The project took residents from the Callon and Fishwick areas in Preston, Lancashire, recognised as some of the most deprived areas in the UK, and trained them as community journalists who contributed to a "hyperlocal" newspaper that was distributed round the estate. The paper also served as a way of collecting "data" for designers who developed digitally connected objects aimed at solving problems identified by the journalists. A process the team dubbed insight journalism (Blum-Ross et al. 2013). One example, the Wayfinder, was a digital display and a moving arrow which users could text to point to events happening in the local area. Another, Viewpoint (Taylor et al. 2012a), was a kiosk, placed in local shops that allowed users to vote on questions from other residents, the council and other interested parties. The questioner had to agree that they would act on the responses they got, a promise that was scrutinised by the journalists.

The idea was developed during the 2012 Unbox festival[10] in India, when a group of designers and journalists applied the model of insight journalism to the issue of sexual harassment on the streets of New Delhi. The solution, built on reports and information gathered by journalists, was to build a device that would sit on top of one of the many telegraph poles that clutter the streets attracting thousands of birds. The designers created a bird table fitted with a bell. When a woman felt threatened or was subjected to unwanted attention she could use Twitter to "tweet" the nearest bird table and a bell would ring. The ringing bell would scatter any roosting birds giving a visible sign of a problem in the area. The solution was as poetic as it was practical, highlighting not just the impact of the physical but the power of journalism as data to help solve a problem.[11]

Stage four: Make data real

Despite its successes sensor journalism is still a developing area and it is not yet clear if it will see any growth beyond the environmental issues that drive many of the examples presented here. Like data journalism, much of the discussion around the field focuses on the new opportunities it presents. These often intersect with equally nascent but seductive ideas such as drone journalism.[10] More often than not, though, they bring the discussion back to the more familiar ground of the challenges of social media, managing communities and engagement. As journalism follows the mechanisms of the institutions we are meant to hold to account into the digital space, it is perhaps a chance to think about how it can move beyond simply building capacity within the industry, providing useful case studies (Gray et al 2012). Perhaps it is a way to for data journalism to help journalism re-connect to the minority of those in society who, by choice or by circumstance, are left disconnected.

Thinking about ways to make the data we find and the data journalism we create physical, closes a loop on a process that starts with real people in the real world. It begins to raise important questions about what journalism's role should be in not just capturing the problems and raising awareness but also creating solutions. In an industry struggling to re-connect, it maybe also starts to address the issue of solving the problem placing journalism back in the community and making it sustainable. Researchers reflecting on the Bespoke project noted that "elements of the journalism process put in place to inform the design process have continued to operate in the community and have proven to be more sustainable as an intervention than the designs themselves" (Taylor et al. 2012b).

If stage three is to make our own data, perhaps it is time to start thinking about stage four of data journalism and make data real.

Notes

[1] See http://www.spatialinformationdesignlab.org/projects.php?id=97, accessed on 23 September b2012

[2] See http://hosted.ap.org/specials/interactives/_international/oly_fea_pollution/index.html, accessed on 1 October 2013

[3] The BBC clearly stated that their sensor had a 20 per cent margin of error

[4] See https://xively.com/http://hosted.ap.org/specials/interactives/_international/oly_fea_p ollution/index.html, accessed on 2 October 2013

[5] See http://makezine.com/2013/04/15/arduino-uno-vs-beaglebone-vs-raspberry-pi/, accessed on 2 October 2013

[6] http://project.wnyc.org/cicadas/, accessed on 2 October 2013

[7] http://www.theguardian.com/uk/series/reading-the-riots, accessed on 2 October 2013

[8] http://airqualityegg.wikispaces.com/AirQualityEgg, accessed on 2 October 2013

[9] https://www.newschallenge.org, accessed on 2 October 2013

[10] http://unboxfestival.comhttp://unboxfestival.com/, accessed on 2 October 2013

[11] http://www.dronejournalismlab.org/, accessed on 2 October 2013

References

Alba, Davey (2013) Sensors: John Keefe and Matt Waite on the current possibilities, Tow Centre for Digital Journalism, 5 June. Available online at http://towcenter.org/blog/sensors-john-keefe-and-matt-waite-on-the-current-possibilities/, accessed on 12 August 2013

Alvarez, Marcelino (2011) 72 Hours from concept to launch: RDTN.org, Uncorked Words, 21 March. Available online at http://uncorkedstudios.com/2011/03/21/72-hours-from-concept-to-launch-rdtn-org/, accessed on 12 August 2013

Ashton, Kevin (2009) That "Internet of Things" thing, *RFiD Journal* 22 pp 97-114. Available online at http://www.rfidjournal.com/articles/view?4986, accessed on 25 September, 2013

Department of Business Innovation and Skills (2009) *Digital Britain: Final Report*, Stationery Office

BBC (2008) In pictures: Beijing pollution-watch, BBC News website, 24 August. Available online at http://news.bbc.co.uk/sport1/hi/front_page/6934955.stm, accessed on 12 August 2013

Blum-Ross, Alicia, Mills, John, Egglestone, Paul and Frohlich, David (2013) Community media and design: Insight journalism as a method for innovation, *Journal of Media Practice*, Vol. 14, No 3, 1 September pp 171-192

Bradshaw, Paul. and Brightwell, Andy. (2012) Crowdsourcing investigative journalism: Help me Investigate: A case study, Siapera, Eugenia and Veglis, Andreas (eds) *The Handbook of Global Online Journalism*, London: John Wiley & Sons pp 253-271

Ellison, Sarah (2011) The man who spilled the secrets, *Vanity Fair*, February. Available online at http://www.vanityfair.com/politics/features/2011/02/the-guardian-201102 , accessed on 13 September 2013

Gray, Jonathan, Chambers, Lucy and Bounegru, Liliana (2012) *The Data Journalism Handbook*. O'Reilly. Free version available online at http://datajournalismhandbook.org/

Howard, Alex (2013) Sensoring the news, O'Reilly Radar, 22 March. Available at http://radar.oreilly.com/2013/03/sensor-journalism-data-journalism.html, accessed on 12 August 2013

Kalin, Sari (2012) Connection central. MIT news magazine, 21 August. Available at http://www.technologyreview.com/article/428739/connection-central/, accessed on 22nd August 2013

Knight, Megan (2013) Data journalism: A preliminary analysis of form and content. A paper delivered to the International Association for Media and Communication Research, 25-29 June, Dublin

Livingstone, Sonia and Lunt, Peter (2013) Ofcom's plans to promote "participation", but whose and in what? LSE Media Policy Project, 27 February. Available online at http://blogs.lse.ac.uk/mediapolicyproject/2013/02/27/ofcoms-plans-to-promote-participation-but-whose-and-in-what/, accessed on 23 September 2013

Moradi, Javaun (2011) What do open sensor networks mean for journalism?, Javaun's Ramblings, 16 December 16. Available online at http://javaunmoradi.com/blog/2011/12/16/what-do-open-sensor-networks-mean-for-journalism/#sthash.yXXlHoa2.dpuf, accessed on 9 August 2013

Oliver, Laura (2010) UK government's open data plans will benefit local and national journalists, Journalism.co.uk, 1 June. Available online at http://www.journalism.co.uk/news/uk-government-039-s-open-data-plans-will-benefit-local-and-national-journalists/s2/a538929/, accessed on 12 August 2013

Rogers, Simon. (2011) *Facts are Sacred: The Power of Data* (Guardian shorts), Cambridge, UK: Guardian Books

Safecast History (no date) Safecast.com. Available online at http://blog.safecast.org/history/, accessed on 25 September 2013

Sopher, Christopher (2013) How can we harness data and information for the health of communities?, Knight Foundation, 16 August. Available online at https://www.newschallenge.org/challenge/healthdata/brief.html accessed on 10 September 2013.

Taylor, Nick, Marshall, Justin, Blum-Ross, Alicia., Mills, John, Rogers, Jon, Egglestone, Paul, Frohlich, David M., Wright, Peter, Olivier, Patrick (2012) *Viewpoint: Empowering Communities with Situated Voting Devices.* Proceedings of the Computer Human Interaction (CHI) conference, New York: Association for Computing Machinery pp 1,361-1,370

Taylor, Nick; Cheverst, Keith; Wright, Peter and Olivier, Patrick (2013) *Leaving the Wild: Lessons from Community Technology Handovers,* Proceedings of the SIGCHI Conference on Human Factors in Computing Systems, New York: Association for Computing Machinery pp 1,549-1,558

Waite, Matt. (2013) How sensor journalism can help us create data, improve our storytelling, Poynter.org. 17 April. Available online at http://www.poynter.org/how-tos/digital-strategies/210558/how-sensor-journalism-can-help-us-create-data-improve-our-storytelling/, accessed on 28 August 2013

Note on the contributor
Andy Dickinson is a Senior Lecturer at the University of Central Lancashire where he teaches online and digital journalism. Based in the Media Innovation Studio, he is interested in the places that technology, journalism and the community meet. He blogs as andydickinson.net.

Hacks, hacking and the NSA: Encryption for the working journalist

Gabriel Keeble-Gagnère argues that – in the light of the recent NSA revelations – journalists, especially those dealing with sensitive topics, should become familiar with encryption techniques. And he provides an overview of the methods reporters can use to protect themselves from the snoopers

The cache of National Security Agency (NSA) documents leaked by Edward Snowden to Glenn Greenwald and Laura Poitras early in 2013 has brought into sharp focus the surveillance efforts of the US government. While it had been assumed for years that the NSA monitored much internet traffic, the leaks have provided documentary proof that these programs are, indeed, operational and in some cases more invasive than previously thought. While the implications for the citizens of the world (since the reach of the NSA is global) are profound, and have been discussed extensively in the media (both on- and off-line), here we focus on the following questions: What are the implications for working journalists, for whom source confidentiality, and the ability to work free of government interference are so integral? And what can they do about it?

We will argue that journalists, especially those dealing with sensitive subjects, must become familiar with elements of computer security and encryption. In light of this, the aims of this chapter are two-fold: to place the Snowden revelations in the broader context of government intimidation and attacks on journalists, discussing the practical implications; and to give a brief overview of the methods and tools journalists can employ to protect themselves.

What this chapter cannot do is detail how to protect oneself absolutely; instead, it hopes to introduce a number of tools and ideas that can be a starting point for working towards a useful knowledge of encryption and computer security. It must be emphasised that perfect security is impossible, especially on the internet, as this can only be achieved by avoiding it completely. Depending on the situation, this may be a prudent choice.

What we now know

Here are some of Edward Snowden's most important revelations.

Many technology companies are actively aiding the NSA access users' data (Greenwald et al. 2013, Ball et al. 2013)

Anyone using services provided by large internet companies such as Gmail, Facebook, Hotmail and Skype should assume that all their communications are being monitored and stored. In many cases technology companies have actively assisted the NSA in their efforts to access user data – even if, as in the case of Yahoo, they initially resisted (Miller 2013). Journalists working on sensitive stories should avoid these services completely.

The backbone of the internet is being tapped directly (MacAskill et al. 2013)

Even if services provided by companies known to be collaborating with the NSA are avoided, this does not mean communications cannot be monitored. It has been revealed that the NSA (and GCHQ) has been given secret access to the network of undersea cables which carry the bulk of international phone and internet traffic. In practice, this means that any unencrypted communications on the internet may be monitored and logged.

Encryption technologies are being attacked (Ball et al. 2013)

It should be assumed that any encryption features built into proprietary software and services are unsafe. In addition, any encryption reliant on keys that have been generated by a third party (for example, HTTPS encryption used by many websites) is also not secure. Even analysts at Britain's GCHQ were shocked when they learned of the NSA's efforts in this space, as *The New York Times* noted: "When the British analysts, who often work side-by-side with NSA officers, were first told about the program, another memo said, 'those not already briefed were gobsmacked!'" (Perlroth et al. 2013).

Many popular proprietary technology platforms are compromised

In many ways one of the most serious revelations with regards to computer security since even the most secure cryptography will be useless on a compromised machine (the sensitive information can be accessed before it is encrypted). It has been reported that the NSA has had backdoor access to all Microsoft Windows operating systems since Windows 95 (Maloof 2013); the NSA also has access to user data on Apple iPhone, Android and Blackberry phones (Rosenbach et al. 2013). Since the source code for proprietary software is not made public, backdoors are always possible. While not completely immune, open-source software, for which the source code can be studied and scrutinised by the development community, is much less likely to be compromised. In light of this, it would be preferable for journalists to learn how to use an open-source operating system such as Linux.

What it means

In short, journalists can no longer rely on internet companies, commercial software, or even the rule of law to protect them or their data. Especially at risk are those who work with whistleblowers – as Julian Assange and Glenn

Greenwald are perhaps the most aware. It goes without saying that whistleblowers themselves must be especially careful, even more so than the journalists they work with; the experiences of Bradley/Chelsea Manning and Edward Snowden have made this clear. Indeed, following an initial (encrypted) exchange with Snowden (who had not revealed his identity at the time), Laura Poitras was given "instructions for creating an even more secure system to protect their exchanges". Snowden had already contacted Greenwald anonymously, with instructions on how to use encryption, but had been ignored (Mass 2013). In the future, unless journalists have a working knowledge of cryptographic techniques, whistleblowers will, rightly, be unwilling to approach them.

Beginning the journey towards encryption

Journalists, not usually known for their computing skills, may be unsure how to go about familiarising themselves with the various techniques for encrypting their communications and data. This section, therefore, hopes to introduce a number of tools and concepts, together with resources for continued learning; hopefully, it can provide the basis for journalists to begin the journey.

All the tools detailed below, unless stated otherwise, are open-source and freely available for Windows, Mac OSX and Linux operating systems. Given the high chance that Windows and Mac OSX are compromised (see discussion above), it is recommended to use Linux in situations where security is critical. Naturally, as with all software, bugs and security problems are constantly being found (and hopefully fixed); it goes without saying that the latest (stable) version of all the following tools should always be used.

For critical applications, one should already be familiar with the tools in question to avoid potential errors which could compromise security. Most of the tools described below provide comprehensive guides which should be studied carefully.

A note on passwords

Many of the encryption methods detailed below involve the use of a password. The importance of using good passwords cannot be overstated. This is true also for passwords linked to email and other online accounts, though one should take particular care in picking good passwords for encryption as this will determine its reliability. For example, using a strong encryption method but with "abc" as password is hardly better than using no encryption at all, at least in situations beyond the most trivial. A good password is one that is relatively long (more than 10 characters), involving upper- and lower-case characters, numbers, special characters such as # and *, and not using any words that can be obviously linked to you. As Snowden allegedly told Poitras in their initial exchange, "assume that your adversary is capable of a trillion guesses a second" (Maas 2013).

Communicating securely

The most widespread tool for encryption of emails is PGP (Pretty Good Privacy, http://www.openpgp.org), and its open-source implementation GPG (GNU Privacy Guard, http://www.gnupg.org). These tools use the encryption algorithm known as RSA, named after its creators Rivest, Shamir and Adelman. This method relies on two keys: one, the *public key*, is usually shared online (for example, via a personal homepage or through key servers such as http://pgp.mit.edu/) and enables third parties to encrypt messages they wish to send; and the *private key*, without which the encrypted message cannot be decrypted and read. Note that the sender of the encrypted message need not have ever met the recipient; however, they must at least trust that the public key (and associated email address) genuinely belongs to them.

It is important to understand that the strength of RSA relies on a mathematical belief: that very large integers (with hundreds of digits) are difficult to factor (that is, reduce to its prime components). While no known method exists to do this in any reasonable space of time, this does not preclude the possibility that one will be found in the future. Still, the Snowden leaks seem to have confirmed that the NSA has not yet been able to "crack" the underlying mathematics of RSA (Simonite 2013).

One important factor in the security of RSA is the key size used (measured in bits), which are generally powers of 2 greater than 1024. To be safe, a key size of 4096 bits or more is advised. Another consideration is the implementation of RSA being used. As discussed in the first part of this chapter, proprietary implementations, especially those on embedded devices, are potentially compromised and should be avoided. A Swiss study found that an alarming number of public keys available on the internet shared common factors; the likely reason being sloppy implementations and small key sizes (Lenstra et al. 2012). Given their wide use and history, PGP and GPG can be assumed to be among the most reliable implementations at present.

Another capability of RSA besides encryption is that of digitally *signing* emails and data (this involves using your private key to encrypt – then your public key can be used by anyone to decrypt it and check that the result is the same as the message in question). Such a signature can be used by the recipient of data to confirm that the email has not been tampered with in transit. This is particularly important if an email account is hacked, as it can be used to prove that an account has been compromised.

For real-time communications, an account on the real-time messaging network Jabber (available at http://register.jabber.org), together with an open-source chat client such as Pidgin (http://www.pidgin.im/), allows encryption of messages using the OTR ("off the record") plugin (http://otr.cypherpunks.ca/).

With both methods described above, communications are only safe once keys have been exchanged and verified via a *different* communication channel (voice-based is preferable as it is difficult to imitate), where the identity of the intended recipient can be confirmed. This is to avoid so-called *man-in-the-middle* attacks, which may best be explained with an example. Say that Alice and Bob[1] wish to communicate securely, and are presently in physically different locations. If Alice emails Bob requesting his public key (in order to send him an encrypted email), Alice has no way of knowing if Bob's email account has been hacked (by Eve, say) and an alternate public key (for which Eve owns the private key) sent in the reply instead.

If Alice simply uses this key to send an encrypted email with sensitive information, Eve will be able to decrypt it. Hence the importance of verifying keys through another channel – in this case, Alice can simply call Bob and verify the key he emailed is, indeed, his own key. Note that this channel need not be encrypted – in fact, even if Eve is listening in, unless she can change Bob's voice in real-time in a way that convinces Alice, there is no problem (so long as this channel is only used to verify keys). In practice, it is not the key that is verified but its *fingerprint*, a much shorter string of characters that is used to identify the key itself.

Encrypting files

In addition to encrypting communications, journalists will often need to encrypt documents they are working on, such as articles in progress or documents passed to them in confidence. Commonly used compression tools often provide encryption support; though as discussed above, commercial tools are potentially compromised and should not be trusted. A reliable open-source compression tool is 7zip (http://www.7-zip.org/), which supports the AES-256 encryption standard. As noted previously, the strength of the encryption will be compromised by a trivial password. The full set of US diplomatic cables leaked to WikiLeaks was distributed as a 7zip-encrypted file; it was decrypted only after the *Guardian* journalist, David Leigh, published the password in a book[2]. Another popular tool is Truecrypt (http://www.trucrypt.org/; not strictly open-source, though the source code is available), which offers a wider range of cryptographic functions, such as encrypting entire file systems.

It is worth noting that extra care may be needed when working with particularly sensitive information. It follows from the first part of this chapter that any computer connected to the internet is *potentially* at risk of being spied on. In such a situation, the sensitive data can be accessed before it is even encrypted. An extra level of care that can be taken – and one adopted by renowned computer security expert Bruce Schneier while working on parts of the Snowden documents (Schneier 2013) for the *Guardian* – is to buy a new computer, which is never connected to the internet, and used solely for the purpose of working on, encrypting and decrypting sensitive files (this is known as "air-gapping"). This way, the plaintext (non-encrypted) data will never be loaded into memory on an online computer.

Accessing the internet anonymously

When connected to the internet, our identity is revealed by a unique IP (internet protocol) address. Each connection we make on the internet (to websites, email servers and so on) may be traced back to us with this address. What this means is that even with prudent use of encryption, the identity of whistleblowers and those they work with can be uncovered (though what they are saying may not be). Because of this, and depending on the situation, anonymous access to the internet may be desired.

One of the simplest ways of achieving this is with the Tor software package (http://torproject.org/), which anonymises connections by sending them through a series of intermediate nodes (computers running the Tor software in "relay" mode), before finally accessing the website through the final node in the chain, the exit node. One important point to note is that while communications within the Tor network are encrypted, the exit node will transmit data as it was at the beginning – in other words, the user is responsible for encrypting their communications. Failure to do so can compromise anonymity. Care should also be taken when links are followed, since external applications (for example, when opening a linked PDF file) opened will not be running through Tor by default and can unmask you.

While there are a number of potential issues with Tor, and new vulnerabilities are often being found, it is still believed to be a reliable way to achieve anonymity online. Indeed, the NSA's own exploits of Tor have focused on the Firefox web browser supplied with the Tor Browser Bundle (these exploits have since been fixed), not the Tor system itself (Schneier 2013). Despite this, the Tor Browser Bundle is still recommended (the website states: "Almost any other web browser configuration is likely to be unsafe to use with Tor") – just make sure to always use the latest version.

Another way of anonymising oneself online is to purchase an account on a VPN (Virtual Private Network) service. In a nutshell, this simply serves as a relay point for your connections; the IP address you appear to be connecting from is that of the VPN server, not your personal computer. Data is encrypted between your computer and the VPN servers (though it should be noted that this is one of the types of encryption that the NSA has worked to compromise). There are a large range of VPN services available, with varying levels of security. One word of caution: many VPN services will log all user activity and hand over this information when pressured by governments and law enforcement (Enigmax&Ernesto 2013). For true anonymity, a VPN provider that does not log user activity is essential; AirVPN (https://airvpn.org/) and PrivatVPN (https://www.privatvpn.se/en/) are two providers that claim not to.

Note that Tor and VPNs can also be used to access websites that have been blocked. In countries which operate particularly aggressive censorship of the internet, such as Iran, China and Saudi Arabia (and let's not pretend that Western governments are exempt – Australia, Italy, France and the UK were placed "under surveillance" in the annual Reporters Without Borders "Enemies of the internet" report in 2010 following moves to implement their own filters), access to sites routinely used by journalists such as Twitter may be restricted; a VPN account allows you to bypass such filters regardless of physical location.

Learning more

In an ideal world everyone would use encryption; in practice, however, it is beyond the technical skills, and patience, of most people. There have been a number of initiatives recently that seek to educate the broader public on cryptography issues. Started more than a year before the Snowden leaks came to light, the now-global Cryptoparty (https://cryptoparty.org/) emerged practically overnight following an exchange on Twitter initiated from Melbourne, Australia (Butt et al. 2012). It aims to provide a space for those interested in learning about cryptography to learn from users who are already familiar with tools and concepts, through talks and workshops. In New York, an encryption workshop was organised by the "Hacks/Hackers" group, with the specific aim of educating journalists (Kirchner 2013). These kinds of initiatives can be expected to become more common in the post-Snowden age. Journalists who are keen to learn should contact local computing groups (such as Linux user groups) or "hackerspaces" (a comprehensive list can be found at http://hackerspaces.org/wiki/List_of_Hacker_Spaces) and try to organise similar sessions.

The limits

While appropriate and careful use of available technologies can protect journalists from many threats, it has limits. Governments will still try to intimidate and interfere with journalists using the means at their disposal. In particular, laws can be passed criminalising methods detailed above; indeed, many Western governments have already made it a crime to refuse to decrypt an encrypted file. While criminalising encryption outright is most likely unworkable in practice, this will not prevent governments from trying. Not that laws need be the limiting factor: the illegal detention of Greenwald's partner, David Miranda, at London's Heathrow Airport, is unlikely to be the last such incident.

These actions are part of a worrying broader movement to start treating leakers (and the journalists they work with) as threats to national security, with governments arguing that terror laws are appropriate in this context. In the US, the National Defense Authorization Act for Fiscal Year 2012 (NDAA) has led to concerns that journalists may be targeted. A lawsuit was filed on 13 January 2013 (Hedges vs. Obama), arguing that Section 1021(b)(2) may authorise indefinite detention of journalists who are suspected of "providing substantial support" to terrorists. The wording is so vague it has raised concerns that the law can also be applied to journalists who interview or simply write about groups or movements the government is opposed to, such as environmentalists or WikiLeaks (Kuipers 2012).

The ongoing case of Barrett Brown is another example. Brown, an American writer and journalist, is facing 105 years in jail – and has been gagged by a Federal Court order – for reporting on hacked private intelligence companies (Goodman et al. 2013). The bulk of the charges against him are related to his publishing of a link in an internet chat room.

Given the above, to what extent are journalists really at risk of being snooped on? How much effort should journalists devote to protecting themselves? The answer depends on individual circumstances. The vast majority of journalists will rarely find themselves targeted by governments. However, with large-scale leaks becoming more and more common, and governments' reactions increasingly extreme, few serious journalists can afford not to have at least a basic knowledge of the tools discussed in this chapter. Indeed, it is possible we would still be in the dark if it wasn't for Poitras's positive response to Snowden's initial contact.

Conclusion

Given what we now know, without careful use of encryption, a journalist cannot honestly guarantee the anonymity of a source – in some cases, this might be a matter of life and death. As Snowden has said himself: "In the wake of this year's disclosure, it should be clear that unencrypted journalist-source communication is unforgivably reckless" (Maas 2013). Put another way, Snowden is saying that journalists cannot do their job properly without encryption. Just as the internet revolutionised journalism and the way journalists work (for better or worse), the Snowden leaks highlight the need for another major shift in practices. Journalistic training should reflect this – university courses should provide at least an option to learn about encryption (for example, in collaboration with a computing or maths department).

Finally, no matter how good your encryption, it is ultimately no substitute for that most essential ingredient in human relations: trust. Journalists and their sources should probably err on the side of caution. As John Young, founder of notorious leaks site Cryptome (http://www.cryptome.org/) puts it: "Best, be creative, imagine a means to triumph over the advice given here. Don't brag about it" (Cryptome 2012).

The Snowden leaks have revealed that there is, indeed, a war going on – an information war in which cryptography is a key weapon. The true role of journalism is to hold power to account; sadly, as we now know, a power that has evidently overstepped. It's time for journalists to fight back.

Notes

[1] Alice, Bob and Eve are common names used in cryptography books

[2] The password, CollectionOfDiplomaticHistorySince_1966_ToThe_PresentDay#, gives an idea of the care appropriate for sensitive situations

References

Ball, J., Borger, J. and Greenwald, G. (2013) Revealed: How US and UK spy agencies defeat internet privacy and security, *Guardian Weekly*, 6 September

Ball, J., Harding, L. and Garside, J. (2013) BT and Vodafone among telecoms companies passing details to GCHQ, *Guardian*, 2 August

Enigmax&Ernesto (2013) VPN Services That Take Your Anonymity Seriously, 2013 Edition, *TorrentFreak*, 2 March 2013. Available online at http://torrentfreak.com/vpn-services-that-take-your-anonymity-seriously-2013-edition-130302/

Butt, C. and Cook, H. (2012) Privacy movement finds strength in crypto night, *Age*, 23 September

Lenstra, A. K., Hughes, J. P., Augier, M., Bos, J. W., Kleinjung, T. and Wachter, C. (2012) *IACR Cryptology ePrint Archive 2012*, No. 64

Cryptome (2012) How to submit material to Cryptome anonymously. Available online at http://cryptome.org/cryptome-anon.htm, accessed on 4 October 2013

Goodman, A. and Gonzalez, J. (2013) Jailed Journalist Barrett Brown Faces 105 Years For Reporting on Hacked Private Intelligence Firms, *Democracy Now*, 11 July. Available online at http://www.democracynow.org/2013/7/11/jailed_journalist_barrett_brown_faces_105, accessed on 5 October 2013

Greenwald, G. and MacAskill, E. (2013) NSA Prism program taps in to user data of Apple, Google and others, *Guardian*, 7 June

Greenwald, G. (2013) The persecution of Barrett Brown – and how to fight it, *Guardian*, 21 March. Available online at http://www.theguardian.com/commentisfree/2013/mar/21/barrett-brown-persecution-anonymous, accessed on 30 September 2013

Kirchner, L. (2013) Encryption, security basics for journalists, *Columbia Journalism Review* website. Available online at http://www.cjr.org/behind_the_news/hacks_hackers_security_for_jou.php?page=all, accessed on 5 October 2013

Kuipers, D. (2012) Activists sue Obama, others over National Defense Authorization Act, *Los Angeles Times*, 18 April

MacAskill, E, Borger, J., Hopkins, N., Davies, N. and Ball, J. (2013) GCHQ taps fibre-optic cables for secret access to world's communications, *Guardian*, 22 June. Available online at http://www.theguardian.com/uk/2013/jun/21/gchq-cables-secret-world-communications-nsa, accessed on 30 September 2013

Maloof, F. (2013) NSA has total access via Microsoft Windows. Available online at http://www.wnd.com/2013/06/nsa-has-total-access-via-microsoft-windows/, accessed on 30 September 2013

Mass, P. (2013) How Laura Poitras helped Snowden spill his secrets, *New York Times Magazine*, 18 August. Available online at http://www.nytimes.com/2013/08/18/magazine/laura-poitras-snowden.html?pagewanted=all&_r=0, accessed on 30 September 2013

Mass, P. (2013) Q. & A.: Edward Snowden Speaks to Peter Maass. Available online at http://www.nytimes.com/2013/08/18/magazine/snowden-maass-transcript.html, accessed on 4 October 2013.

Miller, C. (2013) Secret court ruling put tech companies in data bind, *New York Times*, 14 June. Available online at http://www.nytimes.com/2013/06/14/technology/secret-court-ruling-put-tech-companies-in-data-bind.html?pagewanted=all, accessed on 30 September 2013

Perlroth, N., Larson, J. and Shane, S. (2013) NSA. Able to Foil Basic Safeguards of Privacy on Web, *New York Times*, 6 September

Rosenbach, M., Poitras, L. and Stark, H. (2013) iSpy: How the NSA accesses smartphone data, *Der Spiegel*, 9 September

Schneier, B. (2013) Attacking Tor: how the NSA targets users' online anonymity. Available online at http://www.theguardian.com/world/2013/oct/04/tor-attacks-nsa-users-online-anonymity, accessed on 5 October 2013

Schneier, B. (2013) NSA surveillance: A guide to staying secure. Available online at http://www.theguardian.com/world/2013/sep/05/nsa-how-to-remain-secure-surveillance, accessed on 30 September 2013

Simonite, T. (2013) NSA Leak Leaves Crypto-Math Intact but Highlights Known Workarounds. Available online at http://www.technologyreview.com/news/519171/nsa-leak-leaves-crypto-math-intact-but-highlights-known-workarounds/, accessed on 1 October 2013

Note on the contributor

Gabriel Keeble-Gagnère is Senior Informatics Analyst for the Australia-China Centre for Wheat Improvement at Murdoch University, Perth, Australia. He has a BSc. in Mathematics and Computer Science from Imperial College, London, and a Maîtrise Master's in Pure Mathematics from Pierre and Marie Curie University, Paris, France. While he works in bioinformatics, he has a strong interest in cryptography and topics related to internet security.

Offshore secrets revealed: How the biggest ever leak of data to journalists was handled

When an enormous cash of data emerged exposing the use of offshore tax havens by the world's rich and famous, an international consortium of journalists got to work in an unprecedented, complex, collaborative endeavour. Here Arthur Lashmar shows how they did it – and the extraordinary effects of the revelations

4 April 2013 was not a good day for Scot Young, a 51-year-older fixer for the super-rich who, with his close-cropped hair and trim physique, has a passing resemblance to the thriller actor Jason Statham. Young was sitting in his cell in London's depressing Pentonville Prison serving a six-month sentence and his day was about to get a lot worse. Young had been jailed for "flagrant and deliberate" contempt of court over an acrimonious divorce with his wife, Michelle, by refusing to reveal where he had stashed his wealth.

The wily Scot had risen from working-class origins in Dundee to a £14 million Oxfordshire mansion and was noted for his lavish lifestyle. Scot Young was a property developer and associate of Russian oligarch Boris Berezvosky. He once bought his then wife, and mother of his two children, a Range-Rover filled to the roof with couture dresses. For her 40th birthday, he gave her a £1 million necklace. The marriage broke down in 2006 and in divorce proceedings Scot claimed to having lost his £400 million wealth in a three-month period that coincided with the separation from his wife. There followed an extremely long and bitter court battle deciding the truth of his ex-wife's claims that his money had not been lost but hidden in offshore accounts. She said her husband had been happy and spending vast sums of money on a yacht and private jet just before his alleged bankruptcy, breakdown and attempted suicide. Young's assets had been subject to a global freezing order by the High Court in 2007. This order forbade Young from moving or selling his alleged disputed assets. At the beginning of the year, the High Court jailed Young for refusing to reveal the details of what had happened to his millions.

Probing the secret world of offshore banking

Young may have been in jail but he must at least felt sure his wife would not get any of his money. But on that morning the *Guardian* had produced the first stories from an international investigation that laid bare the inner machinations of the usually highly secret world of offshore banking especially on the British Virgin Islands (see http://offshoreleaks.icij.org/search). In just one of the stories, it was revealed the way Young had moved his assets out of the reach of his wife and the British courts. They appeared to show exactly how Scot Young had used agents to rearrange and merge some of his offshore companies containing his assets in an attempt to hide them further. They included correspondence suggesting Young had interests in a BVI company that owned a potentially lucrative Moscow development with a value estimated at £64m.

Young was just one of those using offshore evasions to be revealed in what is the biggest ever leak of data to journalists. It is also believed to be the biggest collaboration by a team of international journalists and programmers. In the first 24 hours of publication, the *Guardian* was filled with stories from a collaboration between the International Consortium of Investigative journalists (ICIJ), the BBC in the UK, *Le Monde* in France, *Süddeutsche Zeitung* and Norddeutscher Rundfunk in Germany, the *Washington Post*, the Canadian Broadcasting Corporation (CBC) and 31 other international media partners. According to the ICIJ, eighty-six journalists from 46 countries used both hi-tech data crunching and traditional reporting skills to sift through emails and account ledgers covering almost 30 years.

Using offshore accounts to evade tax has an enormous impact on perpetuating poverty. The advocacy group Global Financial Integrity says the illegal channelling of profits offshore cost developing countries almost $6 trillion between 2001 and 2010 (Porteous 2013). In global terms, the Scot Young story was not even a particularly significant one: it just showed how one British millionaire had used offshore banking to hide his assets. Another one concerned the jailed fraudster Achilleas Kallakis. He used fake BVI companies to obtain a record-breaking £750m in property loans from incompetent British and Irish banks. The *Guardian* headlined one of its stories: "More than 100 of Britain's richest people have been caught hiding billions of pounds in secretive offshore havens, sparking an unprecedented global tax evasion investigation" (Neate 2013).

As well as Britons hiding wealth offshore, an odd assortment of government officials and rich families across the world were identified: from the US, India, Pakistan, Indonesia, Iran, China, Thailand and former communist states. The data shows that their secret companies are based mainly in the British Virgin Islands. Just a few of the offshore owners revealed in the leaked files include:

- French Socialist President François Hollande's 2012 election campaign co-treasurer: Jean-Jacques Augier was revealed to keep his fortune offshore. The name of 59-year-old Augier, a businessman, appeared in the documents highlighted by *Le Monde*. These showed that he had shares in two offshore firms in the Cayman Islands through his financial holding company. Eurane Augier said that his actions were fully legal and attributes his participation in these schemes to his "adventurous nature" but has said he does not have "either a personal bank account in the Cayman Islands or any personal direct investment in that territory".

- Mongolian Deputy Speaker Bayartsogt Sangajav set up an offshore company with a Swiss bank account while he served as finance minister of the impoverished state from 2008 to 2012. He said it was "a mistake" not to declare it, and: "I probably should consider resigning from my position." Shortly afterwards he did resign following a vote by 87.5 per cent of the Parliament in favour of his resignation. The disciplinary committee of the SGK had convened earlier to discuss secret accounts after it had emerged the speaker had not disclosed his BVI company title and its Swiss Bank account that had contained $1 million at some time in 2008 (Valencia 2013).

- Maria Imelda Marcos Manotoc, a provincial governor in the Philippines, is the eldest daughter of former President Ferdinand Marcos, notorious for corruption. More popularly known as Imee Marcos, ICIJ said she did not report her offshore trust on asset disclosure statements that she was required to file every year as a public official. At the time of going to press, the Philippines' authorities were investigating the allegations. Imee Marcos said she had referred the matter to her lawyers. "Let's leave that aside for now and let the lawyers take care of it."

- Bankrupt Swedish real estate tycoon Hans Thulin had as much as $17 million sheltered offshore at a time when the Swedish government was pursuing him in court for millions of dollars in unpaid debts, according to secret records obtained by ICIJ and reviewed by *Fokus*, Sweden's leading news magazine.

How the story started
The story started with investigative journalist Gerald Ryle who had spent 26 years as a reporter and editor in Australia and Ireland, including many years at the *Sydney Morning Herald* and the *Melbourne Age* newspapers. A quietly spoken man, he uncovered some of the biggest stories in Australian journalism, four times winning that country's highest journalism award. He is a former deputy editor of the *Canberra Times*, a former Knight-Wallace Journalism Fellow at the University of Michigan and the author of a book based on one of his former investigations, *Firepower* (ICIJ 2013a). As a result of his earlier investigations into offshore banking, Ryle was told by a source he would receive an important package, one that would be a career highlight. "I still remember the day it arrived, there was just the office manager there, I just hugged her and thanked her and walked back to my office. I pulled the package open and there was a hard drive inside," said Ryle.

At first he did not know what it was but it became clear that it was full of an enormous cache of details of confidential emails, documents and files from the offshore world. From what could be made of the scattered and vastly disorganised material Ryle later recalled his thoughts as: "I know it is a potential goldmine but I don't actually know what I'm looking at, I'm not sure how valuable it is" (CBC News 2013). Ryle knew it was information from the secretive offshore world, was authentic and that the next step was to organise extracting the data in some kind of meaningful format. A chance to have access to the resources needed for this type of operation became available when Ryle was offered a continent-changing job heading the International Consortium of Investigative journalists (ICIJ) in Washington DC.

Founded in 1997, ICIJ was launched as a project of the Centre for Public Integrity to extend the centre's style of watchdog journalism, focusing on major international, cross-border crime, corruption, and the accountability of power. Backed by the centre and its computer-assisted reporting specialists, public records experts, fact-checkers and lawyers, ICIJ reporters and editors provide real-time resources and state-of-the-art tools and techniques to journalists around the world (ICIJ *Our Staff 2013*). The ICIJ has been responsible for a number of high profile stories such as the Tobacco Underground Project.[1] With the consortium's resources available to him, Ryle started to organise an international effort to structure the information so that journalists worldwide could analyse and find big names and stories from the data on a safe and secure platform in an efficient and ordered way.

Handling over 250 GB of unstructured data: The problems and the solutions

Ryle knew his job as a journalist was to publish as much as he could without putting any lives at risk or putting inaccurate information into the public domain. The data cache was enormous. As one of the reporters involved commented: "It's the largest amount of mixed data that has come into journalists' hands." With more than 250 GB of unstructured data the leak was over 160 times larger in size than the US cables leaked and published by WikiLeaks in 2010 (Campbell 2013a). The drive contained four large databases plus half a million text, PDF, spreadsheet, image and web files. Analysis by ICIJ's data experts showed that the data originated in 10 offshore jurisdictions, including the British Virgin Islands, the Cook Islands and Singapore. It included details of more than 122,000 offshore companies or trusts, nearly 12,000 intermediaries (agents or "introducers"), and about 130,000 records on the people and agents who run, own, benefit from or hide behind offshore companies (Campbell 2013a). When ICIJ further analysed the data using sophisticated matching software, it found that about 40 per cent of the files and emails were duplicates (ibid). The information also spread across more than 170 countries and territories (ibid). The significance of the data was apparent. The British Virgin Islands, for example, is the biggest provider of offshore entities in the world and notorious for its role in allowing the world's rich to avoid tax. The BVI records identify 30,000 people and more than 500,000 registered companies.

The ICIJ appointed as Data Journalism Manager, in what it dubbed the "secrecy for sale" investigation, to the British journalist Duncan Campbell,[2] a founder member of the ICIJ and an award winning reporter (ICIJ 2013b). Campbell is known for his work into secret surveillance and international espionage with wiretapping and the Echelon satellite interception network. Campbell is also considered to have one of the most brilliant minds in British journalism. He has been at the forefront of using computing and understanding of computing to produce many stories. He was one of three people prosecuted, unsuccessfully, under the Official Secrets Act in the mid-1970s, for revealing how signals intelligence worked at the Government Communications Headquarters (GCHQ), the British version of the NSA. This was just the first of many run-ins with the British state.

Campbell led the effort in the project to sort through and organise the data. Leading a team of journalists and computer programmers to structure the data for further analysis, Campbell describes the process in an ICIJ article (Campbell 2013b). One of the areas Campbell describes is the use of free text retrieval (FTR) software called NUIX which identifies topic-based documents with the use of keywords. This meant that when someone typed in something like a name or address the FTR displays all of the relevant files according to where the keyword is entered on the returned documents (ibid). However, tens of thousands of files did not have readable text, and software was then used on data such as images to write the text and information in the picture. This brought dozens of new files – such as passports and contracts giving deeper insight into the way the offshore system works – to journalists' attention (ibid).

There were more complications with data being in an inconsistent format, such as addresses not being in the order of country, state/county, street etc. (for instance, sorting a Paris Road as being in Paris). Spelling problems also resulted in a large number of leftover misspelt addresses. This prompted a group of the programmers to develop a piece of software that recognised misspelt areas and badly formatted information and corrected it. The four intact databases that were found on the drive were also rebuilt to try to find further insight into how the data was stored and operated. When this was completed it was found that often the offshore agent's company did not appear to comply with the law in their duty to investigate and name the actual beneficiaries of the account and who were really behind the offshore accounts: they had made a system that could facilitate this but the relevant boxes had been left out.

When the database had been completed and all of the previously disorganised and unreadable data had been cleaned up by the international teams, it was put on a platform in which journalists could quickly and securely access the files they needed for their investigations. This program, called Interdata, was developed and deployed in less than two weeks during December 2012. This program proved vital to the success of the project, providing relevant information on countries and areas for certain groups and had made over 28,000 online searches and downloaded more than 53,000 documents as of April 2013 (ibid).

Tackling the various layers of deception in the files

When it came to analysing the data there was already another layer of deception in the files, aimed at attempting to hide the relevant names of shareholders, directors and other key beneficiaries. The main method for this was through the use of nominee directors who sell the use of their names so that they front these companies whilst actually not knowing anything about them. This happens through a three-point process:

- the first was the signing of an agreement to guarantee that they would not take control of the companies in their name and that the secret owners would retain full access to their offshore funds;

- then the nominee would hand all of the management and accounts to the real owner of the business to which the company promised would not get found out;

- finally, the undated resignation letter which gives the nominee the ability to avoid any liabilities of the company if anything goes wrong.

This method led to a variety of fascinating revelations of single people owning vast arrays of businesses. One of the best reported examples is that of Englishwoman Sarah Petre-Mears, based on the tiny Caribbean island of Nevis, who has more than 1,200 companies in her name. With her business partner Edward Petre-Mears as director of at least 1,100 companies as well, this made them appear to be among the biggest international businessmen and women in the world (Ball 2012). However, it is not their entrepreneurial spirit that has seen their success but signing a few papers from a courier in return for cash, making them nominee directors of the large number of companies their names were credited to. The Petre-Mears are just examples of the nominees using a huge web of the 175,000 companies in the British Virgin Islands (Ball 2013).

The ICIJ team had to remove any information that could put any of people identified at risk so data such as passport numbers and home addresses had to be excluded from the database. "But persistently following leads through incomplete data and documents yielded some great rewards: not just occasional and unexpected top names, but also many more nuanced and complex schemes for hiding wealth. Some of the schemes spotted, although well known in the offshore trade, have not been described publicly before. Patience was rewarded when this data opened new windows on the offshore world," said Duncan Campbell (Campbell 2013b). He was supported at the UK end by expert computer programmer Matt Fowler, who had left his highly paid industry job to join the ICIJ team, and Craig Shaw, a journalist.

The "quick and dirty" tactic

As journalists trawled through the offshore accounts for high profile names, the ICIJ, who had teamed up with the *Guardian*, had decided on what David Leigh, the *Guardian*'s then-investigations editor, called a "quick and dirty" tactic by reporting the stories of all of the most famous and prominent beneficiaries in rapid succession instead of waiting for all of the stories to come out of the data and then release them.[3] A number of major stories emerged leading to the resignation of a number of prominent political figures. A large amount of the offshore activities linked back to China, Hong Kong and Taiwan, with a large number also from Russian origins (ibid). Russia and the former Soviet republics are now notorious for corruption and the use of hidden offshore banking. It showed that Russians had recently moved away from using Cyprus as their preferred offshore base in the 20001 to the British Virgin Islands as it gave them (until now) better secrecy.

One of the biggest hits for the ICIJ was on Azerbaijan President Ilham Aliyev after he and members of his family were revealed as shareholders in at least four offshore companies. It is against Azerbaijan law to be involved in business whilst in power. Aliyev was director and shareholder of the company in 2003. After becoming president in October 2003, he and his wife acquired a BVI company, Rosamund International Ltd which was still operating until May of 2004 (Candea 2013). This all appeared to contradict the signed agreements the country's government had made offering more transparency and an end to corruption. Conveniently for Ilham and his wife, Mehriban, they have been given immunity from any criminal prosecution in their lifetimes after a vote in parliament (ibid).

In September 2013, the Organised Crime and Corruption Reporting Project (OCCRP), based in Sarajevo and Bucharest, awarded the title "Corruption's Person of the Year" to Aliyev. "President Aliyev and his family, in fact, along with other persons in his inner circle, are involved in so many secret businesses that we uncovered," says Paul Radu, OCCRP's executive director. "We identified hidden companies that were owned by the first family of Azerbaijan in Panama, for instance, or in the Czech Republic. And we identified assets that they owned back in Azerbaijan via these companies" (Coalson 2013).

Also in September 2013, the family of a former South Korean president convicted of corruption vowed to pay back an estimated $154m (£98m) of corruptly-obtained assets. Former President and dictator Chun Doo-Hwan's son said the family would hand over various assets in restitution to the state. A former military general, Chun was leader from 1979 to 1988 after a coup. In 1996 he was convicted for treason, corruption and mutiny, but pardoned in 1997 and ordered to pay compensation for the slush fund he had amassed. Charges against the 82-year-old former leader included that he collected hundreds of millions of dollars in bribes during his term in office. He was ordered to pay 220bn won ($202m, £129m) in restitution to the state. He paid some of the money, but said he did not have enough to settle the rest. However, the ICIJ's investigation found offshore accounts relating to the family. His youngest son was revealed to have hidden money offshore in 2004 of which some was believed to be from his father's slush fund. Doo-Hwan's oldest son had joined the family business and was found by the ICIJ's leaks to be the director and shareholder in a secret BVI company. Chun's four children will now hand over assets that include valuable art and a house in Seoul, where Chun and his wife are currently living. His son apologised at a press conference to the Korean nation following months of renewed efforts by prosecutors to recover the money.

"I bow my head in apology on behalf of the family for having caused concerns regarding the issue of penalty payment," Chun Jae-kook, Chun's eldest son, said in the capital, Seoul. "The family will co-operate as much as possible so that the authorities' actions to collect penalty payment can be completed smoothly and we will also respond conscientiously to any investigations" (BBC News 2013).

Open access to the Offshore Leaks Database
Anyone can access the Offshore Leaks Database which allows users to search through the 100,000-plus secret companies, trusts at http://offshoreleaks.icij.org/search providing they agree to ICIJ terms and conditions. There is an Offshore Leaks web app, developed by *La Nacion* newspaper in Costa Rica, which displays graphic visualisations of these offshore entities and the networks around them, often including the company's true owners. Gerard Ryle is encouraging anyone recognising names to tip the ICIJ off via email so that they can investigate (Ryle 2013).

The whole offshore data operation has been a huge success for the ICIJ. As one of those involved said: "Offshore secrecy is no longer guaranteed." It has paved innovative methods for journalists to deal with unstructured data. Having such an international team was not without its problems. As Duncan Campbell revealed at the Centre for Investigative Journalism's 2013 Summer School in London, there were tensions in the international team and disputes arose between the UK and Costa Rica computing teams. Another problem has been that a huge number of the entries refer to Chinese nationals. China is not known for its business transparency at the best of times. With investigative journalism being a marginal and potentially dangerous activity in China, the ICIJ have found it hard to get Chinese partners to investigate these commercial networks. It is fascinating that a communist country allows its business people to have offshore accounts. This should produce new revelations though few of the names will mean much to a UK domestic audience.

Duncan Campbell said secure communication was a problem too: "The project team's attempts to use encrypted email systems such as PGP ("Pretty Good Privacy") were abandoned because of complexity and unreliability that slowed down information sharing. Studies have shown that police and government agents – and even terrorists – also struggle to use secure email systems effectively. Other complex cryptographic systems popular with computer hackers were not considered for the same reasons. While many team members had sophisticated computer knowledge and could use such tools well, many more did not," he said (Campbell 2013b).

"The message is simple: If you evade tax, we're coming after you"

Gerard Ryle has not revealed where he got this hard drive but it is known that similar data was supplied to Her Majesty's Customs and Excise in 2010 and other revenue enforcement agencies at about the same time. Ryle, director of the ICIJ, told the *Guardian* he expected the collaboration between tax authorities in the UK, US and Australia to lead to "the largest tax investigation in history". He added: "We know from the data we obtained there are names of people from more than 170 countries. Some are prominent citizens – politicians, celebrities, businessmen, the elite of some societies. To have three major tax agencies collaborating – with the possibility of many more doing the same – is potentially a major blow to the secrecy of offshore jurisdictions." George Osborne, the Chancellor, warned the alleged tax evaders, and a further 200 accountants and advisers accused of helping them cheat the taxman: "The message is simple: If you evade tax, we're coming after you." HM Revenue and Customs warned evaders that they would face "criminal prosecution or significant penalties" if they do not voluntarily disclose their tax irregularities, as the UK steps up its efforts to clamp down on avoidance ahead of the G8 summit in June (Neate 2013).

Ramifications of the leak are likely to continue for months. Faced with threats of sanctions the Premier of the British Virgin Islands, Orlando Smith, admitted his government had entered into talks with the US Treasury over complying with a US law passed to crack down on offshore tax evasion (Porteous 2013). Algirdas Semeta, the EU Commissioner, said the offshore leaks investigation had transformed tax politics and had increased the political will to tackle the problem of tax evasion. "I personally think the offshore leaks investigation could be identified as the most significant trigger behind these developments ... It has created visibility of the issue and it has triggered political recognition of the amplitude of the problem," he told the *EU Observer*. He added that tax transparency overrode the principle of data privacy.

After the September 2013 meeting of the G20 in St. Petersburg (somewhat dominated otherwise with the Syrian chemical warfare controversy), Russia announced new measures to fight offshore tax evasion, including a plan to share tax data automatically among the G20 nations by the end of 2015. The Leaders' Declaration also pledged the G20's assistance to developing countries seeking to establish automatic tax information sharing, but it stopped short of providing a timeline for implementation (ibid). By September 2013 journalists from 190 countries had produced stories from the database about prominent citizens who had hidden offshore accounts. The secrecy that has protected the corrupt across the world is beginning to break down under the pressure of determined, technology savvy and linked global journalism. There is still a long way to go.

Notes

[1] Since multinational tobacco companies profit by turning a blind eye to cigarette smuggling tobacco has become the most smuggled legal drug in the world

[2] Not to be confused with Duncan Campbell, the former *Guardian* crime correspondent

[3] David Leigh has since retired as the investigations editor of the *Guardian* after an illustrious career

References

Ball, J. (2012) Sham directors: The woman running 1,200 companies from a Caribbean rock, *Guardian*, 25 November. Available online at http://www.theguardian.com/uk/2012/nov/25/sham-directors-woman-companies-caribbean, accessed on 7 October 2013

Ball, J. (2013) More than 175,000 UK companies have offshore directors, *Guardian*, 4 April. Available online at http://www.theguardian.com/uk/2013/apr/04/uk-companies-offshore-directors-figures, accessed on 7 October 2013

BBC News (2013) South Korean ex-dictator's family to settle $154m in fines, 10 September. Available online at http://www.bbc.co.uk/news/world-asia-24028798, accessed on 7 October 2013

CBC News (2013) How ICIJ's Gerald Ryle got the offshore leaks files video, 22 May. Available online http://www.youtube.com/watch?v=N8mFjrIDRHA, accessed on 7 October 2013

Campbell, D. (2013a) How ICIJ's Project Team Analyzed the Offshore Files, ICIJ, 4 April. Available online at http://www.icij.org/offshore/how-icijs-project-team-analyzed-offshore-files, accessed on 7 October 2013

Campbell, D. (2013b) How ICIJ's Project Team Analysed the Offshore Files, 3 April. Available online at http://www.icij.org/offshore/how-icijs-project-team-analyzed-offshore-files, accessed on 7 October 2013

Candea, S. (2013) Offshore companies provide link between corporate mogul and Azerbaijan's president, 3 April. Available online at http://www.icij.org/offshore/offshore-companies-provide-link-between-corporate-mogul-and-azerbaijans-president, accessed on 7 October 2013

Coalson, R. (2013) Azerbaijani President Aliyev Named Corruption's "Person of the Year", 2 January. Available online at http://www.rferl.org/content/azerbaijan-ilham-aliyev-corruption-person-of-the-year/24814209.html, accessed on 7 October 2013

ICIJ (2013a) Our staff, Gerard Ryle. Available: www.ICIJ.org/about, accessed on 7 October 2013

ICIJ (2013b) Duncan Campbell journalist profile. Available online at http://www.icij.org/journalists/duncan-campbell, accessed on 7 October 2013

Porteous, K., Hudson, M. and Chavkin, S. (2013) Release of Offshore record draws worldwide response, 2 October. Available online at http://www.icij.org/blog/2013/04/release-offshore-records-draws-worldwide-response, accessed on 7 October 2013

Neate, R. and Ball, J. (2013) 100 of UK's richest people concealing billions in offshore tax havens, 9 May. Available online at http://www.theguardian.com/politics/2013/may/09/100-richest-uk-billions-offshore-tax-havens, accessed on 7 October 2013

Ryle, G. (2013) Why we are not turning over the offshore files to government agencies, ICIJ. 21 August. Available online at http://www.icij.org/blog/2013/04/why-we-will-not-turn-over-offshore-files-government-agencies, accessed on 7 October 2013

Valencia (2013) Deputy speaker Bayartsogt Sangajav resigns, 25 April. Available online at http://www.business-mongolia.com/mongolia/2013/04/25/deputy-speaker-bayartsogt-sangajav-resigns/#sthash.UEo1O4z5.dpuf, accessed on 7 October 2013

Note on the contributor
Arthur Lashmar is interested in data journalism. He is a student at Thomas Hardye School, Dorchester, and attended the Centre for Investigative Journalism Summer School in July 2013.

Hyperlocal media and data journalism

Data journalism is still a nascent concept in the emerging hyperlocal media sector, argues Damian Radcliffe, but examples of activity do exist – particularly in the US – and steps can be taken to make it more mainstream

Background and context

Hyperlocal blogs and websites can offer a valuable service to local communities. Their greatest qualities are their interactivity with their readership and the exchange of local information and discussion that they facilitate. Hyperlocal websites can potentially also be good for maintaining local identity and can provide healthy scrutiny and discussion of local democracy and local issues, which is to be encouraged (House of Commons Culture, Media and Sport Committee 2010).

Hyperlocal media is a small but emerging part of the UK's local media ecosystem. NESTA's landscape report, *Here and Now – UK Hyperlocal Media Today*, defined hyperlocal media as: "Online news or content services pertaining to a town, village, single postcode or other small geographically-defined community" (Radcliffe 2012: 6). Available on all media platforms, this sector has a long history across the print medium and is increasingly becoming more established in the digital space. The number of known websites rose from 432 in May 2012 (Ofcom 2012) to 633 by February 2013 (Turner 2013) and the real picture may be bigger once content on social media platforms is taken into consideration.

In the absence of more detailed data, the *Openly Local Hyperlocal Directory*[1] (from which these figures are derived), serves as our most detailed model for understanding the size and geographic spread of the UK's hyperlocal media scene. Not surprisingly, research suggests that much of this activity is focused on major conurbations such as London and Birmingham. However, Ofcom has also noted: "... some rural areas were well served, with South Gloucestershire having 11 sites, largely aimed at small towns and villages, and Wiltshire having ten" (Ofcom 2012). In contrast to this regions such as the North East, the East Midlands or the three Devolved Nations of Scotland, Wales and Northern Ireland appear to be disproportionately under-served (Ofcom 2012: 110).

Figure 1.105 Comparison of population and hyperlocal website provision

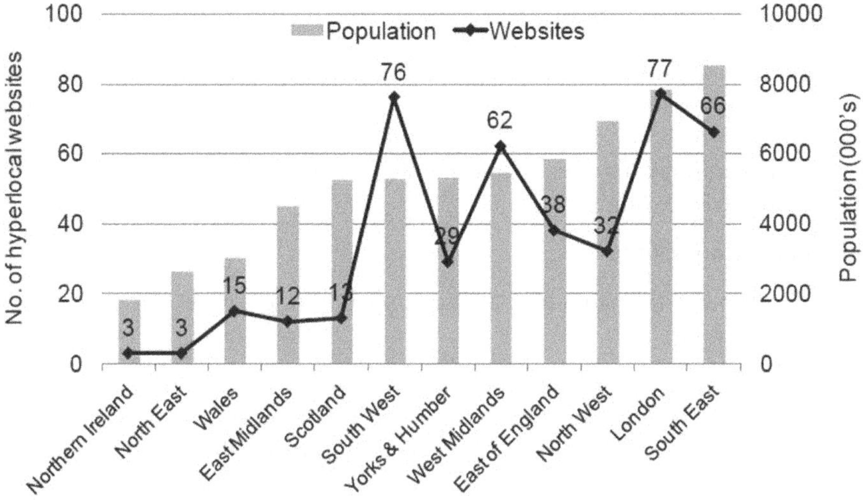

Source: Openly Local / Birmingham City University / ONS / Ofcom (May 2012)

It will be interesting to see if this geographic distribution changes over time, especially as the sector becomes more established, or if devolution – at national and local levels – encourages the creation of more sites, including those designed to hold political institutions to account.

Political encouragement

The Coalition Government has made some positive noises to encourage local accountability, particularly in its desire for citizens to scrutinise public data. However, the results have yet to live up to the hyperlocal hyperbole. Following a decision to open up government data – including local government spending[2] and information "at a level that allows the public to see what is happening on their streets" (Prime Minister's Office, 10 Downing Street 2010) – the Secretary of State, Communities and Local Government, Eric Pickles, enthusiastically called for an army of "armchair auditors" to scrutinise local accounts, arguing:

> Greater openness in spending is the best way to root out waste, spot duplication and increase value for money. That is why I have been asking councils to "show me the money" so local taxpayers can see where their hard earned cash is going (Department for Communities and Local Government 2010).

The move was later accompanied by efforts to ensure that "credible community or 'hyperlocal' bloggers and online broadcasters get the same routine access to council meetings as the traditional accredited media have" (Department for Communities and Local Government 2011). Although no indication was given as to what the criteria were for determining how a community or hyperlocal blogger could be considered "credible" – the rationale for their role was more explicit:

> With local authorities in the process of setting next year's budget this is more important than ever. Opening the door to new media costs nothing and will help improve public scrutiny. The greater powers and freedoms that we are giving local councils must be accompanied by stronger local accountability (ibid).[3]

Disappointing results

> 'I reckon a few armchair auditors might decide to watch telly instead' (Osley 2011).

Despite comments in mid-2011 that the "new wave of local scrutiny by citizen journalists, microbloggers and armchair auditors ... was a triumph" (Department for Communities and Local Government 2011b), the evidence to substantiate this claim is limited. Although there were some initial successes – from Adrian Short's website for the Royal Borough of Windsor and Maidenhead (the now defunct http://armchairauditor.co.uk/) to the successful identification of issues in Barnet (http://wwwbrokenbarnet.blogspot.com/) and Islington[4] – these were exceptions, rather than the rule. The reasons for this mainstream failure are multiple. Perhaps, as Neil O'Brien, the former Director of the Policy Exchange think tank, suggested:

> I think when they were in opposition the Conservatives were a bit naive about the way they thought they could just stick data out there and brilliant people would come and cut it up and make it very useable (cited by Wheeler 2012).

Particular barriers pertinent to hyperlocal publishers include: time, skills and the format in which the data is available (ibid). Time is an especially important consideration for hyperlocal publishers given that these sites are seldom run full time (many practitioners hold down other day jobs). Alongside this, there is also the consideration that data mining may not throw up anything of particular interest, or that it can be difficult to determine the story behind the data – if, indeed, there is one at all (Osley op cit).

Hyperlocal publishers may also come to the conclusion that their limited time is better served focusing on content which is quicker (and often easier) to produce. Certainly they cannot cover everything (Jones 2011) although that is not to say that they do not offer stories related to local government. They clearly do (Williams 2013). It is just that they are not necessarily embracing data – and data journalism – to do it.

Hyperlocal data journalism: Three UK case studies

Despite the presence of a number of inhibiting factors, examples of data driven hyperlocal media do exist. In 2010 Dave Harte produced a map[5] of gritting routes for Bournville News, taking publicly available information but presenting it in a useful way for residents. On his blog he explained the "tedious process of creating the map and why this hyperlocal blogging thing is doomed to failure unless we get a rich supply of local data to feed off" (Harte 2010). He also outlined the motivation behind this effort:

> I thought the potential grit shortage might mean that some roads would stop getting gritted should the cold spell continue and knowing which roads were meant to be gritted would be useful knowledge. "Will my road get gritted?" is an easy question to answer since the City Council has an alphabetical list of all the roads that are gritted in order of priority (ibid).

Later in the year, James Cousins, Conservative councillor for Shaftesbury ward in Wandsworth, did something similar; plotting the location of all grit bins in the borough on a Google map and posting[6] this on his blog. The data, previously only available in a text format – and four clicks deep – on the council website, was now potentially a lot more accessible (Dale 2011).

Alongside presenting existing data in new and creative ways, hyperlocal websites also encourage the creation of new datasets too – covering areas where existing data either does not exist, or fails to provide the level of granularity needed to solve a particular issue. One example of the latter is Bramcote Today. Established following a workshop led by Talk About Local and facilitated by Broxtowe Borough Council, one of site's earliest successes stemmed from online discussions about Hillside Road (Johnson 2011a) – a notorious accident blackspot.

As a result of these conversations, the county council installed equipment to monitor the number and speed of vehicles, later sharing the results (Johnson 2011b) with Bramcote Today readers and involving them in a discussion around potential solutions such as a community speed watch scheme (Austin 2011). A number of these measures were successfully implemented. This result was very much in line with the hyperlocal ethos of Talk About Local founder William Perrin. He described his ambition as being to:

> ... use the web to drive people into local democratic avenues to get things to change ... [The websites are] there to augment real human engagement in the political process. You need representatives to make decisions ... but the web can help them understand better what those issues should be ... we help augment traditional community action (cited in Beckett 2010).

Other UK hyperlocal sites[7] are helping to generate data – and action – using off-the-shelf resources such as mySociety's FixMyStreet widget, which allows people to "report, view, or discuss local problems like graffiti, fly tipping, broken paving slabs or street lighting". Since it launched in early February 2007, more than 350,000 incident reports have been generated[8] with MySociety reporting that over 50 per cent of users have never contacted their local council before; showing that the tool can play a role in promoting active citizenship (FixMyStreet 2013). Some US hyperlocals make use of a similar tool, SeeClickFix[9] – the data it provides offering a means to highlight issues, generate stories and promote discussion, "an example of community news that doesn't necessarily come packaged in story form" (Gahran 2012).

Hyperlocal data journalism: Three case studies from across the pond
Beyond embracing SeeClickFix, a number of American-based US hyperlocal websites have also harnessed data journalism to help tell the stories of the communities they serve. San Jose-based NeighborWebSJ used maps to report on the "Streetlight Shutoff Program", a cost-saving initiative to permanently switch off certain lights. Although it saved the city $77,000 a year – against an electricity bill of $3.5 million a year for streetlights, and a $90 million budget shortfall – many residents and businesses argued the scheme increased the risk of crime. On one road, Alum Rock Avenue, a resident complained that lights were out at 13 bus stops. In response to these community concerns, the website included a Google Map to indicate where lights were out across the city, as well as information on how to report issues to the authorities (Rombeck nd a).

This reporting helped to identify that some lights had been turned off by accident, whilst others were turned back on as a result of public pressure, including those at the bus stops on Alum Rock Avenue. In February 2013 the city agreed to reconnect 900 of the streetlights that had been previously shut off as part of the budget cuts in 2008-2009 (Rombeck nd b). The team at NeighborWebSJ have also produced a Google Map which shows all of the 2012 homicides in San Jose, with data coming from police press releases, and links to other media.[10] This type of activity has been taken a stage further by specialist hyperlocal sites such as Homicide Watch DC[11] which covers every murder in the District of Columbia. The site uses "original reporting, court documents, social media, and the help of victims" and suspects' friends, family, neighbours and others in an effort to "cover every homicide from crime to conviction". It was awarded the Knight Public Service Award by the Online News Association in 2012 in recognition of its efforts to explore a single issue in a single geographic area.[12]

Meanwhile, in California, the Bay Citizen, created an interactive map to show every bike accident reported to police. Users can filter by road conditions, lighting and other requirements such as "who is at fault". The map makes use of data from 14,113 incidents between January 2005-December 2009, allowing cyclists to determine which are the safest routes to use, and which are the ones they should avoid.

Lessons from EveryBlock: Why data alone is not enough

All of these examples involve hyperlocal publishers using data to illustrate particular issues or community considerations; often harnessing maps as a means to tell stories or provide opportunities for audiences to analyse data in a manner which is meaningful to them. The sites are not purely data driven, and they all provide context and interpretation which audiences clearly value.

These are important considerations for publishers, and the failure of the EveryBlock – a US-based website which aggregated local information produced by government and state agencies – helps to reinforce this point. The site, which offered a data-centric approach to hyperlocal, launched in 2008 and was bought by MNBC in 2009. However, in February 2013, the site was closed[13] after NBC decided that they "didn't see a strategic fit for EveryBlock within the [NBC News Digital] portfolio" (Schiller, cited in Sonderman 2013).

As Steve Johnson, Assistant Professor of Electronic Journalism at Montclair State University, noted: "Readers don't care about the raw data. They want the story within the data" (Johnson 2013). By way of an example, he explained what happened when he explored data related to lower Manhattan:

> There were reports on what graffiti the city said it had erased each month, by neighborhoods. But what was missing was context, and photos. If I'm a reporter doing a story on graffiti, I want to show before and after photos, AND, more importantly, I want to know whether the city is successfully fighting the graffiti artists, i.e., who is winning. The raw data didn't provide that.

To some extent, the EveryBlock team acknowledged this when in 2011 they moved the site moved in a new direction, telling their audience:

> As valuable as automated updates of crime, media mentions, and other EveryBlock news are, contributions from your fellow neighbors are significantly more meaningful and useful. While we're not removing our existing aggregation of public records and other neighborhood information (more on this in a bit), we've come to realize that human participation is essential, not only as a layer on top but as the bedrock of the site (Holovaty 2011).

Ultimately however, this pivot was unsuccessful and although some decried the fact that EveryBlock was "clearly the future" (Coates 2013), the site failed to resonate enough with audiences or advertisers to survive.

Moving forward: Five ways to help further grow and embed hyperlocal data journalism

Perhaps we should not be surprised that data journalism – and the armchair auditing that the UK Government has spoken so enthusiastically about – is not more mainstream at a hyperlocal level. After all, this sort of activity is not for everyone:

> … you need to be a particular type of person. Politically, you need to be engaged and interested in local government, understand how local government works and have a driving reason to dedicate yourself to it. To have all these traits in combination is rare (Worthy 2013).

And even with the power of automated technology and feeds, it is clear that audiences still value context and interpretation; activities which can often require quite a lot of leg-work.

> Sure, give me an aggregator that sifts through a Twitter "cloud" and tells me what the conversation is all about in my neighbourhood; but then I still need a grunt to go and knock on doors; make contact; get content (Waghorn 2009).

As we have seen, for time-pressed hyperlocal publishers, regular usage of data journalism may just be one thing too many to accommodate. However, given the increasing wealth of public data being made available, it is not unrealistic to expect that the hyperlocal sector will, over time, need to embrace data journalism more than it has at present.

Below are five ways in which the sector might be able to build upon existing practices, so that data journalism becomes a more mainstream hyperlocal activity.

1. Using data as a day-to-day illustrator

DNAinfo.com New York used maps and infographics to help demonstrate the conclusions of their analysis of the city's 2011 stop and frisk numbers. This enabled them to identify the top 25 locations where people were stopped-and-frisked by the police, as well as the extent to which black and Hispanic New Yorkers are stopped-and-frisked far more than any other demographic. Their analysis also showed that more people are stopped at the Port Authority Bus Terminal – regardless of race – than any other location (Colvin and Harris 2012).

2. Using data to create niche blogs or stories

Given the plurality of news sources increasingly used by audiences (Ofcom 2013) citizens and hyperlocal publishers may want to explore the idea of responding to a major (perhaps even single) issue with a unique series of stories, or potentially even a standalone website. Birmingham City University students showed how this might work when in 2010 they set up a hyperlocal blog – http://birminghambudgetcuts.blogspot.com/ – aimed at the 50,000 public sector workers in the region. The site specifically focused on budget cuts and how they were affecting people (Watt 2010).

3. Using FoI to unlock hitherto hidden data

FoI (Freedom of Information) requests can be a useful means to unearth data which might otherwise not be published. As a result, it can offer great potential as a source for stories. Saddleworth News demonstrated this effectively following an FoI into the cost and usage of the Oldham Says website, revealing that the site had received just 2,548 unique visits in the six months to the end of September 2010.

> With a total of £25,544 having been spent on setting up the site, that's roughly equivalent to an incredible £10 for each and every click. The site's readership has been particularly low in the last two months, with just 268 people logging on in August and 296 doing so in September (Saddleworth News 2010).

4. Unlocking the power of the many (or at least a few): Networked journalism

Given that many hyperlocal websites are run by an individual, or a very small number of volunteers, having the time and skills to embrace data journalism can be a challenge. One solution to this issue may be more networked journalism, bringing together people around specific questions or issues as the Birmingham based website Help Me Investigate did[14]. Working in this way may require a change of approach for some publishers – and, of course, recruiting and managing the efforts of volunteers can be a time-consuming. Nevertheless, as Professor Jeff Jarvis has argued:

> Professional and amateur, journalist and citizen may now work together to gather and share more news in more ways to more people than was ever possible before. Networked journalism is founded on a simple, self-evident and self-interested truth: We can do more together than we can apart ... This, I believe, is the natural state of media: two-way and collaborative (Jarvis 2008).

5. Data driven campaigns and partnership working

Finally there are also opportunities to use data as a tool for partnerships, with hyperlocals identifying stories as a grassroots level which then get escalated at a wider local, regional or national level. Perhaps surprisingly this doesn't happen as often as you might think:

> Thus far, "there's been only one example of collaboration [with local newspapers]. I found statistics on ambulance call-outs in response to assault incidents. They were rising massively but violent crime was only rising a small amount ... The newspaper picked up on my research, ran some more maths on the numbers, and ran a story" (Perrin, cited in Beckett 2010).

Final thoughts

Alongside these five areas of opportunity, I would also like to see the sector come together more to help develop data journalism skills, share best practice and explore opportunities for partnership working with other hyperlocals.

One potential area to do this could be around joint investigations. It would be fascinating to see sites in major cities such as Birmingham or Manchester coming together on a semi-regular basis to jointly explore key datasets around subjects such as crime, public spaces or health. This would enable them to tell the story relevant to their own patch as well as build a city-wide or national picture around topics which always enjoy a strong local dimension.

The second version of Help Me Investigate – which focuses on supporting a network of community editors around specific issues (Bradshaw 2011) – offers a potential model for this and it would be interesting to see if this approach could be expanded to other topics and collaborators. This could be particularly effective if combined with a trade body (Radcliffe: 2013) which can promote training and the sharing of best practice. Such a body could help improve data journalism knowledge and training across the sector and in the process help to take hyperlocal media – as well as hyperlocal data journalism – to the next level.

Whether inter-sector links develop along these lines is perhaps, to some extent, a moot point. I believe that they would help the sector to grow and develop, but irrespective of that it clear is that both data journalism and hyperlocal media are an increasingly established part of the 21st century news and information landscape. As a result, seeing how they evolve and embrace one another will be fascinating journey to observe.

Notes

[1] See http://openlylocal.com/hyperlocal_sites, accessed on 6 October 2013

[2] The Government undertook to publish "new items of local government spending over £500 to be published on a council-by-council basis from January 2011 … and new local government contracts and tender documents for expenditure over £500 to be published in full from January 2011". See: https://www.gov.uk/government/news/letter-to-government-departments-on-opening-up-data, accessed on 6 October 2013

[3] Also see: Access to local council meetings: ministerial letter. Available online at https://www.gov.uk/government/publications/access-to-local-council-meetings-ministerial-letter, accessed on 6 October 2013

[4] The CLG website notes in a July 2011 announcement entitled "Armchair auditors are here to stay" that in Barnet "serious deficiencies in procurement arrangements saw the council spend over £1m of taxpayers' money to hire a private security firm with no tendering exercise, contract or proper invoicing. It was uncovered by local armchair auditors and activist bloggers". They also highlight that "in Islington an independent audit of thirty of the council's top five hundred suppliers found that many invoices had been paid more than once". See https://www.gov.uk/government/news/armchair-auditors-are-here-to-stay, accessed on 6 October 2013

[5] View the map:
https://maps.google.co.uk/maps/ms?hl=en&ie=UTF8&t=p&msa=0&msid=10110999 7956977110556.00047ce1b07baadd30e81&ll=52.426291,-1.949043&spn=0.018318,0.042915&z=14&source=embed, accessed on 6 October 2013

[6] See http://jamescousins.com/2010/12/gritting-wandsworth/, accessed on 6 October 2013

7 For example, Lichfield Live, http://lichfieldcommunitymedia.org/2012/04/26/how-to-add-recent-fixmystreet-reports-to-your-hyperlocal-site/, accessed on 6 October 2013

8 See http://www.fixmystreet.com/ – stats provide on the homepage when accessed on 1 October 2013

9 See http://seeclickfix.com/, accessed on 6 October 2013

10 See https://maps.google.com/maps/ms?msa=0&msid=217123681087309783437.0004c94f4cd9b69d312e5&hl=en&ie=UTF8&t=m&source=embed&ll=37.321732,-121.875501&spn=0.171191,0.205865, accessed on 6 October 2013

11 See http://homicidewatch.org/, accessed on 6 October 2013

12 See http://homicidewatch.org/about/, accessed on 6 October 2013

13 See http://blog.everyblock.com/2013/feb/07/goodbye/, accessed on 6 October 2013

14 See http://helpmeinvestigate.com, accessed on 6 October 2013

References

Austin, Steve (2011) Hillside Road Proposals, Bramcote Today, 4 April. Available online http://bramcotetoday.org.uk/2011/04/04/hillside-road/, accessed on 6 October 2013

Beckett, Charlie (2010) Grassroots networked journalism key to future of local news, says Polis director, Journalism.co.uk, 7 June. Available online http://www.journalism.co.uk/news-features/grassroots-networked-journalism-key-to-future-of-local-news-says-polis-director/s5/a539020/, accessed on 6 October 2013

Bradshaw, Paul (2011) Announcing Help Me Investigate: Networks, Online Journalism Blog, 7 November. Available online at http://onlinejournalismblog.com/2011/11/07/announcing-help-me-investigate-networks/, accessed on 6 October 2013

Colvin, Jill and Davis, Paul (2012) Port Authority is top stop-and-frisk hotspot regardless of race, DNAinfo, New York, 4 June. Available online at http://www.dnainfo.com/new-york/20120604/new-york-city/port-authority-is-top-stop-and-frisk-hotspot-regardless-of-race#ixzz1wrTXMVW5, accessed on 6 October 2013

Coates, Tom (2013) @tomcoates, 7 February. Available online at https://twitter.com/tomcoates/status/299558981007970306, accessed on 6 October 2013

Dale, Robert (2011) Engaging the local population – online, BBC Online, 19 October. Available online at http://www.bbc.co.uk/blogs/blogcollegeofjournalism/posts/engaging_the_local_population, accessed on 6 October 2013

Department for Communities and Local Government (2010) Eric Pickles "shows us the money", 12 August. Available online at https://www.gov.uk/government/news/eric-pickles-shows-us-the-money-as-departmental-books-are-opened-to-an-army-of-armchair-auditors, accessed on 6 October 2013

Department for Communities and Local Government (2011) Citizen journalists and bloggers should be let in to public council meetings, 23 February. Available online at https://www.gov.uk/government/news/citizen-journalists-and-bloggers-should-be-let-in-to-public-council-meetings, accessed on 6 October 2013

Department for Communities and Local Government (2011b) Armchair auditors are here to stay, 8 July. Available online at https://www.gov.uk/government/news/armchair-auditors-are-here-to-stay, accessed on 6 October 2013

FixMyStreet (2013) FixMyStreet – press use. Available online at http://www.mysociety.org/press-area/fixmystreet/, accessed on 6 October 2013

Gahran, Amy (2012) SeeClickFix: Crowdsourced local problem reporting as community news, Knight Digital Media Center, 19 September. Available online at http://www.knightdigitalmediacenter.org/blogs/agahran/2012/09/seeclickfix-crowdsourced-local-problem-reporting-community-news, accessed on 6 October 2013

Harte, David (2010) Data is the New Grit, daveharte.com, January 14. Available online at http://daveharte.com/bournville/data-is-the-new-grit/, accessed on 6 October 2013

Harte, David (2012) cited by Turner, Jerome (2013) Media, Community and the Creative Citizen at the AHRC Connected Communities showcase, Interactive Cultures, 18 March. Available online at http://www.interactivecultures.org/2013/03/media-community-and-the-creative-citizen-at-the-ahrc-connected-communities-showcase/, accessed on 5 July 2013

Holovaty, Adrian (2011) EveryBlock's first major redesign, EveryBlock, March 21. Available online at http://blog.everyblock.com/2011/mar/21/redesign/, accessed on 6 October 2013

House of Commons Culture, Media and Sport Committee (2010) *Future for local and regional media*, House of Commons, London, 24 arch. Full report available online at http://www.publications.parliament.uk/pa/cm200910/cmselect/cmcumeds/43/4302.htm;quote available online at http://www.publications.parliament.uk/pa/cm200910/cmselect/cmcumeds/43/4308.htm, accessed on 6 October 2013

Jarvis, Jeff (2008) Foreword, Beckett, Charlie, *Supermedia: Saving Journalism So It Can Save the World*. Republished on BuzzMachine, 6 June. Available online at http://buzzmachine.com/2008/06/06/supermedia/, accessed on 6 October 2013

Johnson, Mike (2011a) Accidents on Hillside Road, Bramcote Today, 14 March. Available online http://bramcotetoday.org.uk/2011/03/14/accidents-on-hillside-road/, accessed on 6 October 2013

Johnson, Mike (2011b) Accidents on Hillside Road – Traffic Survey Results, Bramcote Today, 29 March. Available online http://bramcotetoday.org.uk/2011/03/29/hillside-road-survey-results-2//, accessed on 6 October 2013

Johnson, Steve (2013) Sorry EveryBlock, you never learned how to write a headline, Hudson Eclectic, 8 February. Available online at http://hudsoneclectic.com/2013/02/08/sorry-everyblock-you-never-learned-how-to-write-a-headline/, accessed on 6 October 2013

Jones, Richard (2011) Thirteen lessons I've learned from running a hyperlocal site, The Richard Jones Journalism Blog, 5 October. Available online at http://richardjonesjournalist.com/2011/10/05/thirteen-lessons-ive-learned-from-running-a-hyperlocal-site/, accessed on 6 October 2013

Ofcom (2012) *The Communications Market 2012*, London: Ofcom. Available online at http://stakeholders.ofcom.org.uk/binaries/research/cmr/cmr12/CMR_UK_2012.pdf, accessed on 5 July 2013

Ofcom (2013) *News Consumption in the UK: 2013 Report*, London: Ofcom. Available online at http://stakeholders.ofcom.org.uk/binaries/research/tvresearch/news/News_Report_2 013.pdf, accessed on 6 October 2013

Osley, Richard (2011) My life as an armchair auditor, March 22. Available online at http://richardosley.wordpress.com/2011/03/22/my-life-as-an-armchair-auditor/, accessed on 6 October 2013

Prime Minister's Office, 10 Downing Street (2010) Letter to government departments on opening up data, London, 31 May. Available online at https://www.gov.uk/government/news/letter-to-government-departments-on-opening-up-data, accessed on 6 October 2013

Radcliffe, Damian (2012) Here and Now: UK hyperlocal media today, London: NESTA. Available online at http://www.nesta.org.uk/library/documents/Here_and_Now_v17.pdf, accessed on 5 July 2013

Radcliffe, Damian (2013) Where hyperlocal media should focus its attention, journalism.co.uk, 16 September. Available online at http://www.journalism.co.uk/news-commentary/-where-hyperlocal-media-should-focus-its-attention-/s6/a554081/, accessed on 6 October 2013

Rombeck, Janice (no date a) Shutoff streetlights worry SJ neighborhoods, NeighborWebSJ. Available online at http://www.neighborwebsj.com/shutoff-streetlights-worry-sj-residents/, accessed on 6 October 2013

Rombeck, Janice (no date b) 900 streetlights shut off to save energy costs will shine again starting in March, NeighborWebSJ. Available online at http://www.neighborwebsj.com/900-streetlights-shut-off-to-save-energy-costs-will-shine-again-starting-in-march/, accessed 6 October 2013

Saddleworth News (2010) Exclusive: Just 10 readers a day for official Oldham website, Saddleworth News, 20 October. Available online at http://www.saddleworthnews.com/?p=3713, accessed on 6 October 2013

Schiller, Vivian, senior vice president and chief digital officer of NBC News, quoted in Sonderman, Jeff (2013) NBC closes hyperlocal, data-driven publishing pioneer, Poynter, February 7. Available online at http://www.poynter.org/latest-news/top-stories/203437/nbc-closes-hyperlocal-pioneer-everyblock/, accessed on 6 October 2013 2012

Waghorn, Rick (2009) The lesson comes from the streets of Baghdad. That our future has to be a "joint operation", you need grunts on the ground, you win no hearts and few minds with just drones in the air, Out With A Bang, 23 April. Available online at http://outwithabang.rickwaghorn.co.uk/?p=283, accessed 6 October 2013 2012

Watt, Andrew (2010) Birmingham budget cuts ... The story so far, Watt's Going On, 20 November. Available online at http://watts-going-on.blogspot.com/2010/11/birmingham-budget-cuts-story-so-far.html, accessed on 6 October 2013 2012

Wheeler, Brian (2012) Government online data ignored by "armchair auditors", BBC Online, 9 November. Available online at http://www.bbc.co.uk/news/uk-politics-20221398, accessed on 6 October 2013

Williams, Andrew (2013) The value of hyperlocal news content, Centre for Community Journalism, 11 January. Available online at http://www.communityjournalism.co.uk/research/the-value-of-hyperlocal-news-content/, accessed on 5 July 2013

Worthy, Ben (2013) Where are the armchair auditors? Open Data Institute, 3 June. Available online at http://www.theodi.org/blog/guest-blog-where-are-armchair-auditors, accessed on 6 October 2013

Note on the contributor

Damian Radcliffe is an Honorary Research Fellow at Cardiff School of Journalism, Media and Cultural Studies. He has written about hyperlocal media for a number of organisations and media outlets including: Ofcom, the BBC College of Journalism, Networked Neighbourhoods, journalism.co.uk and the Democratic Society. In 2012 NESTA published his landscape report, *Here and Now*, the first comprehensive review of the UK's hyperlocal scene. Links to Damian's extensive hyperlocal writing and research can be found via his personal website: www.damianradcliffe.com/hyperlocal.

Old reporting, new methods: How data journalism is keeping an eye on government

Tom Felle interviews a group of international data journalists and finds they all argue their work can play a crucial democratic role in holding the powerful to account

The new frontier

Research methodologies from the social sciences, including quantitative statistical manipulation and analysis, are increasingly being used by journalists to investigative important areas of public interest. The first steps by journalists into this area of investigation came in the 1950s. In recent years the advent of digital and online journalism has given data reporting new momentum. Journalists working in this area have brought creativity and editorial flair in reporting stories to wide audiences, including using multimedia presentation software tools to visualise data for mass consumption, telling often complex stories in easy to understand ways.

Journalists are also using data reporting as an investigative tool to report on issues in the public interest, and hold government – elected officials and bureaucracy – to account. It is a new frontier for journalists interested in the area, and it is becoming an increasingly important research tool when investigating issues such as public spending, procurement, and a range of public services.

Through a series of qualitative interviews with early adopters and regular users working in the national and international media in a number of countries globally, this chapter examines the impact that digital data reporting is having on the traditional role of journalism in holding the executive branch of government to account. Responses suggest strong evidence for the emergence of digital data reporting as a key component in the journalists' toolkit, with a number of key respondents placing data within the domain of investigative journalism, and as an important device when conducting public interest journalism. Unlike many of the criticisms leveled at other forms of "new" journalism, especially around the loss of editorial standards, data reporting requires "old" standards of fact checking, accuracy and "elbow grease" in order to be effective. Those working as data journalists have developed a keen sense of altruism, regularly sharing data and open sourcing their results.

First, what is journalism?

Many hundreds of academics have discoursed at length about what the role of the journalist was, and is, and as a corollary of that what role the news media performs. In general terms, the concept of what is a journalist and what is journalism are very relevant. It can be argued that there is an explicit public interest function for journalists working in the news media, regardless of platform. While most news organisations (save for the BBC, other similar national state broadcasters and a minority of trust-owned newspapers internationally) are commercial enterprises, journalists working for these companies rarely see the pursuit of profit for their owners as their primary motivation.

A comprehensive discussion cannot take place here, but most academics agree that news journalism has an explicit public interest function (Gatlung and Ruge 1965: 64-90; Harcup and O'Neill 2001: 261-280). In contemporary British society, the role of the journalist and the news media might be said to be to entertain and to titillate as much as it is to inform, to engage, to analyse, uncover, to report and to hold power to account. Entertainment scoops, sports, gossip and comment receive as much (and in many cases more) space in newspapers than news receives. Despite this, the public interest role of news organisations in the UK is unquestionable, with virtually all newspapers performing that role in some shape or form.

And what is journalism's role in democracy?

The question of what is the role of journalism – and of the journalist - in a democracy has perhaps received contemporary relevance given the *Guardian*'s publication of classified material in 2013, leaked to it by the former US National Security Agency (NSA) contractor Edward Snowden. The series of reports, which detailed the extent of electronic surveillance undertaken by security agencies in the US and the UK against its own citizens and foreign governments, was an undoubted scoop of international significance. However, the reaction by the security forces in the UK, who used counter terrorism legislation to detain the partner of the journalist who broke the story at an airport, demonstrated on the one hand how important a role journalists play in bringing such stories into the public domain, but on the other hand how difficult that role can be, even in an advanced democracy (Borger 2013; Rusbridger 2013). Put plainly, it is arguable that governments, no matter how democratic, have a penchant for secrecy. There are some secrets – such as areas of national security, counter-terrorism and defence – that are rightly kept undisclosed, but by and large most democratic governments keep information secret for far less than national security concerns. In some cases it is simply to protect their own political interests.

In advanced democratic societies the differing branches of government – an executive that is separate from the legislature and the judiciary – are set up to ensure checks and balances. The news media, in carrying out an investigating and reporting function, in essentially keeping an eye on government and elected office holders, have often been labelled a "fourth estate". The concept was first espoused by Edmund Burke (Schultz 1998: 49). The term was originally applied just to newspapers or "the press" by virtue of the fact that radio, and later television, had yet to be invented; however it is contemporarily understood to encompass all news media. It is arguable, therefore, that the news media have a crucial role as public interest defenders or as "professional citizens" in a democracy (Felle and Adhsead 2009). That role of journalism in democracy is so important that a number of states, including the US, offer some limited privilege and protection to those working in the media.

The First Amendment to the US constitution states: "Congress shall make no law … abridging freedom of the press" (Federal Government of the United States of America 1787). No such explicit protection is offered in the UK, though almost all advanced democracies recognise the right of journalists to investigate and criticise government, and transparency legislation such as FoI is commonplace (Felle 2013). The right to free expression and an implicit right to be informed are laid down in the European Convention on Human Rights (Council of Europe 1950) and in the UN Convention on Civil and Political Rights (United Nations 1966). In a fast-changing media landscape, the right of bloggers and those who work online for non-traditional media to call themselves journalists is disputed, however (Dobuzinskis 2011).

Many will argue that this places the news media on a pedestal, where it does not belong. There have been numerous examples of cases where these high standards have not been lived up to. Most news organisations in the US and the UK collectively failed to question the validity of both governments' claims that the Iraqi regime had weapons of mass destruction in 2003 (Kumar 2006: 48-69). The UK media itself became the story after a series of allegations of criminality against the *News of the World* (Davies 2009). In a number of Eurozone countries including Spain, Greece and Ireland, most news organisations failed to seriously question their governments' economic policies in the mid-2000s (Schechter 2009). The economies of those countries later collapsed with severe social and financial consequences for citizens.

However, despite falling short on occasion, the news media in advanced democracies have developed sophisticated roles as public interest watchdogs. It is to that role of holding power to account that, albeit perhaps an arrogant notion, most news journalists espouse. Not all journalism brings down governments, but human interest investigations that expose the impact of heath cuts, or that uncover favoured treatment or sharp practice in the awarding of public contracts are every bit as valuable to citizens as investigations which lead to political resignations or sackings. News and current affairs journalists, by their nature, do things that annoy those in power, but that is the price those elected to office are expected to pay to ensure democratic accountability.

The news media's presence, then, assures transparency; through their reporting journalists act as public interest champions as much as investigators of corruption. As European Ombudsman Emily O'Reilly and others have argued, reporting has the capacity at least to "keeps government honest" (2008). Sometimes journalists uncover bureaucratic incompetence, and occasionally political corruption. More often no significant wrong may have occurred, but newspapers report on stories that may be embarrassing; may highlight hypocrisy, feather-bedding or pork-barrelling; and sometimes stories that are worthy of airing to generate public debate on the merits and demerits of policy decisions. This, most would agree, is laudable.

What is data journalism?
Using data to report news has been around almost for as long as journalism has been. Newspapers and broadcast organisations have always reported on the latest official statistics from state agencies; business news has contained charts and graphs to visualise the financial stories of the day; editors have commonly used graphics to display rising house prices, or politicians' expenses. Many of these stories have had data as their source. Reprinting a table of figures may be unintelligible for audiences, so journalists have always acted as translators, and story tellers, taking the figures and reporting honestly, analysing what they mean, and giving context to help audiences better understand them.

Computer assisted reporting, or CAR as it became known, was first used by the US television network CBS in 1952 to predict the outcome of the US presidential election (Bounegru 2012: 18-20). For more than 40 years journalists have compiled their own databases, or sought to use official data, when conducting investigations. Rather than simply report on what government press releases said or on spin from private corporations, these reporters sought independently to verify facts and reveal truths, often using social science methods and rudimentary computers to do so. It is noteworthy that this branch of journalism became known as "public service" journalism (ibid).

But while the CAR community has become well established, a newer data reporting community has emerged with the advent of digital journalism within recent years. Loosely defined, data reporting can be described in two ways – data may either be the source of the story; or else data may be the "how" the story is told. Journalists have been able to use software far more effectively in sourcing stories, where large and complex datasets can be mined and cross referenced often proving a rich source for news; and in telling stories. Visualisation software such as Tableau Public and geo-coding with Google Maps can allow for far greater interactivity between the story and the audience, and therefore higher public engagement with the story. As Lorenz and others have argued, this makes the journalism more personally engaging (2012: 4). In that sense, data can uniquely make the news process itself much more individual. Whereas newspapers might report on the headline figures, interactive data stories allow readers to drill right down to the individual level, something newspapers could never do because they simply wouldn't have had the space.

Data's role as a watchdog on democracy

Increasingly, governments throughout the world have been going digital, holding far more information in electronic form. With continued international moves toward greater transparency many governments are publishing far more information. If, as has been previously argued, journalists have a key role to play as watchdogs on democracy, then it is arguable that data journalism has an important part to play in this regard, in reporting on and investigating what is being published. O'Murchu argues a central role for journalists in this space is to be able to operate effectively as data reporters, so they can "scrutinise the world and hold the powers that be to account" (2012: 10). The real power of data journalism lies in its ability to allow journalists verify stories independently, to prove whether reports are true of false, and to be able to move away from reliance on official sources for information.

The "fourth estate" role is also heightened, as possibilities that data creates to tell important stories, as Bradshaw (2013: 2) argues, allows for far more complex investigations using software to find connections. In the past these stories may not have been told fully, or may never be uncovered at all. Whereas previously this was done by compiling databases of their own, now journalists are increasingly using complex statistical software to analyse large data sets. It is worth noting that some, though not all, of the most recent pioneers in this regard have not been from traditional news organisations, but rather from philanthropically supported foundations, many of whom have specific public service remits, and are staffed by former senior journalists, such as Pro Publica in New York. In some cases this was because of a poor record of investigative journalism, and a realisation of its importance for democracy and civil society, such as thedetail.tv in Northern Ireland (Torney 2013).

Though a relatively new breed, the data journalism community espouse high standards, with sharing of tips and ideas commonplace; a culture of open sharing data sources; and of painstaking fact checking stories before publication (Bounegry 2012: 20-22). It can be argued that this pursuit of high standards adds credibility to reporting. However, for journalism to be effective, it needs to have an engaged, and a wide audience. There has been some criticism that data reporting is fast becoming an exclusive domain for the technologically literate. Journalism academics, including Dickinson, have asked if data journalism is really producing tools that people can use in the democratic process.

> Does making a spreadsheet available to users really democratise information? Does making something searchable by postcode really make it more useful on the ground? Isn't it just creating a small, equally

uncountable, data elite? Is it really just a good way to reposition (consolidate) journalism as gatekeepers? (Dickinson 2013).

Those most likely to read "red top" tabloids in the UK are those most likely to be disengaged from politics, and among lower socioeconomic classes (Hansard Society 2012: 4). Rather than acting as a watchdog on behalf of citizens, is data journalism creating a wider gap between those who can afford to be engaged, and large tranches of society that are becoming completely disengaged from the wider political process, and effectively opting out of society? There is some merit in this argument.

Methodology

In order to examine how data journalism is being used by journalists, and what role if any it has in the democratic process, this chapter has gone straight to the source – the journalists themselves – to examine these issues. While this research is bedded in journalism, a best practice approach from social science was taken when conducting the interviews. By a process of examination of output from international media organisations, key players, including leading data journalists, analysts and multimedia editors from various news organisations were identified and contacted. Those contacted were chosen because of their geographic location and the standing of host media organisations. Potential respondents from a mix of broadcasters and "traditional" print newspapers were sought.

In total 14 multimedia journalists and data specialists from major international news organisations were contacted via email and asked to take part in interviews in August 2013. Nine responses were received and eight media professionals were subsequently interviewed. Qualitative interviews were conducted via telephone in English during August and September 2013, and the answers to semi-structured interviews were coded and key themes raised by respondents identified. While it is more common in social science for interviews to be conducted anonymously, in journalism such behaviour is considered anathema to good reporting, save for exceptional circumstances. Given the public interest nature of the discussions there was no reason to promise anonymity, so interviews took place on the record. Respondents are listed in appendix 1.

The reason for conducting interviews was two-fold. Firstly, this research aims to examine if those at the coalface – the multimedia journalists using data as part of their work – see data journalism either implicitly or explicitly as having a democratic function. Do data journalists believe that their work can assure transparency, hold government to account and engage citizens? If so, is there evidence that this is taking place? Secondly, given that data journalism is largely based online, is there a danger that rather than inform and engage citizens, it may contribute to an informed technology literate elite, while further alienating masses from the political process?

A number of contributors to this book have looked at examples of how the *Guardian*, the BBC and other media organisations in the UK are using data. Discussions with UK (except Northern Ireland) data journalists were specifically excluded from this chapter; instead, it will look at the results of interviews with journalists working internationally so as give a global perspective. The threshold for this research is not scientific, rather it attempts to examine current practices, examine the views of professionals, and analyse whether tentative assumptions made earlier in relation to data's role in democratic accountability can be substantiated.

Why data journalism is important

The five "w"s of the inverted pyramid are to reporters what the ten commandments were to Moses. While news reporters are supposed to answer all five, the so-called fifth "w" or "why" is seldom answered in news reports. Why a fire occurred, or why someone was knocked off their bicycle and killed may not be immediately apparent, or answerable for weeks or months until an investigation or inquest has taken place. Data journalism is important because it attempts to answer the "why" question. It allows for better storytelling, argue many respondents. Data reporting has always been part of the journalists' toolkit; however, digital journalism has allowed for a far more meaningful storytelling experience for both the reporter and the reader.

Pamela Duncan, journalist with the *Irish Times*, suggests that digital storytelling using data journalism has allowed reporters to "interpret, contextualise, examine and analyse" news in quite different ways. It may not be always possible to answer the "why", but, she suggests, "it allows reporters to look beyond the surface of news and report much more in-depth on issues. There are important stories to be told, and they are not being told elsewhere" (Duncan 2013). Paris-based Alexandre Léchenet, of *Le Monde*, agrees, arguing that "digital allows for better storytelling. You can turn raw data and turn it into something useful ... [there is an] unlimited number of stories that can be told. Stories can be told that could not be told previously" (Léchenet 2013c).

Respondents suggest that digital data reporting has made the leg work for journalists easier, as Toronto-based the *Globe and Mail*'s Stuart Thompson notes: "Journalists have always used data as part of reporting but the growth of and access to digital tools has make it much easier. Previously what took hours to do with a stack of paper and a strong cup of coffee can be done much more quickly on a computer" (Thompson 2013). Digital storytelling using data visualisations and maps can be far more effective at telling certain types of stories than was the case with traditional newspapers or broadcasters. "Journalism will always be attracted to great stories, and data provides opportunities to tell great stories in a visually appealing way. In particular, the capacity of data that is presented using multimedia to tell very big national stories, as well as individual stories by adding interactivity, is really special," suggests *Spiegel*'s Jens Radue, in Hamburg, Germany (Radue 2013b).

There was strong unanimity among those interviewed that data journalism fulfils a central role in allowing journalists act as watchdogs, and in holding government to account. As discussed earlier, global transparency initiatives have resulted in many governments and international corporations making large datasets available electronically. US National Public Radio's (NPR) news applications editor Brian Boyer points to that accountability role of journalists, suggesting that once journalists realised there were stories to be told, they followed, though he suggests that journalism continues to be slow to react. "During the 2012 [US] presidential campaign both sides were using big data analytics, testing messages. Journalism was on the outside of that, it is really just playing catch up" (Boyer 2013). It is also important to note that data reporting does not tell the whole story. Journalists working with numbers say they often team up with specialist colleagues to report a story, adding interviews, human interest case studies, background and analysis to interactive charts, maps and graphics (Butt 2013; Duncan 2013). Often the data journalism is just the start of the reporting process, with "beat" sources and good old-fashioned reporting still all-important (Thompson 2013).

Data reporters as investigative journalists
The role of the data journalist is individual to each reporter; however, all respondents placed data reporting within the sphere of investigative journalism. Respondents generally agree that data reporting has a role to play in holding power to account, and acting as the "fourth estate" in democracy. While a number of respondents point out that data reporting has the capacity to do so, some suggest the reality was more nuanced in that data reporting is used to tell stories of pitches and plays in sports games as much as it is to report on government. Despite this, the role of the journalist as an agent of democratic accountability is well defined, and journalists working as data reporters and editors strongly identify with this through the interviews. There was universal agreement of the role of journalism generally, and of data journalism, as a watchdog on democracy.

There was also evidence of this in action, through reporting such as election coverage in European countries (Léchenet 2013a; Léchenet 2013b; Radue 2013a) in a great deal political coverage in Canada, such as MPs' expenses and "movers and shakers" in federal politics (Thompson 2013); in Australia with the Melbourne *Age*'s schools performance database (Topsfield and Butt 2012); and gun ownership in Northern Ireland (Torney 2012). An investigation by the *Age* into poker machine usage used datasets on household income and spending by neighbourhood to investigate gambling addiction in socially deprived areas of Melbourne. The story was front-page news, as well as an interactive dataset online (Butt 2012b). The investigation – which showed that the poorest areas reported the highest spend on "pokies" – is a textbook example of journalism in the public interest.

In addition to accountability, many respondents suggested that digital data reporting did have an important role to play in allowing journalists fulfil a public interest and public service function, and was being used quite often by newsrooms worldwide in doing so. In the US, NPR's Washington DC-based data journalist Matt Stiles argues this nuanced role more accurately reflects the day-to-day work of data reporters. "There is an accountability role with all journalism but sometimes it's not so much a question of government accountability as public interest journalism. Not every story will have a political angle or go viral but there is a lot of engagement nonetheless." The broadcaster's "State Impact" series looking at companies engaged in fracking in Pennsylvania (NPR 2012), and their "Playgrounds for Everyone" series (NPR 2012), are examples. It is fair to summarise, then, that respondents viewed data reporting as not necessarily always about holding government to account but about informing the public in a way that government is not. Data reporting is not always about accountability journalism but rather is being used as a tool to verify independently, to serve a public interest, and to allow journalists remain sceptical of government.

Audience engagement

Audience engagement was identified as important for a number of respondents, though in some cases engagement was far greater than in others. This impacted in two ways, both as a motivator to report stories audiences may be interested in, and engaging audiences by asking them to take part in the reporting process, or "crowdsourcing" for stories. NPR has had some considerable achievements in this area: one example is a series they produced on disability accessible playgrounds, which they published admitting it was unfinished. The broadcaster asked listeners to visit the site, and fill in gaps, adding their local playground to the map, and listing whether it was accessible or not (NPR 2013). The story proved extremely popular with audiences (Boyer 2013). In Australia, the *Age* ran a series on bicycle accidents, using both official statistics to map accident danger spots, but also asking readers to add to the map with their own stories and experiences (Butt 2012a). The newspaper also asked readers to suggest stories they would like reported, and have run "hacks and hackers" events to crowdsource for coders to help with reporting (Butt 2013).

However, it hasn't all been easy for media organisations. In Germany, for example, media organisations have had mixed success with crowdsourced stories, with inconsistent responses. Engagement often depended on the story (Radue 2013b), and while some stories such as political campaigns, spending and elections were worthy and ought to have been reported, engagement tended to be low. In other cases, especially stories that personally impacted on audiences, engagement tended to be higher. In Canada, analytics showed that audiences were engaging by reading stories, and in many cases interacting with visualisations, but the *Globe and Mail* has yet to use UGC in data projects (Thompson 2013).

Respondents named crime, health, schools and personal finances/taxes as among the areas that attracted most engagement, along with "local" angles to major national stories (Torney 2013; Duncan 2013; Boyer, 2013). Politics elicited stronger engagement in Canada and Germany than with respondents from most other media organisations worldwide (Thompson 2013; Radue 2013b). However, elections tended to engage wide audiences everywhere, and data series that focused on election results were described as the "nerd super bowl" (Boyer 2013).

How the stories are reported is also important with digital journalism making data much more engaging. Visualisations such as mapping, as well as interactivity, can allow a potentially limitless number of stories to be told. While a newspaper might be interested in telling overall crime figure stories, readers are likely to be much more interested in the crime figures for their local area, which an interactive graphic on crime statistics would allow readers to do. Respondents all agreed that the way stories are presented played a major role in how readers engaged with stories, with visualisations making stories easier to read and understand. Often very large and complex datasets were being written about, and could be displayed in an interactive map extremely easily, and readers could read both the big story (overall picture) and individual (local) stories they may be interested in by using interactivity.

The *Irish Times* (Lally 2012) told the story of national crime figures in the pages of their newspaper, but readers were able to engage at the local level of each police station in their online data series. Similarly, with NPR's "State Impact" fracking series (NPR 2012) and a number of data stories published by *Spiegel* online's data hub (see www.spiegel.de/thema/daten) (Radue 2013b) and the *Age* (Butt 2013), a macro story reported by the media organisation was quite often layered with interactive features that allowed audiences to interact, and tell their own local stories. Interestingly, such stories tended to have a far longer shelf life, with repeated visits for weeks and months after the original story may have been published (Butt 2013; Boyer 2013). There is evidence that – perhaps not surprisingly – many news organisations are aligning their digital data reporting to reflect their traditional strengths, and what their newspaper audiences are interested in. The *Globe and Mail* has a long history of credibility in reporting on politics and business, and their data coverage is also strong in this area (Thompson 2013).

A philosophy of sharing (well, mostly)
Methods used in data reporting are shared with, and come from, the academic social sciences. Publishing raw data is a common occurrence in academic disciplines to add credibility to findings. All respondents point out that a similar culture of sharing in data journalism also adds credibility to their reporting, in that readers can see the source, and those with vested interests have a greater difficulty in arguing or spinning against the story. "Making all source material available allows readers, if they are interested, to see for themselves the source of the story. It gives news organisations a lot of credibility," says *Spiegel*'s Radue (2013).

However, it also puts an onus on news organisations to triple check every detail to ensure there are no mistakes. "The standard bar is set very high," he adds. "The culture of sharing started with the *Chicago Tribune*. We want to be honest with people, so we share. People really like our work, we have a special relationship with our audience. But it's harder for someone else to argue against the figures if you have proof, if anyone can go and do what you did and get the same results. It gives stories added credibility," said NPR's Boyer (2013). Somewhat interestingly, most respondents also pointed out that while they are happy to share their raw data post publication, the "scoop" value of the story is still important, and data is very much close hold until stories are published (Stiles 2013; Torney 2013).

Data for the masses, or just for the elites?

As discussed earlier there is, perhaps with some justification, a perception that data journalism is elitist. Media organisations that have a solid reputation for publishing data related stories tend to be AB publications, rather than low-brow tabloids. Praise-worthy investigations concerning African governments' spending and mineral wealth by the Open Knowledge Foundation (Chambers 2013) or the *Guardian*'s UK riots data series (Rogers 2012), for example, may never be read by many people living in those countries, and directly affected by those stories. Equally, stories previously mentioned in this chapter of social disadvantage, inequality or school performance, for example, may only ever be read by those who have access to the internet, and who are already likely to be from an affluent demographic, given the nature of the likely audiences for news organisations that are reporting these stories. Is that not creating a technologically informed elite?

Journalists working in the area strongly disagree. Respondents argue that, if the logic of the argument that their reporting was elitist was followed, the corollary of that would be not to report the stories at all. A number of respondents argued that all news organisations were moving toward digital because that is where audiences were going. "There have always been people that have been disengaged, or not interested in what newspapers report on. It is not the fault of newspapers, data journalism is not causing that. Most data reporting also appears in the newspaper, so the argument that readers may be missing out doesn't stand," said Thompson (2013). Many point out that all media organisations have a percentage share of the audience, and do not reach everyone with their reporting. *Spiegel*'s Radue (2013b) argued that the internet had made such reporting accessible to a far wide audience of potentially hundreds of millions worldwide, whereas traditional print publishers or broadcasters had much smaller audiences. "A lot of sharing on social media goes on; *Spiegel* online has 11 million unique monthly users. The internet is the motor of democratisation all over the world. Data is accessible, far more accessible than newspapers" (ibid). NPR's Boyer concurs. He also pointed to mobile devices, which he claimed were "game changers". Analytics suggested that far great audiences, from a much wider demographic, were accessing news and data apps on mobile devices than would have traditionally been the case (Boyer 2013).

One tool in the toolkit

Does data reporting have a public interest role? Can using data reporting assure transparency? Does it engage citizens, or is data journalism just creating a well-informed, technologically literate elite and leaving many citizens behind? Evidence suggests such journalism has a public interest and important democratic function. Around the world reporters are finding stories in the numbers, acting in the public interest, and producing better and stronger stories using digital data reporting methods. Data is fulfilling a traditional accountability role, albeit in a more nuanced way than perhaps one might have first imagined. There is strong evidence that an emerging digital data reporting community is starting to engage public audiences in a way that print journalism cannot. Data is never going to replace traditional forms of reporting such as a bank of good contacts. Nor can it tell human stories better than an interview with a person directly. It has an important role to play, but it is just one tool in the toolkit.

References

Borger, Julian (2013) Why the *Guardian* destroyed hard drives of leaked files, *Guardian*, 20 August. Available online at http://www.theguardian.com/world/2013/aug/20/nsa-snowden-files-drives-destroyed-london, accessed on 20 September 2013

Bounegru, Liliana (2012) Data journalism in perspective, Gray, Jonathan, Bounegru, Liliana and Chambers, Lucy (eds) *The Data Journalism Handbook*, California: O'Reilly Media. Available free online at http://openzazu.files.wordpress.com/2012/08/the-data-journalism-handbook-gnv64.pdf, accessed on 12 September 2013

Boyer, Brian (2013) Interview with the author via telephone, 16 September 2013

Bradshaw, Paul (2012) What is data journalism, Gray, Jonathan, Bounegru, Liliana and Chambers, Lucy (eds) *The Data Journalism Handbook*. California: O'Reilly Media. Available free online at http://openzazu.files.wordpress.com/2012/08/the-data-journalism-handbook-gnv64.pdf, accessed on 12 September 2013

Butt, Craig (2012a) Our killer roads, *Age*. Available online at http://www.theage.com.au/victoria/roadtoll, accessed on 12 September 2013

Butt, Craig (2012b) Pokies hit city's poorest, *Age*, 1 August. Available online at http://www.theage.com.au/victoria/pokies-hit-citys-poorest-20120731-23d89.html, accessed on 12 September 2013

Butt, Craig (2013) Interview with the author via telephone, 13 September 2013

Chambers, Lucy (2013) African spending – monitoring the money in Africa, Open Knowledge Foundation blog, 18 March. Available at http://blog.okfn.org/2013/03/18/africanspending-monitoring-the-money-in-africa, accessed on 26 September 2013

Council of Europe (1950) *Convention for the Protection of Human Rights and Fundamental Freedoms*, Strasbourg: Council of Europe

Davies, Nick (2009) Murdoch papers paid £1m to gag phone hacking victims, *Guardian*, 8 July. Available online at http://www.theguardian.com/media/2009/jul/08/murdoch-papers-phone-hacking, accessed on 26 September 2013

Dickinson, Andy (2013) Does data journalism help democracy? www.andydickinson.net online blog post, 13 August. Available online at http://digidickinson.net/2013/08/13/does-data-journalism-help-democracy, accessed on 27 September 2013

Dobuzinskis, Alex (2011) Judge in defamation case rules blogger is no journalist, Reuters. Available online at http://www.reuters.com/article/2011/12/08/us-blogger-ruling-idUSTRE7B72KR20111208, accessed on 12 September 2013

Duncan, Pamela (2013) Interview with the author via telephone, 21 September 2013

Editorial (2013) A shield law is necessary to protect US journalists, *Washington Post*, 22 September. Available online at http://articles.washingtonpost.com/2013-09-22/opinions/42299450_1_u-s-journalists-journalist-shield-law-federal-judges, accessed on 26 September 2013

Felle, Tom (2013) FoI and the Irish parliamentary system, Adshead, Maura and Felle, Tom (eds) *FOI@15*, Manchester: Manchester University Press

Felle, Tom and Adshead, Maura (2009) *Democracy and the Right to Know: 10 years of the Freedom of Information Act in Ireland*, University of Limerick: Limerick Papers in Politics and Public Administration

Galtung, Johan, and Ruge, Mari Holmboe (1965) The Structure of Foreign News: The Presentation of the Congo, Cuba and Cyprus Crises in Four Norwegian Newspapers, *Journal of Peace Research*, Vol. 2 No. 1 pp 64-90

Hansard Society (2012) *Audit of Political Engagement 9: The 2012 Report Part 2: Media and Politics*, London: House of Commons

Harcup, Tony, and O'Neill, Deirdre (2001) What is news? Galtung and Ruge revisited, *Journalism Studies*, Vol. 2, No. 2 pp 261-280

Kumar, Deepa (2006) Media, war and propaganda: Strategies of information management during the 2003 Iraq war, *Communication and Critical/Cultural Studies*, Vol. 3, No. 1 pp 48-69

Lally, Conor (2012) Crime in a recession, *Irish Times*, 24 August. Available online at http://www.irishtimes.com/debate/crime-in-a-recession-1.542359, accessed on 12 September 2013

Léchenet, Alexandre (2013a) Comment les parlementaires ont utilize leur reserve en 2012, *Le Monde*, 8 June. Available online at http://www.lemonde.fr/politique/article/2013/08/06/comment-les-parlementaires-ont-utilise-leur-reserve-en-2012_3458300_823448.html, accessed on 20 September 2013

Léchenet, Alexandre (2013b) Le montant de la reserve parlementaire enfin devoile, *Le Monde*, 10 July. Available online at http://www.lemonde.fr/politique/visuel_interactif/2013/07/10/le-montant-de-la-reserve-parlementaire-enfin-devoile_3445469_823448.html, accessed on 20 September 2013

Léchenet, Alexandre (2013c) Interview with the author via telephone, 16 September 2013

Lorenz, Rirko (2012) Why journalists should use data, Gray, Jonathan, Bounegru, Liliana and Chambers, Lucy (eds) *The Data Journalism Handbook*. California: O'Reilly Media.

Available free online at http://openzazu.files.wordpress.com/2012/08/the-data-journalism-handbook-gnv64.pdf, accessed on 12 September 2013

National Public Radio (2012) "State Impact" Pennsylvania fracking database. Available online at http://stateimpact.npr.org/pennsylvania/drilling, accessed on 17 September 2013

National Public Radio (2013) "Playgrounds for Everyone" data series. Available online at http://apps.npr.org/playgrounds, accessed on 17 September 2013

O Murchu, Cynthia (2012) An essential part of the journalists toolkit, Gray, Jonathan, Bounegru, Liliana and Chambers, Lucy (eds) *The Data Journalism Handbook*. California: O'Reilly Media. Available free online at http://openzazu.files.wordpress.com/2012/08/the-data-journalism-handbook-gnv64.pdf, accessed on 12 September 2013

O'Reilly, Emily (2008) Freedom of Information: The first decade, *10th Anniversary Conference of Freedom of Information in Ireland conference proceedings*, Dublin: Office of the Information Commissioner

Radue, Jens (2013a) Reden von Merkel und Steinbrück: Die Sprache der Macht. Available online at http://www.spiegel.de/video/reden-von-merkel-und-steinbrueck-die-sprache-der-macht-video-1296111.html, accessed on 9 October 2013

Radue, Jens (2013b) Interview with the author via telephone, 19 September 2013

Rogers, Simon (2012) Riots broken down: Who was in court and what's happened to them? *Guardian* online datablog, 4 July. Available online at http://www.theguardian.com/news/datablog+uk/london-riots, accessed on 26 September 2013

Rusbridger, Alan (2013) I would rather destroy the copied files than hand them back to the NSA and GCHQ, *Guardian* online http://www.theguardian.com/world/video/2013/aug/20/alan-rusbridger-miranda-snowden-nsa-gchq-video, accessed on 9 September 2013

Schechter, David (2009) Credit crisis, how did we miss it, *British Journalism Review*, Vol. 20, No. 1 pp 19-26

Schultz, Julianne (1998) *Reviving the Fourth Estate*. Cambridge, England: Cambridge University Press

Stiles, Matt (2013) Interview with the author via telephone, 12 September 2013

Thompson, Stuart (2013) Interview with the author via telephone, 3 October 2013

Topsfield, Jewel and Butt, Craig (2012) At Maribyrnong College, build it and not only will they come, they'll excel, *Age*, 20 December. Available online at http://www.theage.com.au/national/education/at-maribyrnong-college-build-it-and-not-only-will-they-come-theyll-excel-20121219-2bnah.html, accessed on 20 September 2013

Torney, Kathryn (2012) Who owns Northern Ireland's 153,000 legally held guns, thedetail.tv, 23 August. Available online at http://www.thedetail.tv/issues/116/firearms/who-owns-northern-irelands-153000-legally-held-guns, accessed on 21 September 2013

Torney, Kathryn (2013) Interview with the author, 5 September 2013

United Nations (1966) *International Covenant on Civil and Political Rights*, Geneva: United Nations Publications

United States Government (1787) *Constitution of the United States of America*, Washington DC: US Government Printing Office

Appendix 1: Interviewees

Brian Boyer, National Public Radio and formerly the *Chicago Tribune*, USA

Craig Butt, *Age*, Melbourne, Australia

Pamela Duncan, *Irish Times*, Dublin, Ireland

Alexandre Léchenet, *Le Monde*, Paris, France

Jens Radue, *Der Spiegel*/Spiegel.de, Hamburg, Germany

Matt Stiles, National Public Radio, Washington DC, USA

Stuart Thompson, *Globe and Mail*, Toronto, Canada

Kathryn Torney, theDetail.tv, Belfast, Northern Ireland

Note on the contributor

Tom Felle is a former Independent News and Media reporter and correspondent. He is contributor to a number of books on local journalism, democracy and the press, press regulation, FOI and new media. He started his career with the *Connacht Tribune* in the West of Ireland and briefly worked for Associated Newspapers. He has worked as a journalist in Australia and in the Middle East and has contributed to a wide range of international publications on foreign affairs and political issues. In 2006 and 2007 was Beirut Bureau Chief of the Lebanon News Agency. He is a lecturer in Journalism and New Media at the University of Limerick, Ireland. Email: tom.felle@ul.ie.

The advent of the statistician journalist

John Burn-Murdoch highlights the way in which journalists have used statistical methods to uncover a series of exclusives for the *Financial Times*

"Social science done on deadline" – Stephen Doig

Behind the interactive news desk at the *Financial Times* is a well-stocked bookshelf on which sits a copy of Joseph F. Healey's *Statistics: A Tool for Social Research*. Opening the book on any page reveals a reassuring mix of highlighting, underlining and annotations, for the *FT*'s is not a newsroom where statistics is the preserve of a special interest group, but one where it forms the backbone of the journalistic process.

The *FT* may not be the first news organisation to have woven statistical methods into its journalism but it is one of a growing group of media outlets for which the particular branch of mathematics has become invaluable. Data journalism is an art as old as newspapers themselves and, in fact, many argue that treating it as a distinct discipline is fallacious. But the statistician journalist is an emergent role and a clear example of where a specialist skillset – quite different to specialist subject knowledge – opens up entirely new journalistic avenues.

To summarise the role of the statistician journalist, I must borrow a phrase from Stephen Doig, the Knight Chair in Journalism at the Walter Cronkite School of Journalism and Mass Communication at Arizona State University, who refers to precision data journalism as "social science done on deadline" (Remington 2012). Doig's reference to social science is particularly important because of the images of scientific rigour and academic standards that it invokes. There is a danger with data journalism, as with any job title *du jour*, that there will be some who rush to declare themselves data journalists without actually having the requisite expertise. Stories based solely on cursory exploration of aggregate statistics, often making no attempt to ask questions of statistical significance or sample representation, have abounded in recent years and it is vital that we data journalists hold ourselves to Doig's standards and only hit publish when we know a story would pass peer review if submitted as a social science paper.

To me, three recent examples demonstrate perfectly the power of statistics in journalism. Nate Silver's resounding success in predicting the outcome of the 2012 US election upended – perhaps forever – public opinion of the relative strength and trustworthiness of statistical modelling and "in the know" punditry. Even before Silver's success, Chris Giles and Chris Cook (since appointed Policy Editor of the BBC's flagship news and current affairs show *Newsnight*) were each honoured by the Royal Statistical Society for their use of statistical methods in uncovering entirely separate exclusives for the *FT*.

Adding statistical rigour into the equation

Cook, the *FT*'s executive comment editor but previously its education correspondent, began by obtaining access to the National Pupil Database (NPD), a comprehensive set of anonymised records comprising the longitudinal academic performance of every one of England's school pupils from the age of four to 18, as well as contextual demographic data for each individual. The database was obviously a potential goldmine, but Cook rightly set out to answer specific questions rather than simply running exploratory analyses on its entire contents (a common mistake among aspiring data journalists is to go after interesting datasets without knowing what questions to ask of them beforehand). At the time of writing, Cook's analysis of the NDP has yielded more than 20 stories, every one unique to the *FT* and, unsurprisingly, they have tended to stimulate high levels of reader engagement and discussion below the line.

In this chapter, I will look at three of Cook's stories in particular: one on the effectiveness of the English grammar school system, a second on the education idiosyncrasies of London and a third on the always controversial topic of ethnicity in education. All three of these make use of the same statistical technique – multivariate regression, or the use of statistics to identify and tease apart the individual correlations between pairs of variables in a complex system. Using this method allows you to account for – or effectively ignore – the effects of any variables deemed unimportant or unhelpful to a particular piece of analysis, resulting in the ability to create simple models from complex multivariate systems.

In one of his earlier NPD articles, "Benchmarking school systems", Cook explains: "One question I get asked a lot is: 'You say that Frewmanackshire is a terrible local authority. How do you know? Do you know what we are working with?' It is true that schools with radically different intakes cannot be usefully compared" (Cook 2012a).

He then goes on to introduce the model he uses to deal with the issue of intake, explaining that it accounts for each child's ethnic group, their test scores at 11 years old (and the squares and cubes of those scores, to allow for the possibility a non-linear relationship), their first language, poverty level and whether or not they have any special educational needs. At the other end it spits out the *FT* Score– a value calculated by awarding points based on test scores at 16 in English, Maths and their three strongest other subjects. In effect, by restricting his model's input variables to information about the child themselves, Cook is subsequently able to ascribe any variations in academic performance to external forces exerted on the child as they progress through the education system. Put simply, the model allows Cook to identify under- and over-performing children as compared to the model, and to delve deeper into the data to ask what might be causing this deviation from the projected norm. As Cook states, this is "the kind of exercise one hopes the Department for Education (DfE) is undertaking to identify small areas where schools can be rapidly improved with a small intervention ... and areas where school improvement needs more work ... It also tells you where reform will have diminishing returns" (ibid).

Uncovering London's hidden advantage and giving the lie to grammar schools

In the second of Cook's articles that I will discuss, he uses the model to answer a clearly defined question: "How well do children perform in England's boroughs?" (Cook 2013a). In this case, Cook uses almost exactly the same model but breaks down their score by local authority, or the area responsible for the provision of education within its perimeter. As explained above, the key here is that by already accounting for the background circumstances of each child, the model will now compute scores that can be read as measures of the impact of the local area. Cook himself is quick to point out that "This is not all about schools. Nor does it mean borough councils at the top are very good: academies, families and culture may be doing all the work" (ibid). But it is certainly a much more rigorous approach than simply performing a univariate analysis on local authority, an approach which is not foreign to a number of newsrooms in Britain and around the world.

In this case, Cook was able to conclude that children in London's schools tended to outperform those from other English regions right through from the most disadvantaged one per cent to the least. Not only that, but the extent to which attending school in London improved a child's score was greatest among those below or close to the poverty line.

Another specific use of Cook's model was in his answering an age-old debate in British education circles about the impact of grammar schools on children's academic performance – namely whether or not the process of selecting pupils based on a test at age 11 results in a better education for those who make it through (Cook 2013b). The process was similar to that used in the local area example, except this time Cook created an area into which he grouped the regions with the highest proportions of grammar schools and compared this with the other areas of England. Taking a narrative approach to both his statistical and written analysis, Cook used his model to show:

- that the selective regions ranked 7th out of 11;
- that they dropped to 8th when looking only at children eligible for free school meals – the poorest group of pupils;
- and that looking across the entire range from the most to least disadvantaged children, all other things being equal, children on the most deprived half of the spectrum fared worse in selective than non-selective regions, and only those in the top five or so per cent consistently fared better.

Tackling the causation question

Perhaps the most notable of all Cook's work using the NPD was his report "Race to the top", where he examined the academic performance of children of different ethnicities (Cook 2012b). Using the same model as above but this time breaking down the *FT* Score by ethnicity, Cook showed that children self-identifying as white British and below the median level of deprivation scored considerable worse than any other ethnicity, and especially so at the most disadvantaged end of the scale. Showing a social scientist's curiosity, though, Cook saw that there were further questions to ask: given children from ethnic minorities score so well, and London has England's highest proportions of these children, are they driving London's high performance or is London lifting them above their white British counterparts? He ran the regional analysis again, but split out London's white British children. They scored markedly worse than the London average right through to the least deprived upper echelons, but still notably better than children outside London. In an attempt to answer the causation question, Cook then referred back to the original model, showing that regardless of ethnicity, a child attending school in London in 2011 typically scored three or four GCSE grades higher (across the five subjects comprising their *FT* Score) than counterparts outside the capital. He concluded: "That's a *big* effect, and it persists after taking account of ethnicity. So the difference between London and the rest is not ethnicity, but it certainly helps" (ibid).

In the development of the regression model and the three specific examples, Cook demonstrated how making the decision to actively elevate the quality of his analysis, to set the standard of statistics in journalism, can produce work of the highest standard, provide its authors with exclusive headlines and not only question but rewrite accepted truths.

Playing government finance analysts at their own game

While Cook was carrying out his work on the NDP, another Chris at the *FT* was using statistics to set the national news agenda. On 18 September 2011 Chris Giles, the economic editor, broke the news that the British government's structural deficit (the component of the budget deficit that exists independently of the economic cycle and as a result is typically managed with fiscal policy) was £12bn larger than thought – 25 per cent higher at £61bn than the previous estimate of £49bn – and he did so using nothing more than official figures and a publicly available government briefing document (Giles 2011a).

In April 2011, the Office for Budgetary Responsibility (OBR) – the body charged with providing economic forecasts in the lead up to the UK budget – published a 21-page document detailing how it had calculated its estimates for spare capacity in the UK economy, or the amount of slack in terms of labour or manufacturing capacity that can expedite a recovery until used up. The document outlined not only the data inputs used by the OBR but also the precise formulae used to arrive at the official estimate, allowing Giles and colleagues at the *FT* to replicate the official analysis but using more up-to-date inputs – data on the labour market, recruitment and capacity in the manufacturing and service sectors for the final quarter of 2010 and the first two of 2011 had not been published in time for the earlier forecast, but had become available by September.

The OBR chairman, Robert Chote, had declared that spare capacity in 2011/12 would be 3.9 per cent of national income. But using the new data Giles found that the figure was actually 1.7 per cent using one of the OBR methods and 3.5 per cent using the other, giving 2.6 per cent using the OBR's standard procedure of averaging the two figures (Giles 2011b). The significance of these findings was that this reduction in the output gap would mean a smaller amount of government borrowing that would simply be displaced by economic rebound, and thus a greater amount that would have to be financed by tax rises or spending cuts. Unsurprisingly, considering it had simply been played at its own game, when the OBR was shown the *FT*'s calculations it said they were consistent with its methodology (Giles 2011a).

Giles's analysis yielded three separate stories immediately and was followed up by further reports and analysis in the following days. Yet again it was an exclusive for the *FT* that had required no laborious cultivation of sources, no frantic scrabbling to be first but, instead, expert subject knowledge and a careful analysis of public data and documents. In recognition of his work, Giles was awarded the 2012 prize for statistical excellence in journalism for work published in print. Cook was specially commended in the same category for his exposing and analysis of white British underperformance in England's schools.

Nate Silver: the celebrity statistician

Nate Silver is the first name that springs to mind today when the topic of statistics in journalism is raised, and is likely to remain so for some time. Silver's work in the lead-up to the 2012 US Presidential Election was the most prominent example in living memory of the predictive power of statistics. It had all the right ingredients to do what few pieces of journalism do – transcend the media conference circuit and become a major news story in its own right. Not only was Silver's work tied to weeks of coverage of a global news event, it was breathtakingly simple to understand at a basic level and it could be used by a public that had grown tired of the partisan punditry to which it represented a new and refreshing alternative.

At the heart of Silver's work was Bayes' Theorem – a branch of probabilistic mathematics concerned with incorporating dynamic evidence into predictions about future events. Where the traditional frequentist approach to probability is centred around the idea that any single event is one in an infinite series of events that have or will take place within the same parameters, and thus there is a constant and observable frequency, the Bayesian approach uses the frequencies of ongoing observations to continuously adjust previously-held beliefs concerning probability. In Silver's case, pre-existing beliefs governing the impact of macroeconomic indicators and overall approval rating on national and state-specific voting outcomes were combined with ever-changing polling figures – as well as changing assumptions about the reliability of those figures – to arrive at the overall likelihood of a candidate winning the election at any give time, under any given set of circumstances.

Silver's success was not only in using relatively complex modelling to predict the outcome of the election but in communicating to the wider public the clarity and other advantages that a mathematical approach offers over more traditional discussion based analysis of developing news stories. His decision to leave *The New York Times* and launch FiveThirtyEight as a standalone brand – hiring a band of statistically minded journalists along the way – drew raised eyebrows from many, but the announcement from his former employers that David Leonhardt would head-up a new team specialising in data-driven news and analysis shows that *The Times* is in no doubt as to the direction in which the industry is going.

Preparing the newsroom for a statistical revolution: A warning and an opportunity

Underpinning any strategic venture into data journalism is the creation of a numerate staff, a newsroom just as comfortable working with spreadsheets as articles, just as adept at crafting a formula as writing an intro. The *FT* regularly hosts workshops in data journalism reaching hundreds of staff around the world both within and outside the organisation. Perhaps more importantly it also operates an admirable policy of seconding front-end developers from the IT department to the newsroom, which allows journalists to quickly increase their technical skillset and makes developers feel they are playing a valuable role in the creation and communication of news

Silver, Giles and Cook show what can be achieved when the right people with the right skills are set loose on the wealth of data available to journalists today. And as governments become more open and open data become more rich, the need for the statistically adept journalist is only going to grow. Using data to add depth, colour or context to a story is one thing, but creating a story *ex nihilo* is where the real value lies. The modern news organisation is faced with a trade-off between being first, fast but perhaps wrong, and being right, thoughtful but second place. Statistical journalism offers a third way: first, right and leaving rivals scrambling to report on your story.

Data journalism has achieved the recognition it deserves as a specialist discipline in the 21st century and that is to be applauded, but talk of it revolutionising the industry remains premature while there are still newsrooms where statistical methods are seen as dark arts and proficiency with spreadsheets and visualisation tools – let alone the command line – is viewed with suspicion. Even today journalism internships and postgraduate courses are overwhelmingly the domain of arts graduates who dropped maths and the sciences as early on in their education as possible. Gradually, the number of analytical types seeing journalism as a legitimate career will grow, but attitudes in the upper editorial echelons must change in order to expedite this transition. The editors of tomorrow face a simple question: "Is it enough for my journalists to keep throwing anecdotes at the wall in the hope that something sticks, or should they be carrying out social science on deadline?"

References

Remington, Alex (2012) "Social science done on deadline": Research chat with ASU's Steve Doig on data journalism, Journalist's Resource, 21 August. Available online at http://journalistsresource.org/skills/research/research-chat-steve-doig-data-journalism-social-science-deadline, accessed on 12 October 2013

Cook, Chris (2012a) Benchmarking school systems, *Financial Times*, 5 November. Available online at http://blogs.ft.com/ftdata/2012/11/05/benchmarking-school-systems/, accessed on 9 October 2013

Cook, Chris (2012b) Race to the top, *Financial Times*, 6 August. Available online at http://blogs.ft.com/ftdata/2012/08/06/race-to-the-top/, accessed on 10 October 2013

Cook, Chris (2013a) How well do children perform in England's boroughs?, *Financial Times*, 16 January. Available online at http://blogs.ft.com/ftdata/2013/01/16/how-well-do-children-perform-in-englands- boroughs/, accessed on 9 October 2013

Cook, Chris (2013b) Grammar school myths, *Financial Times*, 28 January. Available online at http://blogs.ft.com/ftdata/2013/01/28/grammar-school-myths/, accessed on 10 October 2013

Giles, Chris (2011a) £12bn hole in UK public finances, *Financial Times*, 19 September. Available online at http://www.ft.com/cms/s/0/f5981c68-dee0-11e0-9130-00144feabdc0.html, accessed on 12 October 2013

Giles, Chris (2011b) Spare capacity doubt clouds growth picture, *Financial Times*, 18 September. Available online at http://www.ft.com/cms/s/0/772709f4-def2-11e0-9af3-00144feabdc0.html, accessed on 12 October 2013

Note on the contributor

John Burn-Murdoch is a data journalist on the *Financial Times*'s interactive news desk and visiting lecturer at City University's Department of Journalism. His role at the *FT* involves analysis, visualisation and interrogation of data as well as reporting on innovative uses of data analytics by companies and governments. Before joining the *FT*, he was editor of the *Guardian*'s big data and analytics site and was awarded the Opinion Panel Prize in 2012 for creative use of journalism.

Data journalism in China: A comparative perspective

Yaneng Feng and Qian Li, in comparing the state of data journalism in China with its current position in Western media organisations, conclude: "It is essential for the Chinese government and media to encourage data journalism – and for society to embrace the change"

Introduction

What is the definition of data journalism? Academics, professionals and practitioners all have different views. Jonathan Stray, a professional journalist and a computer scientist, points out: "Data journalism is obtaining, reporting on, curating and publishing data in the public interest."[1] Paul Bradshaw, a data journalism trainer and writer, says: "Data journalism is ... the convergence of a number of fields – from investigative research and statistics to design and programming."[2]

From the perspective of the practical journalism, data journalism, also called "data-driven journalism", is applying technical software to the procurement and analysis of data, and presenting them in a visualised form. Many media organisations contract the visualisation out to the designers. Others such as the *Guardian, Washington Post* and some independent news agencies have built their own teams processing and visualising the data.

Guo Xiaoke, a Chinese scholar, wrote in his article titled *Development Status and Functions of Data Journalism*: "Data journalism is a discipline that shows the news facts by adopting rich and interactive effects of visualisation in a background of multi-disciplinary techniques, displays the complex relationship between individual and social data to the public, or reports public issues in an objective, easy-to-understand way in order to stimulate the public's concern and participation."[3]

Developments and present status

As a development of "precision journalism", data-based news production is more sophisticated, requiring not only the traditional skills to produce audio, video, pictures and text, but also the knowledge in social research method, computer science, programming, visualisation, interactive design and arts to be able to make use of data.[4] Now the concept of data journalism is being accepted in the international media world due to its profound impact on media and other areas, and every news organisation without exception wants to give data journalism a try.

In China, data journalism is in the ascendant with academic institutes and universities offering relevant courses. In the media industry, companies such as Netease.com and Sohu.com have also established dedicated platforms for a deeper exploration of data journalism. At present, the traditional media in China do not use data journalism as the primary form in news reporting. When data is applied, it is generally presented in static forms such as charts and graphs as a supplement to text-concentrated news reports. In the new media, on the other hand, data journalism is adopted as part of the main news reporting, including more interactive design and dynamic effects, with less text descriptions and more attention to the visual design.

Netease.com started a new section in its News Channel called "Data blog" on 13 January 2012. Almost every news report or article in the section is in the form of colourful charts with various styles, along with text to explain the data charts. So far data news hot topics have included politics, the economy, the military, culture, education – both in China and abroad.

Sohu News set up a new column called "The Figures" in March 2011. It released its first data report "Fiscal Revenue: Financial Sample of the System of Tax Distribution", in which the visualisation of the data played a crucial role. So far data infographics have been used in reports covering the China economy and current affairs.

Comparative analysis with the Western media

One of the most famous recent cases of journalists using complex data analysis tools was during the London-based *Daily Telegraph*'s investigation of MPs' expenses in 2009. "Chart of the Day", of Bloomberg News, is a column integrating Bloomberg News, Bloomberg data and Bloomberg analysis to present complex financial data in accessible ways.[5] Similarly, both the BBC and *Financial Times* publish their budgets in interactive charts regularly on their websites.

In China, Netease News produced a special report on the Spring Festival called "Tenth of the Chinese people" in 2011, telling the story of migrant workers from all provinces on a map of the country. Again, during the Yushu Earthquake in April 2010, four of China's main websites showed different techniques in data reporting.

1. Sohu News

Sohu News set up a special website for the earthquake. A red dot on the map represented a location where an earthquake had recently occurred. Readers could click each red dot to see a pop-up screen describing the earthquake in detail: time, casualties, specific reason, etc. The information was simple and straightforward.

Figure 1. Sohu News

2. Tencent News

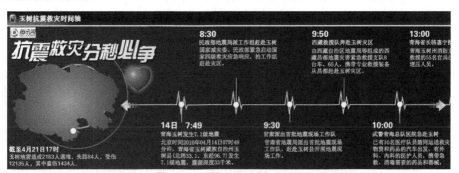

Figure 2. Tencent News

Tencent News presented a timeline to show the development of the earthquake. By clicking the event points on the time axis, readers could extract the information at that time.

3. Sina News

Figure 3. Sina News

Sina News made full use of multimedia. There was not only concise text and vivid pictures, but hyperlinks on the data map through which readers could access other websites to watch the related videos or read more background information.

4. Netease News

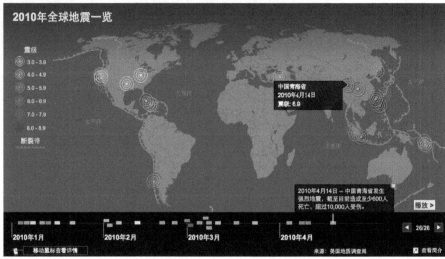

Figure 4. Netease News

The quake was reported via both a timeline and a world map. Readers could interact with the two dimensional presentation not only to obtain the relevant data of the Yushu quake but also to access the other quakes occurring around the world. Netease News, in effect, took an approach similar to that adopted by the London *Guardian* in its reporting of the London riots in August 2011.

Media organisations in China have realised some of the potential of data in news reporting. However, they need to improve their practice. For instance, data journalism tends to focus on major disasters such as earthquakes and rarely on everyday events happening around us daily.

Summary and comparative analysis

The pioneers of data journalism have come from traditional media in Western countries such as the *Guardian, New York Times* and the BBC. In China, although CCTV and other mainstream media have tried data news for a long time, the serious practitioners of data journalism are online media organisations such as Sohu News and Netease News.

When major events happen, both traditional media and new media have to quote the press releases of the Xinhua News Agency, causing news homogenisation. In order to attract more readers, media organisations need to present the news in original formats. Therefore, data journalism is increasingly becoming the "weapon" taken by news websites to fight and win the fierce battle for audiences.

On the other hand, since one key characteristic of data journalism is to present the data through graphic design, online media organisations have an absolute advantage compared with traditional media organisations. It is, therefore, no surprise that news websites lead the way in data journalism in China.

a. Content and source

In the West, data journalists are involved not only in covering everyday economic news and social events but also in in-depth reporting on issues such as budgets, environment pollution, law, education, consumer products and so on. In China, subjects suitable for data news are relatively narrow. They generally focus on economic news as well as big social events. News involving government agencies rarely appears in data journalism reporting.

In Western countries, journalists and citizens can access information relatively easily through the internet. In China, however, accessing certain data is limited. Data from official websites is severely restricted while information from governmental/unofficial sources is often unreliable.

b. Platforms

A lot of data news is published through the official websites of the mainstream media in the West. For example, the *Guardian* set up a "data store forum" on its website, with big data, news, blog and so on – gaining a lot of attention through social media sharing, commenting and reposting.

In China, data news is mainly released on the websites of non-professional, online media. Groups or individuals with professional backgrounds may also produce data news and post it on to their own websites. Currently both platforms have not yet reached wide audiences since they are treated more as "beautiful pictures" rather than serious news reports.

c. Design and form

Data journalism in China is usually presented basically in the form of static diagrams with different colours or shapes. Most infographics are often just experiments in condensing a whole set of information on to one single page, rather than performing the difficult task of selecting the useful facts, simplifying them, and sorting them into a meaningful sequence.[6]

Forms of data news in Western media are much more diversified. There are data maps, timelines, interactive charts and videos to help readers understand the news. In addition, readers are given full access to all the data. The *Guardian*, for instance, publishes all the data that it uses on "Data blog" page so the public can download it freely for reference or further analysis.

Constraints on the development of data journalism in China

- Source constraints: Besides the daily news reports, the significance of data journalism also lies in covering the news that is important but less well known to the public. In China, media organisations usually work with the official data that has been released online. Thus the limited data sources directly restrict data journalism development and narrow the scope of subjects it might cover.

- Design constraints: In China, the text is still the mainstream form in news coverage. Journalists lack the consciousness of putting data or multimedia design into news coverage.

- Audience constraints: It's difficult in China to find audiences receptive to the exciting possibilities of data journalism.

- Educational constraints: Chinese education is still failing to produce sufficient graduates specialist in modern mass media skills such as visual communication or graphic design.

The future of data journalism in China

Firstly, there will be more diverse forms of data collection – with citizens often playing crucial roles. Secondly, data news will be developed by more and more media organisations in the future, especially Chinese mainstream media organisations. Thirdly, data news content diversification will expand people's horizons. In the early days of data news, journalists preferred everyday topics to attract more readers. But the power of data will be applied to many more subjects in the future. The charm of data journalism comes from its ability to simplify complicated issues. Compared to the written report, data journalism has the power to interact far more effectively with its audience. With the development of reporters' skills and a rise in readers' demand, data journalism will expand and could well become a dominant form of reporting.

Finally, data journalism will be particularly attractive on mobile terminals. Touch-screen technology used by mobile terminals can meet the demands of data readers who search for data by tapping their fingers. According to the statistics, 56.3 per cent of Chinese owned mobile phones in the first half of 2013.[7] It has become popular for the most ordinary mobile phone user to access to news through their mobile phones. Along with the growth of the mobile phone users, media organisations will target their data news service to this huge and still growing group.

Conclusion

Foreign media are always more sensitive than Chinese domestic media when a new technology or idea emerges. Data journalism could fundamentally change the way people read the news. To some considerable extent, the social and political environment in China is restricting the development of this new form. Yet it is essential for the Chinese government and media to encourage data journalism – and for society to embrace the change.

Notes

[1] Jonathan Stray, A computational journalism reading list. Available online at http://jonathanstray.com/a-computational-journalism-reading-list, accessed on 12 October 2013

[2] Paul Bradshaw, How to be a data journalist. Available online at http://www.theguardian.com/news/datablog/2010/oct/01/data-journalism-how-to-guide, accessed on 12 October 2013

[3] Guo Xiaoke, *Development Status and Functions of Data Journalism*, Editorial Friend 2013

[4] Guo Xiaoke, *Big Data*, Beijing: Tsinghua University Press, 2013

[5] Matthew Winkler, *The Bloomberg Way*, US: Wiley

[6] Cyrille Vincey, Why We Hate Infographics (And Why You Should). Available online at http://insights.qunb.com/why-we-hate-infographics-and-why-you-should, accessed on 12 October 2013

[7] Mobile phone users rate has reached 56.3 per cent in the first half of 2013. Available online at http://www.16wifi.com/beijinggongjiaoWIFIdongtai/2013/0922/1220.html, accessed on 12 October 2013

References

(Gray, Jonathan, Chambers, Lucy and Bounegru, Liliana (eds) (2012) Why Is Data Journalism Important? *The Data Journalism Handbook*, O'Reilly Media. Available online at http://datajournalismhandbook.org/1.0/en/introduction_2.html#sthash.e9uVDyRV.dpuf, accessed on 19 October 2013

Note on the contributors

Yaneng Feng is a postgraduate student of School of Journalism of Communication University of China majoring in New Media supervised by Prof. Junqi Yan. She is interested in new media and her research interests include data journalism and infographics in China. Contact details: feng462@hotmail.com.

Qian Li is a postgraduate student of the School of Journalism of Communication University of China, having studied engineering at undergraduate level. She is supervised by Prof. Junqi Yan. Her interests lie in the reform of journalism and data journalism. Contact details: 4451590li@sina.com.

Section 4:
Data journalism and journalism education

So there we have it – the primer comes to an end. Hopefully, ignorance has been eradicated or at least assuaged. But how do we train or educate future generations of journalism student not to be afraid of the big bad data wolf?

In the first section of this book, Jonathan Hewett, in a chapter exploring the development of data journalism, also outlined how its learning and teaching began in higher education and in the industry more broadly.

Professor Chris Frost is one of the grand old men of British journalism education, author, along with one of the editors of this volume Richard Lance Keeble, of many of the standard texts. Frost sets his first year undergraduates a simple numeracy test. Too many fail it much to his dismay as he realises they will have to spend much of their professional life decoding the numbers to get to the stories. Without that numeracy they will be lost in the new world of journalism.

Liz Hannaford, of the University of Salford and the BBC, has a simple answer: drop shorthand in undergraduate journalism courses and replace it with modules in computing and coding. She talks to journalists and developers actively working in code in newsrooms, looks at the debate in the academy over the need to re-programme curricula towards computers and the trend especially in J. Schools in the US to teach computing as a matter of course. Should that cross the Pond? Hannaford puts a strong case for it as students need to face the future not the past.

Journalism ethics through accuracy in numbers

Chris Frost highlights the "numeracy crisis" amongst journalism students – and provides a few guidelines on how they may be inspired to become more familiar with figures

"Hands up all those who can't do maths?" It's a question I use at the start of my first year lecture on writing to figures. The depressing truth is that nearly every hand is raised and I'm left with the same question every year: if I'd queried their abilities about other basic skills such as reading or writing that should have been learned in kindergarten then of course the answer would have been very different.

We need to be clear straight away, of course, that my question was not actually about their ability with maths but about basic arithmetic. I was not asking if they were able to handle imaginary numbers, work out differential equations or develop complex trigonometric proofs. I simply want to be sure that people who may spend much of their professional life reporting on government statistics, company balance sheets or academic or consumer surveys have sufficient skill with figures to avoid being bamboozled and are able to explain the truth to their readers, listeners or viewers. The truth is that with one or two exceptions – who are rarely prepared to boast about their basic competence to their peers – most students not only can't handle basic mathematical concepts but are actually rather proud of this disabling incompetence.

I am not alone in seeing this as a matter of concern. The Royal Statistical Society appointed a project worker two years ago to try to raise understanding of the importance of figures to journalists and amongst other things he arranged for a group of scientists to visit journalism schools throughout the UK to explain simple statistics in an entertaining and understandable way. Some celebrities are also trying to raise people's consciousness of figures with comedian Dara Ó Briain being one of the best known.

This widespread ignorance of maths has also been a cause of concern to government and to the world of teaching. Various reviews have been carried out and action plans executed in an attempt to improve the situation. The *Review of Mathematics Teaching in Early Years Settings and Primary Schools*, led by Sir Peter Williams, was launched in 2007 by the Secretary of State for Education and had the aim of examining the evidence to find ways to raise standards of mathematics teaching in schools. The report identified several problems including the need for more specialised teaching in school and the damaging effect that negative parental attitudes towards maths had on their children. Sir Peter said in his report that despite considerable progress in attainment since the introduction of the National Numeracy Strategy:

> ... issues regarding the teaching and learning of mathematics remain, and the United Kingdom is still one of the few advanced nations where it is socially acceptable – fashionable, even – to profess an inability to cope with the subject. A parent expressing such sentiments can hardly be conducive to a learning environment at home in which mathematics is seen by children as an essential and rewarding part of their everyday lives. The review has therefore considered carefully the role of parents and families and their influence on the young learner, with examples of best practice in this regard highlighted (http://webarchive.nationalarchives.gov.uk/20130401151715/https://www.education.gov.uk/publications/eOrderingDownload/Williams%20Mathematics.pdf, accessed on 7 September 2013).

Sir Peter went on to point out the importance of basic arithmetic skills to survive in everyday life. The BBC identified Professor Michael Reiss, of the Royal Society, as another academic who is concerned about standards. In response to the report, he said:

> We cannot hope to succeed in life as individuals or as a nation if we do not have a good grasp of maths. Despite some encouraging recent signs, there is still a pressing need to improve the quality of mathematics education for primary school children. This interim report is to be welcomed as a significant step in the right direction. By placing teachers at its heart it has the potential to inspire teachers and in turn their pupils (http://news.bbc.co.uk/1/hi/education/7306632.stm, accessed on 7 September 2013).

Government has tried to change things. In addition to the report, changes were made in recent years so that in order to gain qualified teacher status trainees had to pass a maths skills text but this has been criticised because it can be resat until the candidate passes.

Educating for science and maths in schools

In the early days of journalism in the UK there was no real formal training of journalists either at college or on the job. Young men (for back in the 1800s it was almost exclusively men) of good education would be employed as reporters. Systematic, formal training and education of journalists outside of the workplace is much more recent. Training in the 19th century was non-existent, although towards the end of the century some thought was given to its development and one of the first books about journalism to be published in the UK was printed in the 1860s by T. A. Reed under the title of *The Reporter's Handbook*. Another early book was *Newspaper Reporting* by J. Pendleton. He makes clear the skills divide with today's technological world:

> ... one of the most detestable of reporting experiences is to attend a similar political meeting far away and be obliged to get back the same night. It is head-aching, eye-straining work for the reporter to transcribe his shorthand notes, for instance, in the guard's van of a fish train jolting over forty miles of railway, especially when he is expected at the office soon after midnight with his copy "written up" ready to hand to the printers (Pendleton 1890: 188).

Shorthand was seen as an important skill for such early reporters and Pendleton presents an entire chapter discussing its history, importance and various systems as does Reed but few other requirements were needed other than a good general education and the need to be "courteous to high and low" (ibid: 158). A century later and 1991 saw the launch of the first journalism undergraduate programmes in the UK and the expansion of such programmes together with the postgraduate programmes already in existence has made journalism in the UK a graduate entry career by default.

Educating young journalists

This upsurge of journalism education and training over the past thirty years has brought with it a concern that the new generation of young journalists should be more professional. The pursuit of truth and the determination to provide accurate information is now more important than ever to the younger generation of journalists. In order to ensure a high level of accuracy a journalist has to take care with source material. First the good journalist must ensure the source is reliable and is who or what he or she claims to be and therefore whether the story is worth using at all. Is it actually news? The reporter must check that the information given is accurate, or at the very least that the source claims it to be accurate, even if this may be in doubt. The reporter must be able to challenge the information and find sources that will challenge it and hold it to account, attempting to provide balance to the account given by the primary source. Finally the reporter should be offering sufficient information to allow the reader or viewer to put the information into context.

This basic professional requirement of ensuring accuracy and seeking truth applies to all sources and many sources these days include figure-based material such as balance sheets, surveys and statistics. A quick scan of newspapers on any day shows the heavy reliance on such sources for stories – sources that many journalists brought up in this culture of "maths doesn't matter" are unable to properly analyse, criticise and put into context. This can lead to two main problems for journalists. First that their inability to handle numbers means they miss stories or are unable to identify the magnitude of a story, either carrying stories that are not in fact very newsworthy as though they are or failing to identify that the event is a potential news story because they have failed to see its significance. This makes them easy game for unscrupulous PR practitioners and spin doctors able to use figures to present a case or cover up a story. The second problem is that even if the journalist does serve his or her audience properly and identify a story, they may not have the arithmetical skill to present it accurately.

Common errors
Journalists, through lack of skill or interest, tend to make a number of basic errors that make analysing the types of figures commonly used in stories very difficult.

Averages
The first and most obvious is the use of averages. Averages, modes and medians are useful ways of presenting figures and deciding whether something departs from what might be considered a typical value. Unfortunately a typical journalist is not certain how to use these or what they mean. To take a fictitious example, whilst it might be inflammatory copy worthy of many a redtop lead to say that the average school child commits a crime every week, it is less newsworthy when we explain that of 100 children, one commits sixty crimes a week most of them minor vandalism, another child manages 30 and a third 10. The other 97 – the mode, the most commonly met statistic, commit no crimes at all. There are some statistics where the average, the mode and the median (the point at which half are a greater number and half fewer) are very similar. The height of adult British males is, according to the Department of Trade and Industry's *Handbook of Anthropometric and Strength Measurements*, 5 foot 9 inches. This will also be pretty close to the mode and the median as few men are taller than 6 foot 3 inches and few shorter than 5 foot 3 inches (although there are a few both taller and shorter). The range of heights generally sits within six to nine inches either side of the median.

But the same is not true of the number of Britons who smoke. The vast majority do not smoke with only 21 per cent of males and 19 per cent of females smoking in the UK according the smoking campaign group ASH (Action on Smoking and Health: http://www.ash.org.uk/files/documents/ASH_106.pdf, accessed on 16 September 2013). That means that four in every five adults does not smoke in the UK, yet averages would give us the figure that they all smoke on average three cigarettes a day and the typical smoker (1/5th of the population) smokes 13 cigarettes a day. This inability to use average and mean properly can lead to bizarre stories with below average performers, whether they are schools or hospitals or airlines being castigated for poor performance. But in any group, no matter how good they are, there are bound to be some who perform below average and there always will be.

Significance

Statistical significance is another important element to a story. Every reporter should always check whether a figure is statistically significant. Variances in death rate are a type of story that often attract big headlines: "New birth pill doubles risk of death" was a story that sparked serious alarm in 2011 (see for instance: "Newer contraceptive Pills 'double the danger of blood clots' compared with older versions": http://www.dailymail.co.uk/health/article-1379357/Newer-birth-control-pills-double-danger-blood-clots.html, accessed on 17 September 2013 or "New types of contraceptive pill double blood clot risk": http://www.telegraph.co.uk/health/women_shealth/8848486/New-types-of-contraceptive-pill-double-blood-clot-risk.html).

These kind of stories risk causing many women to immediately quit using their contraceptive pills putting many of them at the much greater risk of injury or death that pregnancy brings. The same articles said the study also showed the pill reduced the risk of ovarian cancer by 45 per cent. Whilst the statistics may have been right (and some medical researchers still dispute this) raising the risk of death from one in 100,000 to two in one hundred thousand is virtually meaningless. A moment's lapse in concentration reading your Twitter account whilst crossing the road would put you at far more risk.

Often the figures reporters are presented with are just wrong anyway, so not only can the figures show insignificant risks, they may just be plain incorrect and misleading. There are many urban myths about; zombie statistics, as the excellent BBC Radio Four programme *More or Less* describes them: false statistics that refuse to die. These are often figures that have little or no basis in fact and that just a little thought and research would soon show to be false or at least unlikely. One such is the myth that left-handed people are likely to die seven years earlier than right-handed people. Hannah Barnes of BBC News set out to find if this was true. She approached Chris McManus, Professor of Psychology and Medical Education at University College London and the author of *Right Hand, Left Hand*, who quickly told her that it was not at all plausible:

> If this were true it would be the largest single predictor we had of life expectancy – it would be like smoking 120 cigarettes a day plus doing a number of other dangerous things simultaneously. It really is highly implausible that an epidemiologist wouldn't have spotted it previously.

He went on to explain that the researchers made a "very subtle error". The study was conducted in Southern California, which publishes lists of all deaths. The researchers contacted their families to discover if the deceased was right- or left-handed. They found that the average age at death of the left-handers was about nine years younger than of the right-handers. However, Chris McManus explained that left-handers were more common now because of discrimination during the Victorian period. That meant far fewer of those who died would be classed as left handed and this would artificially skew the results.

In order to understand this, imagine there were no left-handers at all born before 1973 – 40 years ago. Any left-handers who died would have to have been born after 1973 and so would be younger at death than the average. If we now look at death records for 2013 all left-handers would have died before the age of 40 as all those older than 40 would be classified as right-handed, yet we could not claim that left-handers only live to a maximum age of 40 (see http://www.bbc.co.uk/news/magazine-23988352, accessed on 7 September 2013).

Michael Blastland and Andrew Dilnot in their excellent book *The Tiger that Isn't* (2007) explain that one question a journalist should always ask is: "Is that a big number?" Indeed, governments often make claims about investing large sums of money in some key policy or another but a quick look at the figures often shows that this is just another meaningless gesture. For instance, investing £100 million to improve school buildings sounds great, until one realises this will be spread over almost 25,500 schools in the UK giving each school approximately £400, little more than the cost of replacing a few windows or painting a few rooms. A number can also often appear very small making it a good story but again we need to check figures. *The Sunday Times* ran with a story in 2012 that said: "Only 100 adult cod in the North Sea." To the newspaper's credit, it later (on 16 September 2012) printed a clarification on its website:

> Clarification: The headline of this article over-simplifies a compex issue. It refers to a fall in the number of fully mature cod over the age of 13, indicating that this is the breeding age of cod. In fact they can start breeding between the ages of four and six, in which case there are many more mature cod in the North Sea. CEFAS, the government fisheries laboratory, says the cod stock remains severely depleted but has been gradually improving. We regret the over- simplification (http://www.thesundaytimes.co.uk/sto/news/uk_news/Environment/arti cle1127310.ece).

The story had made it clear that Atlantic cod start breeding at 4-6 years but did not make it clear that a 13-year-old Atlantic cod would be a rarity despite over-fishing. BBC Radio Four's *More or Less* later commented: "We shouldn't be surprised that there are very few cod aged over 13 (in fact fewer than 60 have been recorded in the North Sea in past 30 years) just as we shouldn't be surprised there aren't very many humans over 100."

So where did *The Sunday Times* get its figures? According to *More or Less*, Dr Tom Webb, a marine ecologist, says this age comes from the website fishbase.org. He points out this is a reliable site, but that the maximum age of cod, given as 25, was not from the North Sea but from the Barents Sea. "The only estimate for a North Sea cod of maximum age is 11." *More or Less* calculated that this meant there were more like 436,900,000 mature cod left in the North Sea – perhaps, it said, a new record for the most inaccurate headline ever covered by *More or Less*.

Facility with numbers means a good journalists can spot when information is likely to be wrong or at least misleading. Ethical professional behaviour requires that a good journalist does his or her best to ensure that we do not mislead readers or accidentally pass on incorrect information. The example above enraged fishing leaders who claimed that stocks were regenerating and these figures gave an entirely misleading picture. Some stories could have even more damaging effects.

Statistics generally are a problem for a journalist seeking to tell the truth or to be as accurate as possible. Even if the figures are correct, they may not mean what they appear to mean. A story that was widely reported after *Panorama* (BBC1) first broadcast it was that more British soldiers or veterans died from suicide in 2012 than died in action in Afghanistan. This is true. *Panorama* identified 50 suicides or suspected suicides in 2012 whilst 44 died in action, of wounds or from some other cause linked to their service (https://www.gov.uk/government/uploads/system/uploads/attachment_data/ file/240279/20130917-Op_Herrick_casualties_upto__31_August13.PDF, accessed on 16 September 2013). The MoD confirmed that seven serving soldiers killed themselves, 14 died in suspected suicides and 29 veterans also took their lives.

Whilst every death is a tragedy, this may not be the staggering story it first appears. Virtually every war since at least Vietnam has seen more suicides that deaths in action. However, a comparison between the number of soldiers and veterans committing suicide and the civil population shows that the rate of suicides amongst soldiers is significantly lower than the rate amongst a similar age and gender group of the civil population So, while campaigners may well be justified in calling on the MoD for more help with post traumatic stress for veterans, serving in Afghanistan as a soldier may actually be safer than being an unemployed young person at home. I suppose it all depends on which you think is the better story.

Finding out the truth behind the figures can sometimes be difficult but it should always be attempted in pursuit of accuracy. The Office of National Statistics is one good place to go to get background information that will help identify if a statistic is likely to be correct. There are two final ways in which journalists' nervousness with figures can lead them astray. The first is to confuse correlation with causation and the second is to fail to understand regression to the mean.

Correlation

Often when producing a story, we want to seek causation – that is to say that this event causes that. For instance, it might make a good story to say that living under electricity pylons may cause cancer, a rumour that has circulated for many years. It might easily be possible to find little clusters of cancer victims living in such places. However, unless you can prove that no such clusters exist elsewhere, you cannot claim one causes the other. It may simply be a correlation. People who live under pylons, for instance, may be more likely to smoke; a known cancer hazard. Living under pylons may not be the cause of their cancer, but merely a correlation.

Regression

Similarly we can often spot patterns: roads that have more traffic accidents or hospitals that have higher death rates than the norm. Often this is correlation rather than causation. Blackpool has a higher than average number of retired citizens so it would hardly be surprising if its local hospital had a higher than average death rate. But we also need to remember that such statistics vary. No matter how careful hospitals are, some people are going to die whilst in their care; it's what often happens to the seriously ill or injured. Some years the number of dead will be higher than others purely by the action of random chance. Often we get very concerned that figures seem to be rising or occasionally jubilant that they are falling.

However, it may simply be that the figures are regressing to the mean. So, if a hospital has an average death rate of eight in one thousand, one year that might rise to 11 and another it might fall to six. It might carry on rising for several years and then fall sharply. Is that a marked improvement? Well, it may be that the hospital has been able to introduce a new medical procedure that has dramatically improved its figures or it could simply be a regression to the mean. An average inevitably means that some years the figures will be lower and some years higher. The same is true with league tables. Inevitably some hospitals or schools are going to be below average and some above. The key question is by how much are they above or below. If all hospitals had a mean death rate of between 7.98 and 8.02, then it probably wouldn't mean very much being in a below average hospital. It might well be above average the following year.

Percentages

Percentages are the final computational method I want to discuss. Many journalists have trouble with percentages and the good ones use fractions rather than percentages where possible as readers tend to understand them better. A 100 per cent increase in traffic means that it doubles whilst a 200 per cent increase would mean that it triples. Many journalists get this and other percentage examples wrong. It's not helped by the idea one can have more than 100 per cent of something. Footballers who give 110 per cent effort for instance. Misuse of percentages and a failure to understand what they can mean can lead to serious inaccuracies in stories as well as seriously misleading and possibly panicking readers.

Conclusion

I have not included any examples in this piece about finance largely because the same rules apply. Journalists are supposed to provide their readers with as close to the truth as we can manage and certainly with accurate information that has been tested as best we can.

With so many stories these days using financial or statistical information it is vital that journalists know how to do that testing, how to challenge the statistics with which they are often presented by those with a particular agenda to press. If they do not have the requisite skills to carry out that testing and ensure they are passing on accurate information, there really isn't much point in being in journalism.

References

Blastland, Michael and Dilnot, Andrew (2007) *The Tiger that Isn't*, London: Profile Books

Livingstone, Charles and Voakes, Paul (2005) *Working with Numbers and Statistics: A Handbook for Journalists*, New Jersey: Lawrence Erlbaum Associates

Pendleton, J. (1890) *Newspaper Reporting*, London: Elliot Stock

Reed, T. A. (1873) *The Reporter's Guide*, London: F. Pitman

Seife, Charles (2010) *Proofiness: The Dark Arts of Mathematical Deception*, New York: Penguin Group

Note on the contributor

Professor Chris Frost is Head of Journalism at Liverpool John Moores University. He is the author of *Journalism Ethics and Regulation* (Pearson Education 2011, third edition), *Reporting for Journalist* (Routledge 2010, second edition) and *Designing for Newspapers and Magazines* (Routledge 2011, second edition). He is also chair of the NUJ's Ethics Council, a former President of the NUJ and Chair of the Association for Journalism Education.

Recalculating the newsroom: The rise of the journo-coder?

Through a series of interviews with journalists and developers working at the BBC and *Financial Times* plus some key players outside of major newsrooms, Liz Hannaford aims to find out about data journalism's special role today. And she tackles the crucial question: Must all journalism students be programmers?

"Why all your students must be programmers" was the provocative title of one of the liveliest panel discussions at the August 2013 Conference for the Association for Education in Journalism and Mass Communication in Washington DC. On Twitter, it was dubbed the #AEJMCBattleRoyale (Hernandez 2013). The panellists talked passionately about how their programming skills enabled them to take their journalism to a whole new level – interrogating data to find the stories nobody else could or turning static, text-based web pages into dynamic, interactive tools. There was less agreement about what level of "programming" knowledge is actually useful to a journalist. There was even less agreement about how to teach it to students in an already tightly-packed course schedule. What do you throw out?

In the United States, the idea of the journo-coder, programmer-journalist, hacker-journalist, journo-programmer (the terminology is undecided) is gaining ground as data journalism develops and the possibility for interactivity on news websites expands every year. Programmers are coming into newsrooms and journalists are venturing further into programming and there is some blurring where the two meet.

A small number of academic studies have tracked the rise of this phenomenon in American newsrooms. For example, Cindy Royal conducted a case study of "Journalists as programmers" in *The New York Times*'s Interactive News Technology Department, suggesting guidelines for other news organisations to follow (Royal 2010). Sylvain Parasie and Eric Dagiral's study focuses specifically on the city of Chicago and suggests that bringing programmers into the newsroom challenges some journalistic ideals (Parasie and

Dagiral 2012). But here in the UK, much less has been written about the "journo-coder" and whether he/she even exists although there are some excellent short case studies in the *Data Journalism Handbook* (Gray, Chambers and Bounegru 2012).

This chapter is, therefore, an exploratory look at how newsrooms here are bringing together these two professions to produce different kinds of data-driven, interactive journalism. Is the goal to create hybrid journo-coders who can write great stories one day and build a website the next? Or is it to nurture teams of "tech-savvy journalists and news-savvy technologists?" (Leimdorfer cited in Herrmann 2011).

Through a series of interviews with journalists and developers working at the BBC and *Financial Times* plus some key players outside of major newsrooms, this chapter aims to find out how journalists and developers are working together. The way technology is adopted in newsrooms is shaped not by the technology itself but by existing organisational structures, work practices and how the end-user is perceived (Boczkowski 2004b). So this chapter also looks briefly at how their work is incorporated into the newsroom structure. Perhaps more importantly from an educational point of view, it examines which technical skills journalists need now and in the future. Must all journalism students be programmers?

The product

The BBC's Visual Journalism Team creates a range of data-driven features for the BBC News website. It consists of a team of journalists, developers and web and television graphics designs which carries out complex data projects and produces visualisations, maps and interactive features.

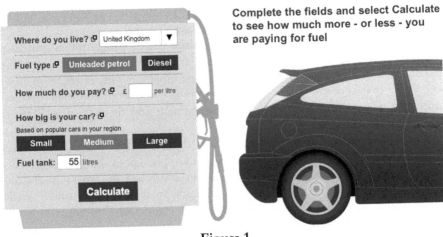

Fuel price calculator: How much do you pay?

The average price of petrol in the UK is about £1.35 a litre or £1.40 for diesel - but how much you pay can vary from street to street and town to town. So how much do you pay and how does it compare with the national average or what people are paying in other countries?

Figure 1

The fuel price calculator is a typical example. The user types in their own details and compares the price for fuel with the price around the world. The developers worked with the journalists to turn all the different data sets on global fuel prices into an interactive feature. At the same time, the designer on the project visualised the information in a way that encourages the user to engage, play and share.

Not all the Visual Journalism team's output relies on crunching data sets. The news that Nasa's Voyager 1 spacecraft may be about to leave the Solar System led to the creation of an interactive journey timeline to convey the vast distances of space. The user is invited to input details of a familiar journey – duration and distance.

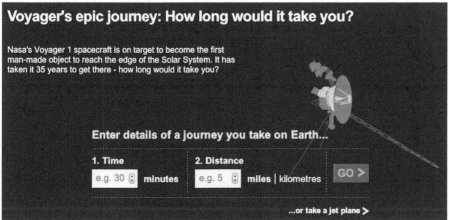

Figure 2

The tool then uses that small piece of data to calculate how long it would take the user to complete each stage of Voyager's journey past the planets. Each stage is illustrated with key quotations and historic footage to create an interactive, multimedia experience. As Andrew Leimdorfer, the Technical Product Manager in the Visual Journalism team, explains: "We could have put all of this in a standard news story and laid it out differently. But the added design finesse makes it a nicer experience for the user."

Two to three weeks is the usual timescale for the team's projects although that is getting stretched now that the audience is fragmented across different platforms. So creating new, bespoke interactive features like this for breaking news is tricky. The team is more likely to use existing tools for a breaking news story and then innovate online with a background feature a few days after a big story initially breaks. For example, following the Japan earthquake of March 2011, the team used data from the US Geological Survey to put together a dynamic map which shows the frequency and size of aftershocks.

Japan quake: Tremor timeline

Hundreds of aftershocks have continued to shake Japan, days after the massive magnitude 9 earthquake that triggered a devastating tsunami on Friday, 11 March.

Press the play button or use the slider to see the spread, size and frequency of earthquakes in Japan greater than magnitude 5 since 10 March.

2200 Hrs 10 March

▶ ◀◀ < > ▮──

Earthquake magnitude

5
6
7
8
9

Magnitude 9
1446 hrs 11 March

Minamisanriku ●
Sendai ●
Fukushima ●

JAPAN

Tokyo ●

Figure 3

The Interactive News team at the *Financial Times* is similar in that it brings together journalists, developers and designers to combine multimedia, interactivity and data visualisation. For example, the interactive map in Figure 4 uses data obtained from Freedom of Information requests showing the London Fire Brigade's response times.

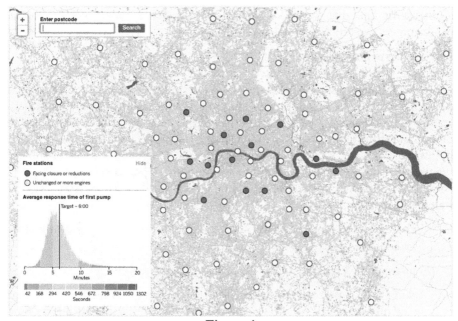

Figure 4

One of the most innovative digital journalism projects to date at the *Financial Times* has been the Austerity Audit – a dynamic piece of storytelling which combines multimedia, data visualisation and long form text. "The stuff we do is quite flashy and involves a lot of coder time," says Martin Stabe, the Head of Interactive News at the *Financial Times*.

Figure 5

Much of that coder time is concentrated on the "front-end" – building the interface that creates the user experience, the interactivity. That involves HTML (the structure of the webpage), CSS (the style of the webpage) and crucially JavaScript which builds the interactivity and manipulation. So where does the journalist fit into this team? Do they need to acquire coding skills? Do the programmers need to acquire journalism skills?

Hybrid or specialist?

Only one of the respondents interviewed at the BBC and *Financial Times* was comfortable being described as a journo-coder or any of the other hybrid job descriptions. "I'd like to think that any developer that works on any journalism team is a journalist," said one. Another respondent identified himself as a programmer but felt he was "becoming more journo". However, he didn't feel he would ever be a complete journalist. All other respondents identified themselves strongly as either a journalist or a developer. They were sceptical about the possibility of combining both skill-sets in one person. Typical statements include:

> I've never met a journalist who is particularly adept at coding in my fairly limited pool.

> I just say I'm a journalist who specialises in maps and charts.

> I don't think a person can straddle both. To make an interactive requires so many different areas of knowledge, you need years of experience just doing that. And journalism is a whole other area of expertise so you'd be lacking in focus on one side.

Andrew Leimdorfer, at the BBC, says that journo-coder hybrids are not essential on his team as long as there are highly talented specialists who can work together. Martin Stabe, at the *Financial Times*, does not believe truly hybrid journo-coders currently exist in the UK. Instead, both news organisations have adopted a team approach, bringing together journalists, developers and designers.

The dream team – and the importance of technical skills

All the respondents at the BBC and *Financial Times* who identified as developers were highly proficient in HTML, CSS and JavaScript and tended to see these as their most important skills. Other key skills included "back-end" programming languages such as PHP and Python which can be used, for example, to access databases. Additionally, they described data and statistical skills to analyse and organise large datasets such as SQL, SPSS and R.

Although Martin Stabe insists that the team approach is the only way to create the "journo-coder", he also believes that for a team like that to work, you need journalists who can at least understand what is technically possible…

> …who can write just enough code to understand what the developers are doing, who can do good data management and the data sourcing aspect of the interactive, investigative project.

Journalists in these teams are not involved in front-end programming and describe their expertise in using software rather than creating it through coding. Analysing information rather than developing interactivity is the key technical skill. One respondent described his skills in "simple things" such as Excel or using mapping software such as ArcMAP. When asked which technical skills journalists *should* have in an ideal world, all respondents emphasised analysing and cleaning up data and a good knowledge of statistics. For Andrew Leimdorfer, the aspiration for journalists should be to be as technically self-sufficient as possible.

> If a person who discovers an interesting data-set then scrapes it from the website, cleans it up to make it usable and visualises it using an online technology – then they are going to be in a much stronger position going to an editor to pitch a story based on that data than someone who found a data-set but has to pitch for a developer's time to try and do something with it. You can see how the first guy would be in a much better position.

This is an important point which was emphasised repeatedly. In a newsroom, developers are a rare and precious resource. So the more basic coding skills a journalist can perform, the more time the developers can spend on the highly specialised tasks. For example, Martin Stabe believes it is reasonable to expect journalists to be able to write simple programming scripts which scrape data from the web and store it on a database.

> From a full time developer's point of view, these are fairly trivial, simple tasks they wouldn't mention on their CV. If you asked a top-notch developer what their skill set is, they probably wouldn't mention they could write complex Excel functions or that they can manage a database using SQL or write a really simple scraper in Python. For a journalist those are exceptional skills and definitely accessible skills and skills that an increasing number of journalists have.

Learning the skills

The respondents came from a variety of backgrounds with only two having degrees in computer-oriented subjects. The rest had gained their knowledge through a variety of informal, self-directed means.

> Basically, it's asking people around you. It saves time. If you try to literally teach yourself, that's very time-consuming. People are often very willing to help.

> I've learnt so much from fellow colleagues – how to build code that is robust and can scale without breaking.

A major part of learning comes from tapping into the community of developers and journalists working in similar areas either online or through informal meet-ups where knowledge is shared.

> There's a huge online community of programmers so you need to absorb yourself in that. You can go to GitHub, download someone else's code and read how they did it. That's the best way to learn - reading the code and

181

seeing how somebody else made it. Otherwise, people blog about how they made something so you keep abreast of what people in similar roles are doing through Twitter.

Often the best training is not from software manufacturers but from journalists using the software.

Knowledge-sharing and the need to continually learn is a distinguishing feature of the developer community and one which it is bringing in to newsrooms to problem-solve on each new project. All respondents said they were constantly learning new skills and pushing the boundaries of their knowledge. In fact, the developers interviewed consistently said 20 to 25 per cent of their work time was spent learning.

You learn by always coding at the edge of your understanding ... It's about constantly throwing yourself into a slightly uncomfortable situation then learning your way out of it.

Every year there's a different way of doing things, producing graphic or interactive, so you have to constantly look at what you know about how to do your job.

However, for the developers, there was no requirement to learn the traditional journalism skills. Instead, they talk about "absorbing" a better understanding of journalistic storytelling.

I have a better instinct now for what journalists need, what the reader wants to see. But I think the roles are split quite nicely ... There's a huge amount I don't need to know – law, editorial guidelines, style. I just don't get involved in that kind of thing.

Working together

Although journalists and developers have their own specialist knowledge and expertise, they need to understand each other's requirements. Andrew Leimdorfer describes his team constantly "bouncing bits of knowledge off each other" and developing a shared language. Journalists on his team, he says, are very different from traditional newsroom journalists.

They're the interface. They understand what the UX (User Experience) guys and developers do. They're web natives. But there is still specialisation. Similarly a developer coming in from outside, it's a tremendous culture shift for them, sitting with journalists. But they quickly adopt the newsroom lingo. What's the top line? What's the peg?

Ideas very often come from outside the interactive teams, from specialist news desks who need a complex, data-driven story told in a compelling way. But ideas also come from journalists within the team. The journalist's first job is to find the data and analyse it to see if it says anything newsworthy. The journalist might then try out some simple visualisations to better understand the data and think about how they might want to tell the story. Having established that the story merits valuable developer time, the process becomes highly collaborative with journalist, developer and designer working closely together.

> The developer is not a deli counter and the reporter doesn't just come up and order what sandwich they want.

> It's not something where one person's job starts therefore another person's job stops ... That collaboration continues right till you've finished.

The journalist takes on a project management role, overseeing the process right through to completion. This means understanding the problem from the developer's point of view, accepting what can and cannot be achieved in the timescale, discussing technical trade-offs and making sure they get the user experience they want for their story.

Coding for fun

So why do journalists choose to work in this highly technical area? And what draws developers to a newsroom? For the journalists, the attraction is the constantly changing nature of the challenge and the ever-expanding possibilities for storytelling. So the interest comes from having to always reframe the way they do things. They are also excited by the power of numbers to reveal a story.

> I got into this broadly through election coverage and being interested in the numbers coming out of opinion polls. They were a really good way to see what was going on and so different from how politicians talk.

When the developers were asked to explain why they wanted to work in a newsroom with a bunch of journalists, the word that came up repeatedly was "fun". Typical responses include:

> When I leave the office, I have a sense of satisfaction. I've done something good. Whatever I've worked on, quite a lot of people are going to benefit from it.

> Because it's a bit unconventional, firstly. It's a very dynamic environment ... I've worked on all kinds of applications that aren't that interesting in terms of what they actually do but the technical side is interesting. In the newsroom, the content of the thing we're making is interesting to me.

> The newsroom is a very good fit for my style ... I'm not a good enough developer to do things that impress other developers. I know just enough to make whatever it is I want to make in the way an ordinary audience would appreciate it.

> The immediacy is a real challenge – making stuff people are going to get something from instantly and will deepen their understanding.

So, the tight deadlines of a newsroom are part of the appeal. For developers, it is like being on a permanent Hackday, constantly building quick prototypes with like-minded people. But they also talked about the creativity of coding in a newsroom.

> It's a very creative process, coding, and there's a big non-technical space – working with people, understanding their problems and solving their problems through building systems.

> We as developers, we do things because they excite us … I might be playing around with a dataset … to find out "I wonder what I can actually do with this data. I wonder how I can make this display on a page … in a way I haven't seen done before. …It's more about fun."

Beyond the mainstream

So far this chapter has looked at how journalists and coders are working together as a team in mainstream newsrooms. But at the fringes of media production, the idea of the hybrid journo-coder is much more attractive. Away from large news organisations, specialisation is a luxury few can afford, says Sarah Marshall, the technology editor at journalism.co.uk. She estimates there are fewer than twenty people in the UK whom she would describe as "journo-coders" but believes their numbers are on the increase.

> Actually, a lot of us in newsrooms are working by ourselves so learning skills is really helpful. For those who really skill up, there are clear advantages.

Benji Lanyado is one example of a journalist who has "skilled up" and has no hesitation in describing himself as a "journo-developer". He started out as a travel writer at the *Guardian*, then left to learn how to code. At the end of his first programming course, he created the Reddit Edit, a snapshot of what's trending on Reddit. He also creates interactive stories for news organisations as a freelancer.

> The reason they say [journo-coders can't exist] is because that's the reality right now. There are very few journalists who code and very few developers who can write good copy or edit a story or oversee an editorial product … I guarantee that the journalists of the future will be more code proficient.

That's certainly the mantra at the London chapter of HacksHackers – a global grassroots network of informal meet-ups stretching from Buenos Aires to Johannesburg. It brings together journalists (the hacks), developers (the hackers) and all sorts of geeky permutations in between. Most don't describe themselves using traditional job titles. Instead words like "creative", "interactive", "storytelling", "multimedia", "data analysis", "entrepreneurship" crop up time and again.

What brings them to a converted brewery in East London is a belief that technologists and journalists belong together and, just sometimes, can exist within the same person. HacksHackersLondon, founded by the *Guardian*'s Joanna Geary, started out as a small gathering in a pub for a few journalists who wanted to learn to code and a few developers who were happy to teach them. It has evolved into a monthly meet-up that has outgrown the pub and regularly packs well over a hundred people into a room.

The conversation is all about the intersection of technology and storytelling and the need to be a part of that. Journalists discuss ways to upgrade their digital skills and look for developers they can learn from. One attendee describes how she was forced to reassess her dream of becoming a journalist when she saw the traditional industry shrinking. Now she's working hard to develop new skills in interactive media, data and programming believing these are the skills that journalism needs today. It's about networking and collaboration, finding like-minded people who can work together across disciplines on investigative projects. These are the people Sarah Marshall, who co-organises HacksHackersLondon, believes will blur the line between journalist and programmer in the future.

A bit of every journalist wants to be a developer and a lot of developers want to be journalists.

Conclusion - Ditch shorthand and learn to code?

There seems little doubt that an understanding of programming is an increasingly useful skill in the journalist's toolkit and one which is valued in the newsroom. It was interesting to note that in July 2013, the advertisement for the *Guardian*'s Digital Journalism Scheme included "coding" on its list of selection criteria. (*Guardian* 2013). An "understanding" of programming obviously covers a broad spectrum. It is unlikely that journalists could also acquire the expertise to write production code for a global news brand whose website is put under huge scrutiny. That is likely to remain the preserve of experienced developers. But the journalists working with these developers need to know enough programming to understand what is possible within the constraints of budgets and timescales.

But a journalist looking to work on a B2B or a hyperlocal website where a team of developers is an unaffordable luxury may well find that a reasonable confidence with HTML, CSS and JavaScript is attainable and would be a highly desirable item on their CV. This is where there could be a real area of opportunity for student journalists looking to find a niche in an era when traditional newsroom jobs for graduates are becoming rarer.

How should journalism departments at our universities respond? Should they ditch shorthand and teach code instead?! Certainly, this is happening to some extent in the States. Columbia Journalism School offers a dual MSc in Computer Science and Journalism. The Medill School of Journalism at NorthWestern

University offers scholarships to students with computer science backgrounds to study on its Masters programme. Here in the UK, the launch of the Interactive Journalism MA at London's City University in 2011 has done much to increase the number of people with these highly technical skills.

Obviously, you do not need to be able to program in order to be a great journalist. But learning some coding skills opens up so many exciting opportunities. It is about creating intellectual curiosity, learning outside your comfort zone. Yes, full-on programming can be daunting but students can dip their toe in the water, at least, by scraping a bit of data off a website into a spreadsheet. That can often produce the fist-pumping moment of achievement that gets them hooked. They've taken the first step on the road to programming. Universities could try to create a HacksHackers-type environment that brings journalists and technologists together and encourages them to collaborate across disciplines to see where it takes them.

Most importantly, we need to foster the curiosity that drives people to constantly seek new knowledge and expand their skills, always thinking about where journalism is going rather than where it has been. All journalists of the future are going to be working on a digital product. They need to be at least curious about how things work behind the scenes.

Figures

1. See http://www.bbc.co.uk/news/business-21238363 (fuel price indicator), accessed on 31 July 2013

2. See http://www.bbc.co.uk/news/science-environment-21937524 (Voyager), accessed on 31 July 2013

3. http://www.bbc.co.uk/news/world-asia-pacific-12748215 (Japan earthquake), accessed on 31 July 2013

4. See http://www.ft.com/cms/s/2/851bed28-7077-11e2-a2cf-00144feab49a.html#axzz2ai1eBcb4 (London fire brigade), accessed on 1 August 2013

5. See http://ig.ft.com/austerity-audit/ (Austerity audit), accessed on 1 August 2013

References

Boczkowski, Pablo J. (2004) The processes of adopting multimedia and interactivity in three online newsrooms, *Journal of Communication*, Vol. 54, No. 2 pp 197-213

Gray, Jonathan, Chambers, Lucy and Bounegru, Liliana (2012) *The DaTa Journalism Handbook*, Sebastopol, CA: O'Reilly Media

Hernandez, Robert (2013) Why all your students must be programmers – The #AEJMCBattleRoyale, Web Journalist Blog, 11 August. Available online at http://blog.webjournalist.org/2013/08/, accessed on 26 August 2013

Herrmann, Steve (2011) Knight Mozilla and BBC News, *The Editors*, 4 November. Available online at http://www.bbc.co.uk/blogs/theeditors/2011/11/welcoming_a_knight-mozilla_fel.html, accessed on 26 August 2013

Parasie, Sylvain and Dagiral, Eric (2012) Data-driven journalism and the public good: "Computer-assisted-reporters" and "programmer-journalists" in Chicago, *New Media and*

Society. Available online at
http://nms.sagepub.com/content/early/2012/11/15/1461444812463345.full.pdf+html,
accessed on 26 August 2013

Royal, Cindy (2010) The journalist as programmer: A case study of *The New York Times*
interactive news technology department. Paper given at the International Symposium in
Online Journalism, University of Texas at Austin, April

Note on the contributor
Liz Hannaford is a former senior broadcast journalist at BBC World Service and has
worked extensively in Russia, Ukraine and Uzbekistan making radio programmes,
reporting, working with local media and training journalists. She currently teaches
journalism to both undergraduates and postgraduates at the University of Salford as well
as continuing her audio work and writing. She runs an after-school club to teach basic
programming skills at her local primary school but expects the children to overtake her
very soon.

Lightning Source UK Ltd.
Milton Keynes UK
UKHW02f1922301117
313661UK00007B/519/P

9 781845 496166